The Divine Master

Life and Teachings of
Guru Nanak Dev

THE DIVINE MASTER

Life and Teachings of Guru Nanak Dev

Sewaram Singh

Foreword by

Dr Gopal Singh

GIAN PUBLISHING HOUSE

NEW DELHI

ISBN : 978-81-212-0286-2

Reprint 1989

Published by

Gyan Publishing House
5, Ansari Road
Daryaganj, New Delhi-110002
Phone: 011-47034999, 9811692060
www.gyanbooks.com
E-mail: books@gyanbooks.com

Printed at: G. Print Process, Delhi.

FOREWORD

Sardar Sewaram Singh's biography of Guru Nanak (first published in 1904) is a unique book in many ways. It is perhaps the first-over volume in the English language, dealing with not only the remarkable life of the founder of the Sikh faith, but also his philosophy of life, inan authentic and scientific way. The writer did have the benefit of Dr. Ernest Trumpp's all-too-literal - and partisan - part - translation of the Adi Granth, together with the biography of Guru Nanak based on the India Office **Najamsakhi.** The learned author must have seen some other histories of the Sikhs as well, like Cunningham's, M 'Gregor's & Malcom's, which gave all - too - brief accounts of the life of Baba Nanak. Bhai Santokh Singh's **magnum-opus,** the **Gur-Partap Surya Granth** and **Nanak Parkash** were also available to him, as also Bhai Bala's hagiography in its various versions. Mr. M.A. Macauliffe's monumental — though uncritical-work on "Sikh Religion" had yet to appear.

It is, therefore, a pioneer's biography. Written by a man of faith, the account is supported by reason and scientific analysis of events. The 100-page chapter on the Master's Creed is really masterly and gives a bird's eye view of the Sikh philosophy in the context of the old creeds—mainly Hindu and Muslim—then prevailing in India. Though over 80 years have passed since the work first saw the light of day, its freshness of appeal is apparent for anyone who goes through the text. The language is simple and concise, got moving, and inspotres the reader by the spiritual, and not merely technical or historical, approach to the life of a world-prophet.

I am glad this beautiful work has been republished. I am sure, everyone who is interested in reading about the Sikh faith and its protestant founder, who influenced the five centuries of India's history after him, will profit by the visions and masterly expositions of the devout and learned author. I salute his worthy memory.

Raj Bhavan
Goa

Dr.Gopal Singh

The Divine Master

ੴ

ਸੰਸਾਰ ਰੋਗੀ, ਨਾਮ ਦਾਰੂ

(ਧਨਾਸਰੀ ਮ: ੧, ਛੰਤ)

TO

THE SUFFERING HUMANITY,

NAME is the Cure.

The Divine Master.

੧ ਓ

ਰਾਖੁ, ਰਾਖੁ, ਰਾਖੁ ਪ੍ਰਭ ਮੇਰੇ,
ਮੈ ਰਾਖਹੁ ਕਿਰਪਾ ਧਾਰੇ ।

ਨਾਨਕ ਮੈ ਧਰ ਅਵਰ ਨ ਕਾਈ,
ਮੈ ਸਤਿ ਗੁਰੁ ਗੁਰੁ ਨਿਸਤਾਰੇ ।

ਨਟ ਮਹਲਾ ੫,੬ (੮).

Save me, Save me, Save me,

Oh. Save me of Thine Own Grace, My Lord,

No other Refuge have I, O Nanak.

Deliver me, my Master, my Divine Master.

Guru Ram Das, the Fourth Master.

ੴ

ਧੰਨਿ ਧੰਨਿ ਤੇ ਧੰਨਿ ਜਨ,

ਜਿਹ ਕ੍ਰਿਪਾਲੁ ਹਰਿ ਹਰਿ ਭਯਉ ।

ਹਰਿ ਗੁਰੁ ਨਾਨਕੁ ਜਿਨ ਪਰਸਯਉ,

ਸਿ ਜਨਮ ਮਰਣ ਦੁਹ ਥੇ ਰਹਿਓ ।

ਸਵਯੇ ਸ੍ਰੀ ਮੁਖ ਬਾਕ ਮਹਲਾ ੫ (੫.)

Blessed, Blessed, Blessed are they,

On whom the Lord hath bestowed His Grace.

Birth and Death touch him not,

Who have knelt to Lord Master Nanak.

Guru Arjan Dev, the Fifth Master.

Servants of God !—or Sons
Shall I not call you ? because
Not as servants ye knew
Your Father's innermost mind,
His, who unwillingly sees
One of His little ones lost–
Yours is the praise, if mankind
Hath not as yet in its march
Fainted and fallen and died !

Matthew Arnold.

PREFACE

Nearly a quarter of the century has passed when I first ventured to publish what I then called "A Critical Study of the Life and Teachings of SRI GURU NANAK DEV, the founder of Sikhism;" and I then expressed that I should "feel myself satisfied and amply remunerated if the little book which I then presented to the Public served the useful purpose of setting the movement for a closer research into the Life and Mission of Guru Nanak Dev agoing." The reception which my book was given by the Sikhs as well as others was very encouraging, and apart from a *Khilaat* in cash which was sent to me by His late Highness Maharaja Sir Hira Singh Malvindra Bahadur of Nabha, I received a large number of letters from Sikhs and Europeans alike, appreciating the attempt that I had made. The whole edition was sold out during a comparatively short period, and the book has now been out of print for nearly twenty years. During this long period, I have unfortunately been busy, at first with my professional work and then with my official duties, and I confess that I have not been able to devote sufficient time to the work of research, which was necessary before another edition could be brought out. I had expected that some Sikh Professor of History and Religion might take up the task with advantage, but it appears that no attempt in this direction was made.

During this period a lot of further material has become available; and some of the older manuscripts have been printed and annotated, and considerable literature of an instructive and inspiring character written in Punjabee, by the Father and Poet-Artist of the modern Punjabee Literature, Bhai Sahib Bhai Vir Singh Ji of Amritsar, at whose feet I have often had the privilege of sitting for instruction and guidance. I was myself roused from my lethargy, when I received an official letter, from the Secretary of the Chief Khalsa Diwan about two years ago, asking me that if I could find no time to prepare a second edition of the book, I might permit the original book to be reprinted by the Diwan, without any revision whatsoever, as the Diwan daily received requests for supply of some literature in English on the Sikh Religion, and more particularly regarding the life of its Divine Founder. The book, however, was not, in my opinion, and in view of the further information and knowledge that had become available, fit to be reprinted without considerable revision, and I promised that I should undertake the work during the time at my disposal. Not that there was any thing in the earlier book, which I need have regretted or have sought to withdraw. It was too brief and dealt with certain aspects of the Master's Life, which, for want of spiritualistic and psychic science which has since become firmly established by the experiences of some Western Professors, were then not quite clearly understood. A thorough revision of the book was hence inevitable, if it was to present the Life of the Master in its full significance.

The work of revision was thus undertaken by me two years ago, but I soon found out that most of the book should have to be entirely re-written, and that the task was much more heavy than I could accomplish in my leisure hours. It could not at any rate be done to my satisfaction, without finding some relief from my official duties. It was thus that I availed of an opportunity last year to obtain leave from my duties, and the result of my labours is now offered to the indulgent public. The book has had almost entirely to be rewritten, and can lay no claim to be a mere second edition of the old work. It has therefore been given a new title altogether. For an explanation of the new Title, see the Fourth Chapter, headed The Master's Master.

SEWARAM SINGH.

PREFACE TO THE PREVIOUS BOOK.

When at first I took my pen in hand
Thus for to write, I did not understand
That I at all should make a little book
In such a mode ; nay, I had undertook
To make another ; which, when almost
done,
Before I was aware I this begun.

Bunyan.

In offering to the public a volume on the Life and Teachings of Sri Guru Nanak Dev, the Founder of Sikhism, no customary apology is needed. The importance of Sikh History is being felt more and more keenly every day. Sikhism, as one of the religious systems of the world, has perhaps the most recent origin, and yet the remarkable progress which it made in the land of its birth within three short centuries is quite unique. The Western mind was first directed towards it when, more than half a century ago, the British extended their frontier to the River Sutlej, beyond which existed a Kingdom, till then unnoticed by the British occupiers of the rest of India, but which the latter had to fight against in a short interval. In their contest with the Sikhs, the British, though victorious, had to respectfully acknowledge the strength, valour and zeal of their enemies, and, ever since the annexation of the Kingdom of the Sikhs by the British, the Khalsa have supplied soldiers to the British Army, who have been next to none in the world in soldiery qualities, which have been put to test not only in India and its borders, but also in China, Africa and other foreign countries.

It was with the object of explaining what real Sikhism, in all its pristine glory, at the time of its Great Founder, was, and how it gradually developed into a Church Militant, that this work was originally started. My idea in the beginning was to write a brief essay on the subject, but, afterwards, its re-writing, on the suggestion of certain friends, resulted in the adoption of the bigger and by nature permanent scheme.

The time and labour which I had to spend on the preparation of this work have been enormous, as compared with my capacities. My only excuse in taking up the self-imposed task was in the fact that a good deal of misunderstanding prevailed regarding the origin and development of the Khalsa Church. The words of Malcolm and McGregor, and the excellent volume from the pen of Captain Cunningham on Sikh History, do not afford much assistance in the solution of the points at issue, perhaps because these writers have devoted too little space to the so-to-say ancient History of the Sikhs. They have mostly dealt with the Political History of the Khalsa which, however, does not really begin till after the demise of the Tenth and Last of the Gurus. I have, therefore, had to fall back upon the original sources, but here too the task was arduous. The History of the Sikh Gurus lies much in obscurity. The materials at our disposal are very chaotic and misleading. The authenticity of the few extant *Janamsakhis* (the biographies in vernacular of Guru Nanak), the original source of all present-day information about the life and work of the first Guru, has been seriously called in question. This much at any rate is certain that they cannot be accepted in their entirety as they stand. Many of them are full of mythological descriptions and fictitious tales. I need only point out regarding them that their use must of necessity be very cautious. The most extant *Janamsakhi*, going under the title of *Bhai Bala's Janamsakhi* exists in so many different versions that none appears to be quite authentic. Dr. Trump has the credit of unearthing an old manuscript *Janamsakhi*, in the India Office, London, which also, though very brief and free from many later-day inventions, cannot be vouchsafed as perfectly correct. It was this huddle muddle sort of material that I had at my disposal. But the task, the more arduous it was the more worth attempting it appeared to me; and the result I offer to the public, in the hope that it may be able to remove certain wrong notions which have hitherto been cherished about Guru Nanak and his work. Whether the critical public will be harsh on me or will look to my work leniently, I cannot say. But here, once for all, I ask the reader's indulgence, inasmuch as I have had to work during hours stolen from my daily task and the means at my disposal to make the book more thorough were rather scanty. I shall feel myself satisfied and amply remunerated if this little book serves the useful purpose of setting the movement for a closer research into the Life and Mission of Guru Nanak Dev agoing. I will be glad to correct any mistakes or supply any omissions, which may be pointed out to me, in the next edition, should it be called for.

In the last chapter I have not been able to resist the temptation of adopting certain expressions from Renan's Life of Christ, as those expressions most fitly applied to the subject in hand. I therefore record here my grateful acknowledgments to the author of the said work.

I am sorry that a number of misprints have crept into the work by oversight, and a list of errata is, therefore, given herewith for the reader's use.

RAWALPINDI CITY,
The 12th October, 1904. } S. S.

I.

Birth and Times.

Of Thy Own Grace, O God, Save the World in agony!

Raise all unto Thee, whichever way they mayst be raised!*

Thus prayed the Master when He saw the world full of ceaseless pain and conflicting creed, warring, each with the other, for supremacy.

More than twenty centuries before Him, a Sage, also born in India, was similarly moved by the misery existing round him and is recorded to have cried out:

O! suffering world:
O! known and unknown of my common flesh;
Caught in this common net of death and woe,
And life which binds to both;

---

* Var Bilawal M. 4, *Sh*: 10; *Sh*: M. 3.

ਜਗਤਿ ਜਲੰਦਾ ਰਖ ਲੈ, ਆਪਣੀ ਕਿਰਪਾ ਧਾਰ ।
ਜਿਤੁ ਦਵਾਰੈ ਉਬਰੈ, ਤਿਤੈ ਲਿਹੁ ਉਬਾਰ ॥

I see, I feel
The vastness of the agony of earth,
The vainness of its joys, the mockery
Of all its best, the anguish
Of its worst..............
I would not let one cry
Whom I could save..........*.

He put the question to himself, "how could it be that Brahm would make a world and keep it miserable," and, without attempting to solve or answer this last question, he found all human cravings as the cause of pain, and laid stress on the suppression of these cravings as the principal remedy for the evils to which human flesh is subject. He laid down an admirable Code of Ethics as the Eightfold Path to Nirvana, about the exact nature of which so much diversity of opinion still exists. Whenever, however, he was questioned about the existence of Brahm, he is recorded to have declared :

Om, Amitya. Measure not with words
The Immeasureable, nor sink the string of thought
Into the Fathomless. Who asks doth err,
Who answers errs. Say naught.†

About six centuries after him, another sage appeared in the extreme west of Asia,

* *Arnold's Light of Asia.*

† *Ibid.*

where the Indian missionaries are stated to have already carried the message of Buddha, and, following most of the moral code of the Indian sage, he announced the universal Fatherhood of God and Brotherhood of man as constituting the Kingdom of Heaven, where all pain must be unknown. He claimed to be the Son of God, who had descended upon earth to carry the burdens of men. He was persecuted, condemned and crucified for what he preached, but his disciples, after him, carried his message far and wide. His simple teachings, however, got immensely transformed, in form and practice, before many centuries had elapsed.

About six centuries still later, however, another teacher appeared in the most idolatrous and superstitious south west of Asia, who, while ridding his country of these degrading professions, asserted the supremacy of God, and, though not listened to and cared for at first, except by the lowly few, pursued his mission with a rare persistence, and, though persecuted and banished from the place of his birth, lived long enough to see his doctrines, involving the principle of the Unity of God and a social system based on the equality of man, conquer and take root. He threatened those, who persecuted him and his followers, with the wrath of God, and thus the Deity he had come to teach about was clothed with attributes, which, in his spiritual mood, he would never have ascribed to God. He declared himself to be the last of the Prophets, which he apparently was amongst the Semitic saints and holy men, and the sole mediator between God and man for all time to come. This last doctrine seems to have led his enthusiastic followers, who were undoubtedly smarting under the grievance of an unjust persecution, to refuse, when they themselves grew in number, to permit that liberty of conscience to their erstwhile persecutors, which the Prophet himself had claimed and been denied. They carried the awe of the scimitar to the countries all around, and centuries of bloody conflict of man against man, tribe against tribe and nation against nation, followed, of which the history is written, as if, in human blood.

In India, the mild and peaceful doctrines of Buddha had already been seriously undermined by the revival of the rigidity of Brahman exclusiveness, when it came in conflict with Muhammadan militantism. Buddhist *Viqharas* were desolated as much as Hindu temples, and the mild non-violent cult of the Indian Sage practically ceased to exist in the country of its birth. The Arabian conquerors of Sindh were followed by hordes of Afghan plunderers, who, according to Wheeler, in his *Short History of India*, "were bitter persecutors of Hindus and "their religion. They broke down temples "and built mosques in their room, as in "the days of Mahmood of Ghazni. A Brahman

"was put to death by a Sultan of this dynasty "for maintaining that the religions of Hindus "and Muhammadans were equally acceptable "in the eyes of God......................
"The Afghans have left a bad name in India. "Their passion for revenge has become a pro-"verb. No man is said to be safe from the "revenge of an elephant, a cobra, or an "Afghan."

Guru Nanak himself has described the political condition of India in the following pathetic terms:

> Kings are butchers, cruelty their knife,
> Sense of duty has taken wings and vanished.
> Falsity prevails like the darkness of the
> darkest night,
> The moon of Truth is visible nowhere.
> I have tired myself in Search, but,
> In the darkness of the Age,
> No path (of righteousness) is visible.
> In Ego, the world is suffering endless pain.
> How shall it be saved, saith Nanak ?*

---

*Var Majh, M. I, *Shlok* 16 (1).

ਕਲ ਕਾਤੀ, ਰਾਜੇ ਕਾਸਾਈ,
ਧਰਮੁ ਪੰਖ ਕਰਿ ਉਡਰਿਆ ।
ਕੂੜੁ ਅਮਾਵਸ, ਸਚ ਚੰਦਰਮਾ,
ਦੀਸੈ ਨਾਹੀ ਕਹਿ ਚੜਿਆ ।
ਹਉਂ ਭਾਲਿ ਵਿਕੁੰਨੀ ਹੋਈ,
ਅੰਧੇਰੈ ਰਾਹ ਨ ਕੋਈ ।
ਵਿਚ ਹਉਮੈ ਦੁਖ ਰੋਈ,
ਕਹੁ ਨਾਨਕ ਕਿਨ ਬਿਧ ਗਤਿ ਹੋਈ ॥

Society was hopelessly disorganized during this period of early Muhammadan invasion and settlement Apart from the invading hordes, whose main object was destruction, massacre and plunder, six dynasties attempted to set themselves up, one after the other, as Sultans of Delhi, during a period of a little over three centuries, but none of them was able to establish a settled government. India's modern historian, Vincent Smith, remarks about this period that "the bloodstained annals of the Sultanate of Delhi, extending over nearly three centuries and a quarter (1206—1526), are not a pleasant reading. They do not repay minute study in detail, except for special purposes. The episodes of Chenghiz Khan and Timur are filled with sickening horrors, and the reigns of several Sultans offer little but scenes of bloodshed, tyranny and treachery. All the Sultans, without exception, were fierce bigots. Even Feroze Shah Tughlak, who exhibited a certain amount of kindly humanity, and felt some desire to do good to his people, was by no means free from the savage intolerance of his contemporaries." Hordes of lawless Afghans over-ran the country, uncontrolled by the Sultans, who nominally held the governance of the country in their hands, and each of them did what was right in his own eyes, and whatever he could do with impunity appeared to him right. The people could find no help against their powerful neighbours, who divided up their lands amongst themselves, as and whenever they pleased, and honour of no woman, whether married or unmarried, was safe, irrespective of age. The so-called Government at Delhi was powerless, even if it desired, to check the misdeeds of these desperados, and it was itself so much disrupted by mutual jealousies and intrigues that it had little time or inclination to exercise any control over them. The annals of this period constitute the darkest page of Indian History.

The indigenous populations of the country, on the other hand, were hopelessly divided amongst themselves. Sunk low in the depths of ignorance and superstition, they had become spiritual slaves. In consequence of the rigidity of the caste system, under the influence of the Brahmanic revival that had turned Buddhism out of India, it had become a horrible sin for a *Shudra* to hear a *Vedic hymn*, which could be adequately punished only by pouring moulten lead into his ears. Hindu could not associate with Hindu. It was an act of pollution to partake of food prepared by another, or to eat inside the same enclosure with him, irrespective of his caste or creed. Intermarriage, which was a common feature in ancient India, became an institution, not existing even in the domain of thought. No man under this system could make his position. His ambition could not be higher than to follow the profession his fathers had followed and to work in it exactly on the same lines as they did. No improved methods of work could be introduced. "Thus life and energy were fettered. Nature had for ever settled for him.... Into his caste a man was born, and was bound to it for life, without regard to poverty or riches, talents, character or skill..... Human dignity and human feelings were bound up in separate castes, and political progress was impossible."* It was amongst these people that the hordes of Afghan freebooters had settled themselves, rendering them political as bad as social, religious as bad as spiritual, slaves.

Mental and moral slavery of the subject races, no less than the exercise of unchecked power and uncontrolled licentiousness of their own, seem to have adversely affected the religious thoughts of the victors as well. Both Hinduism and Muhammadanism were thus corrupted. Purity of heart was no longer one of the essentials of religion. Both the systems had degraded into sets of formalities and ceremonials, which were performed by their votaries like mere automatons. Their objects were no longer understood or sought to be understood. God was no longer an object of faith or worship. The Hindu degenerated into the worship of stocks and stones, and the Muhammadan, with his fanatic tenacity to his professed faith, deemed it enough to repeat certain formulæ

* Sanderson's *Outlines of the History of the World.*

in a language which he no longer understood or cared to understand and began worshipping tombs. While each pretended to be righteous, religious and pious, like the Pharisee of old, neither understood the spirit of religion. Hindu had ceased to be Hindu, whom Krishna of *Bhagwat Gita* would not care to own, and Muhammadan had ceased to be Muhammadan, whom Muhammad himself, if he had somehow reappeared on earth, would have failed to recognize as his followers. Hypocrisy prevailed all round.

Bhai Gur Das, the Sikh Savant and poet, under the Fifth Guru, describes this religious confusion in the following forceful stanzas of his *Vars:*

19. There was quite a confusion in the world when four castes and as many *ashrams* got crystallized. There were *Sanyasis* of ten different denominations, and the *Yogis* set up twelve paths. The *Jangams* and the *Jains* indulged in self-deception and mutual bickering. The Brahmans set up various contests between the *Vedas*, the *Shastras* and the Puranas. The six schools of Philosophy were mutually at daggers drawn, and the thirty-six books added conflict all round. The mystical and magical formulae and alchemy blackened the surface all round by their miraculous pretensions. One was divided up in many and those in very

horrible forms. Thus all were sunk low in superstition in this *Kaliyuga*.

20. Many were the paths that were set up in the world, and thus Muhammad also appeared. He founded what was ruptured into seventy-two sects, and thus was spread enmity and jealousy all round. Fasting, prayers and *eeds* were set up, and the people were thus bound up with further formalities. Then followed *peers*, *prophets*, *walis* and *ghounses*, in many garbs, who produced many *books*. They pulled down temples and built mosques in their places. The heretics and others fought against each other. Sin prevailed all round.

21. Hindus have four castes and Mussalmans four schools. Selfishness, abuse, vanity and useless struggle rage amongst them. Hindus go to the Ganges in Benares, and Mussalmans to the *Kaaba* in Mecca. Mussalmans take to circumcision, while the Hindus are zealous for their thread and forehead mark. These call on Ram and those on Rahim. God is One and both are wandering away from Him. Both have forgotten their *Vedas* and the *Kuran*. The world is lost in avarice. Truth has remained aside and the Brahmans and Mullahs are dying in useless struggles. The order of metempsychosis is not shaken off their heads. *

* *Varan* Bhai Gurdas. I. 19, 20, 21.

The Master himself described this social degeneration in the following hymn :—

Those who pose as benefactors amass wealth by sinful means and give away in charity ;

Those who pose as Gurus wander house to house to impart what they call spiritual formulæ.

Love between man and woman is based on dollar :

They meet at pleasure and depart at will.

None followeth holy scriptures :

Each worshippeth as pleaseth him.

Kazi occupieth seat of Justice,

Counteth beads and repeateth Name of God,

Accepteth bribes and passeth unjust orders,

And, when questioned, he quoteth scripture.

Look at the Hindu:

Who deemeth himself pure for keeping inside kitchen floor;

Taketh advice of the Moslem (oppressor),

And carrieth false tales to persecute his brother.

Yogi hath wives and yet groweth plaites of hair and rubbeth ashes,

Is surrounded by cries of his bastard children :

Yog he hath not attained and path (*juggat*) he hath lost ;

What for he should besmear his head with ashes ?

Such is the condition of the Kaliyuga, saith Nanak,

Self-deception prevaileth everywhere.*

In another hymn the Master remarked thus :—

They devour men alive, and yet they go and bow down to God in *Nimaz* (Moslem prayer) ;

They wear the sacred thread who kill with butcher's knife.

The Brahman cometh to the houses of those slaughterers and bloweth conche and beggeth bread,

He too relisheth the butchery.

Falsehood is their capital,

In Falsehood they trade,

---

* Var Ramkallee, Sh. M. I.

ਸਤੀ ਪਾਪੁ ਕਰਿ ਸਤੁ ਕਮਾਹਿ। ਗੁਰ ਦੀਖਿਆ ਘਰਿ ਦੇਵਣ ਜਾਹਿ।
ਇਸਤ੍ਰੀ ਪੁਰਖੈ ਖਟਿਐ ਭਾਉ। ਭਾਵੈ ਆਵਉ ਭਾਵੈ ਜਾਉ।
ਸਾਸਤੁ ਬੇਦੁ ਨ ਮਾਨੈ ਕੋਇ। ਆਪੋ ਆਪੈ ਪੂਜਾ ਹੋਇ।
ਕਾਜੀ ਹੋਇਕੈ ਬਹੈ ਨਿਆਇ। ਫੇਰੇ ਤਸਬੀਹ ਕਰੇ ਖੁਦਾਇ।
ਵਢੀ ਲੈਕੈ ਹਕੁ ਗਵਾਏ। ਜੇ ਕੋ ਪੁਛੈ ਤਾਂ ਪੜਿ ਸੁਣਾਏ।
ਤੁਰਕੁ ਮੰਤ੍ਰੁ ਕਨਿ ਰਿਦੈ ਸਮਾਇ। ਲੋਕ ਮੁਹਾਵਹਿ ਚਾੜੀ ਖਾਹਿ।
ਚਉਕਾ ਦੇਕੈ ਸੁਚਾ ਹੋਇ। ਐਸਾ ਹਿੰਦੂ ਵੇਖਹੁ ਕੋਇ।
ਜੋਗੀ ਗਿਰਹੀ ਜਟਾ ਬਿਭੂਤ। ਆਗੈ ਪਾਛੈ ਰੋਵਹਿ ਪੂਤਿ।
ਜੋਗ ਨ ਪਾਇਆ ਜੁਗਤਿ ਗਵਾਈ। ਕਿਤੁ ਕਾਰਣਿ ਸਿਰ ਛਾਈ ਪਾਈ
ਨਾਨਕ ਕਲਿ ਕਾ ਇਹ ਪਰਵਾਣੁ। ਆਪੇ ਆਖਣੁ ਆਪੇ ਜਾਣ

They indulge in Falsehood,
And thereby make a living.

Dharam and *Sharam* (sense of duty and honour) have vanished from the country.

Saith Nanak, falsehood prevails all round.

With *Tilak* on forehead and ochre-coloured *dhoti* round waist

(The Hindu) hath dagger in hand and slayeth men,

Weareth blue robes to look respectable,

And accepteth gifts from the *Malechh* (evil minded) to worship the holy books;

Eateth prohibited meat, slaughtered by *Zibah*,

And yet letteth no one to step on the kitchen floor:

Kitchen floor is plastered and prescribed lines drawn around,

And the hypocrite sitteth thereon,

And crieth he, "pollute it not, pollute it not,

Lest this food of mine be defiled and get uneatable."

Their bodies are defiled and they indulge in evil deeds.

Their minds are corrupt, and they wash their mouths (to get pure).

Nanak saith, Remember the Truth,
Be pure that Truth may be realised.*

Such was the condition of Society, which gave rise to a protest of Reform some years before the advent of the Master. This religious

---

* Asa di Var. M. I. 16 (2).

ਮਾਣਸ ਖਾਣੇ ਕਰਹਿ ਨਿਵਾਜ,
ਛੁਰੀ ਵਗਾਇਨਿ ਤਿਨ ਗਲਿ ਤਾਗ।
ਤਿਨ ਘਰਿ ਬ੍ਰਹਮਣ ਪੂਰਹਿ ਨਾਦ,
ਉਨਾ ਭੀ ਆਵਹਿ ਓਈ ਸਾਦ॥
ਕੂੜੀ ਰਾਸਿ ਕੂੜਾ ਵਾਪਾਰੁ।
ਕੂੜੁ ਬੋਲਿ ਕਰਹਿ ਆਹਾਰੁ॥
ਸਰਮ ਧਰਮ ਕਾ ਡੇਰਾ ਦੂਰਿ।
ਨਾਨਕ ਕੂੜੁ ਰਹਿਆ ਭਰਪੂਰਿ॥
ਮਥੈ ਟਿਕਾ ਤੇੜਿ ਧੋਤੀ ਕਖਾਈ।
ਹਥਿ ਛੁਰੀ, ਜਗਤ ਕਾਸਾਈ॥
ਨੀਲ ਬਸਤਰ ਪਹਿਰਿ ਹੋਵਹਿ ਪਰਵਾਣੁ।
ਮਲੇਛੁ ਧਾਨੁ ਲੈ ਪੂਜਹਿ ਪੁਰਾਣੁ॥
ਅਭਾਖਿਆ ਕਾ ਕੁਠਾ ਬਕਰਾ ਖਾਣਾ।
ਚਉਕੇ ਉਪਰ ਕਿਸੈ ਨ ਜਾਣਾ॥
ਦੇਕੈ ਚਉਕਾ ਕਢੀ ਕਾਰ।
ਉਪਰਿ ਆਇ ਬੈਠੇ ਕੂੜਿਆਰ॥
ਮਤ ਭਿਟੈ ਵੇ ਮਤੁ ਭਿਟੈ।
ਇਹ ਅੰਨ ਅਸਾਡਾ ਫਿਟੈ॥
ਤਨਿ ਫਿਟੈ, ਫੇੜ ਕਰੇਨਿ,
ਮਨਿ ਜੂਠੇ ਚੁਲੀ ਭਰੇਨਿ॥
ਕਹੁ ਨਾਨਕ ਸਚੁ ਧਿਆਈਐ।
ਸਚਿ ਹੋਵੈ ਤਾ ਸਚੁ ਪਾਈਐ॥

upheaval, in the words of the late Mr. Justice Mahagovind Ranade of the Bombay High Court, " was heterodox in its spirit of protest against forms and ceremonies and class distinctions based on birth, and was ethical in its preference of a pure heart and of the law of love to all other acquired merits and good works. This religious revival was the work also of the people, of the masses and not of the classes. At its head were saints and prophets, poets and philosophers.

" A few of these saints were women, a few more Muhammadan converts to Hinduism, nearly half of them were Brahmans, while there were representatives in the other half from among all other castes, Marhattas, Kumbhis, tailors, gardeners, potters, goldsmiths, repentant prostitutes and slave girls, even the outcaste Mahars. Much of the interest of this religious upheaval is centred in the facts we have noticed above, as they indicate plainly that the influence of higher spirituality was not confined to this or that class but permeated deep through all strata of society, male and female, high and low, literate and illiterate, Hindu and Mahomedan alike. These are features which the religious history of few other countries can match or reproduce, unless where the elevating influence is the result of a widespread popular awakening. In northern and eastern India a similar movement manifested itself, much at the same time.

Nanak stirred up the Punjab to rise, and made a supreme effort to reconcile Hinduism and Mahomedanism. Chaitanya, in the far east, sought to bring men back from the worship of *shakti* and *kali* to the faith of the Bhagwat, while Ramanand and Kabir, Tulsi Das and Sur Das, Jayadev and Rohi Das, contributed, each in his own way, to the work of spiritual enlightenment."

It may here be pointed out that Ranade seems to have had rather poor knowledge about the Punjab saints, among whom several like Farid were Mohamedans. A few of these saints flourished before Guru Nanak's birth, but none seems to have been able to make any substantial and lasting improvement in the masses. The spirit of protest was, notwithstanding, there. Captain Cunningham speaks of them in relation to the Master as follows :—

"Thus, in the beginning of the sixteenth century, the Hindu mind was no longer stagnant or retrogressive; it had been leavened with Mahometanism and changed and quickened for a new development. Ramanand and Gorakh had preached religious equality and Cheitan had repeated that faith levelled caste. Kabir had denounced images and appealed to the people in their own tongue, and Vullubh had taught that effected devotion was consistent with the ordinary duties of the world.

But these good and able men appear to have been so impressed with nothingness of this life that they deemed the amelioration of man's social condition as unworthy of a thought. They aimed chiefly at emancipation from priestcraft, or from the grossness of idolatry and polytheism. They formed pious associations of contented Quietists, or they gave themselves up to the contemplation of futurity in the hope of approaching bliss, rather than called upon their fellow creatures to throw aside every social as well as religious trammel and to arise a new people freed from the debasing corruption of ages. They perfected forms of dissent rather than planted the germs of nations, and their sects remain to this day as they left them. It was reserved for Nanak to perceive the true principles of reform and to lay those broad foundations which enabled his successor Govind to fire the minds of his countrymen with a new nationality and to give practical effect to the doctrine that the lowest is equal with the highest, in race as in creed, in political rights as in religious hopes."

Such were the times when the Great Master took birth. Political lawlessness, social confusion, religious corruption, moral degradation and spiritual slavery: these were the order of the day. In spite of the periodic appearance of prophets and reformers, who had set high ideals before mankind, the brute in man had still predominated. The galaxy of saints, which appeared in the country a few years before his birth, were obviously the precursers of the Master who came down to warn people against their iniquitous lives, and proclaim the advent of the new Spirit.

The Fourth Guru subsequently sang:

> **From age to age, the Saint appeareth on the earth,**
>
> **Ever to exalt the Righteous.***

Sri Krishna had proclaimed the advent of the Divine Soul on this earth in the following terms:

> **Whenever Dharm declines**
> **And sinfulness becomes ascendant**
> **To protect the Virtuous:**
> **To destroy the Sinful:**
> **To re-establish Righteousness:**
> **From age to age,**
> **I take birth, O Bharat's Son.†**

The Master took birth at Talwandi Rai Bhoe, since called Nankana Sahib, in the Central Punjab, on the Full Moon night of the Kartik lunar month, Sambat 1526 of the era of

---

*Rag. Asa M. IV, *Chhand* (6) 4.

ਜੁਗ ਜੁਗ ਭਗਤਿ ਉਪਾਇਆ ਪੈਜ ਰਖਦਾ ਆਇਆ
ਰਾਮ ਰਾਜੇ ।

†Bhagwad Gita, Discourse IV. 7 and 8.

Vikrmaditya, corresponding to November, 1469. of the Christian era.*

Bhai Gur Das, whose description of the times has been referred to above, subsequently sang :

Sat Gur Nanak hath appeared,
Lo ! Mist hath vanished,
And Light hath shone in the world.

Even as, when the Sun riseth,
The stars disappear,
And darkness gets resplendent with Light.†

His father, *Mehta* Kalu, son of Shiv Ram Das, and mother, Tripta, were middle class Hindus of the Bedi Section of the Khshatrya caste, and were much respected in their community. He was named Nanak, probably after the name of his elder sister, *Bibi* Nanki, who was so called as she was born in her *Nanka* home, the family abode of her maternal grandfather.

---

* One *Janamsakhi* of Guru Nanak fixes the date of birth on the 3rd of Baisakh, Sambat 1526, which date falls in the middle of April 1469. I have adopted the one in November in the text for the reason that the full moon day of *Kartak Paksh*, which fluctuates from year to year in the month of November, and not the April day, is, to this day, observed as Guru Nanak's birthday, wherever there are Sikhs in this province or elsewhere.

† Vars of Bhai Gur Das, I.

ਸਤਿਗੁਰ ਨਾਨਕ ਪ੍ਰਗਟਿਆ, ਮਿਟੀ ਧੁੰਧ, ਜਗ ਚਾਨਣ ਹੋਇਆ ।
ਜਿਉ ਕਰਿ ਸੂਰਜ ਨਿਕਲਿਆ, ਤਾਰੇ ਛਪੇ, ਅੰਧੇਰ ਪਲੋਇਆ ।

Legend says that, at the time of his Birth, which took place at about 1 o'clock at night, when the moon was at its zenith, there were visible some supernatural signs, and the nurse was struck with the beaming face of the Baby, surrounded by a resplendent halo, as the Divine Baby smiled on His advent into this world. It is also recorded that the Pundit Gopal, who was called by *Mehta* Kalu to draw up the new Baby's horoscope, predicted His future greatness. Whatever credence may be given to these traditions, and it must be stated that there is scope for difference of opinion between the believers and non-believers in this respect, we are certain that the Master showed signs in his childhood of a Divine origin and supernatural intelligence. During his infancy he used to melt on seeing misery, and when he was able to walk, the author of Nanak Parkash records instances of his carrying away from home articles of diet and clothing and bestow them on the needy. Instead of taking part in childish sports, He invented new games involving a realisation of the Presence of God, and instructed his companions to practise in them. His parents often got alarmed at his thus getting engaged in the Games of Silence, and called in the village Physician, but nothing abnormal was found in his constitution. These playgrounds are the site of a shrine, called the *Bal Leela* (the Child's frolics), even as His Birth place is the site of a big and beautiful shrine, visited annually by millions of Sikhs.

There was, in those days, a nobleman in Talwandi, Rai Bular by name, the direct eldest descendant of Rai Bhoe, the founder of the village, who was the owner and virtually the ruler of the *Tappa* or District. He was Bhatti Rajput by caste and Muhammadan by religion. The Master was yet in His early age when this nobleman developed a respect for Him, and in him the Master ever afterwards found a faithful and useful friend and disciple.

II.

EARLY LIFE.

The Master was still a boy, when those who had eyes to see and ears to hear, found in him unmistakable signs of a Divine origin. He eschewed all ceremonials and mundane pursuits which led people away from the Lord. At the age of seven, his father put him to the village school, and when the *Pandha*, as the village teacher was called, gave him the first lesson, the Master asked him what he himself knew that he was going to teach him. The question rightly astonished the teacher, but, instead of resenting it, as most of the village school masters are apt to do, the good *Pandha* mentioned all the branches of learning which he had studied and was capable of teaching, and promised that, after the pupil had learned his alphabet, he would be introduced into a knowledge of all of them. This knowledge would make him a useful member of society and enable him to earn wealth. "But have you the knowledge of God, O man," the Master asked. "This learning of thine shall be of no avail to thee in the hereafter. It pertains to matter and is acquired merely to obtain the enjoyments of this world." He then proceeded to tell him what the Divine Knowledge to which he had referred was. "Learn, then, to overcome thy earthly cravings, and let thy heart be filled with devotion to God. Thy mind, thus purified, may be constantly fixed on the Lord, and this shall save thee from punishment for thy past sins." The hymn which the Master sang to the *Pandha* may be translated thus :

Burn thy cravings and mix the ashes into ink ;
Take up thy pure mind for paper ;
Make Devotion thy pen, and thy heart the scribe ;
Take instruction from the Guru and write :

Write the Name, Write the Praise ;
Write of The Endless and The Limitless !

Write, Baba, write, and know how to write ;
Where thy soul shall suffer for writings,
This shall be thy true beacon light.

There, shall they be honoured,
Ever happy and complimented shall they be ;
Selected shall be they,
In whose minds dwelleth the True Name !

By Grace may it be attained,
  All else is talk in vain.

One cometh, another goeth,
  One is called a Governor,

Another is born a beggar, another holdeth
  Royal Court :

It shall be realised hereafter that
  Without the Lord's Name, all hath been
    vain.

Fear Lord. Be afraid of the Future ;
  Thy body shall perish and dissolve.
Those who were called Sultans and Khans
  Have been seen mixing in dust,
Nanak saith, when thou goeth from hence,
  All false attachments shall split.*

---

*Sri Rag; M. I, Sh. ੬.

ਜਾਲ ਮੋਹਿ, ਘਸ ਮਸ ਕਰ,
  ਮਤ ਕਾਗਤ ਕਰ ਸਾਰ,
ਭਾਉ ਕਲਮ ਕਰ, ਚਿਤ ਲਿਖਾਰੀ,
  ਗੁਰ ਪੁਛ ਲਿਖ ਬੀਚਾਰ;
ਲਿਖ ਨਾਮ, ਸਲਾਹਿ ਲਿਖ,
  ਲਿਖ ਅੰਤ ਨ ਪਾਰਾਵਾਰ।

ਬਾਬਾ! ਇਹ ਲੇਖਾ ਲਿਖ ਜਾਣ,
ਜਿਤ ਲੇਖੇ ਤਨ ਪੀੜੀਏ, ਤਿਥੈ ਹੋਵੇ ਸਚਾ ਨਿਸਾਣ ॥
ਜਿਥੈ ਮਿਲਹਿ ਵਡਿਆਈਆਂ,
  ਸਦ ਖੁਸ਼ੀਆਂ ਸਦ ਚਾਉ।
ਤਿਨ ਮੁਖਿ ਟਿਕੇ ਨਿਕਲਹਿ,
  ਜਿਨ ਮਨਿ ਸਚਾ ਨਾਉ।

The teacher was astonished when he heard these words of wisdom, and bowed. The Master attended school no more.* This sudden and unexpected close of the Master's schooling disappointed Kalu, but he hoped that the matters would improve with years. A little later, we find the Master sent to the Persian *Maktab* in the vicinity, but with no better result, from Kalu's point of view, though here, or during the period, the Master seems to have been able to read and write.

At the age of nine, the Master was sent out to graze cattle, belonging to his father. The

---

ਕਰਮਿ ਮਿਲੈ ਤਾਂ ਪਾਈਐ,
ਨਾਹੀ ਗਲੀ ਵਾਉ ਦੁਰਾਉ ॥
ਇਕ ਆਵਹਿ, ਇਕ ਜਾਹਿ ਉਠਿ,
ਇਕਨਾ ਰਖੀਅਹਿ ਨਾਵ ਸਲਾਰ।
ਇਕ ਉਪਾਏ ਮੰਗਤੇ,
ਇਕਨਾ ਵਡੇ ਦਰਵਾਰ।
ਅਗੈ ਗਇਆ ਜਾਣੀਐ,
ਵਿਣੁ ਨਾਵੈ ਵੇਕਾਰ ॥
ਭੈ ਤੇਰੈ ਡਰੁ ਅਗਲਾ,
ਖਪਿ ਖਪਿ ਛਿਜੈ ਦੇਹ।
ਨਾਵ ਜਿਨਾ ਸੁਲਤਾਨ ਖਾਨ,
ਹੋਂਦੇ ਡਿਠੇ ਖੇਹ।
ਨਾਨਕ ਉਠੀ ਚਲਿਆ,
ਸਭਿ ਕੂੜੇ ਤੁਟੇ ਨੇਹ ॥

* The Gurdwara *Patti Sahib* marks the site of the Village School where the Divine pupil taught the teacher.

sun was hot and the Master lied down under the shade of a tree, to take his mid-day rest, while the cattle were grazing. He had just stretched himself on the ground when sleep overcame him. So long as he was asleep, the shade of the tree remained stationary, while shadows of other trees had moved off with the advancing sun. Rai Bular was about this time returning home after his usual round of appraisement of rents of lands, and he and his companions witnessed this phenomenon. On another occasion, Rai Bular saw the Master similarly asleep and a huge cobra piled up close to his head, with its hood spread out to shade the Master's forehead. He called the Master from his sleep and the cobra crawled away. The Rai embraced the boy and kissed him. These spectacles made a deep impression on the nobleman who, ever afterwards, remained one of the most devoted friends and disciples of the Master. On reaching home, Rai Bular sent for Kalu and told him all that he had seen. He advised Kalu never to offend his son and be always respectful to him. Kalu, however, had received complaints that the cattle, whom the Master had taken out for grazing, had ruined the neighbouring crops. The complainants appeared before the Rai and complained of their losses and threatened proceeding to Lahore to prosecute their case, if satisfaction was not meted out to them there. The Master was called and when the complaints were repeated in his presence and the Rai advised payment of the losses, the Master said, "Go and see what losses they have sustained." Rai Bular sent out his men to accompany the complainants and ascertain the loss. These people soon returned and reported, to the astonishment of all, that there had been no damage done to the crops at all. The *Van* tree, where the Master had rested and was guarded by the cobra, is still preserved and close to it stands the shrine, *Malji Sahib*, to commemorate the event, while the Gurdwara *Kiara Sahib* marks the site of the crops which were miraculously restored.

About this time, the occasion came, when according to the tenets of the Hindus, the Master was to wear the sacred thread. The usual preparations were made for the important ceremony, and the family priest, Har Dyal, came to administer the thread to him. "What is this thread and why should I wear it?" questioned the Master, when the *prohit* offered the sanctified thread to him. "It is the sacred *yagyopwit*, by wearing which thou shalt enter upon a new birth in spirit. It would make thee *Dwij* or twice born, and all men of higher castes are enjoined by the *Vedas* to wear it."

"Nay," said the Master, "it is not then the proper thread that you are administering to me and which is to initiate me into a higher life. Thread symbolises man's binding down his passions. If men and women do not check their passions and indulge in shameless sins every day; if their feet, hands, tongue and eyes are not restrained (from committing sins); of what value is this thread? You go threadless then, O Brahman! and having spun one from cotton administer it to others. You perform ceremonies on happy occasions, having received wages for the same, and you pretend to show the way to others from your calendars. Listen and look, O people, this sort of greatness! This man's mind is blind, and still he calls himself a sage!* This thread is purchased from the *bazar*, and is administered by a Brahman, who whispers some teachings into the ears (of the candidate) and claims to be his *guru* (spiritual leader). But when the man dies, this thread is left behind and his spirit goes away threadless. All his thefts, debaucheries, falsehoods, abuses, robberies and scandals follow him, night and day. The thread is spun from cotton by a Brahman, and, on a happy day when a goat is killed for

---

* Asa di Var, M. I, *Shlok* 15 (4).

ਤਗੁ ਨ ਇੰਦ੍ਰੀ, ਤਗੁ ਨ ਨਾਰੀ,
ਭਲਕੇ ਥੁਕ ਪਵੈ ਨਿਤ ਦਾੜੀ,
ਤਗੁ ਨ ਪੈਰੀ, ਤਗੁ ਨ ਹਥੀ,
ਤਗੁ ਨ ਜਿਹਵਾ, ਤਗੁ ਨ ਅਖੀ,
ਵੇੱਤਗਾ ਆਪੇ ਵਤੈ,
ਵਟਿ ਧਾਗੇ ਅਵਰਾ ਘਤੈ ।
ਲੈ ਭਾੜਿ ਕਰੈ ਵੀਆਹੁ,
ਕਢਿ ਕਾਗਲੁ ਦਸੈ ਰਾਹੁ ।
ਸੁਣਿ ਵੇਖਹੁ,, ਲੋਕਾ, ਇਹੁ ਵਿਡਾਣੁ !
ਮਨਿ ਅੰਧਾ, ਨਾਉ ਸੁਜਾਣੁ ॥

a feast, all say, 'Wear.' When it is worn out, it is thrown away and a new one is worn. Look, ye people, this thread should not break, if it has any force or efficacy."*

This baffled the *Pundit*, and he enquired if Nanak would not wear it ; to which the Master replied as follows :—

" Yes, get the thread of contentment from the cotton of compassion, by giving it twists of truth and ties of self-control, and administer it to me, if you can ; for this is the *yagyopwit* which the spirit is in need of. This shall neither be broken, nor get soiled, neither be burnt nor get worn out. Blessed is the man who goeth with this Thread on his person."†

---

* Asa di Var, M. 1, *Shloks* 15 (1) and (2).

ਚਉਕੜਿ ਮੁਲਿ ਅਣਾਇਆ, ਬਹਿ ਚਉਕੇ ਪਾਇਆ,
ਸਿਖਾਂ ਕੰਨਿ ਚੜ੍ਹਾਈਆਂ, ਗੁਰ ਬ੍ਰਾਹਮਣ ਥੀਆ,
ਓਹੁ ਮੋਆ, ਓਹੁ ਝੜਿ ਪਇਆ, ਵੇਤਗਾ ਗਇਆ ।
ਲਖ ਚੋਰੀਆਂ, ਲਖ ਜਾਰੀਆਂ, ਲਖ ਕੂੜੀਆਂ, ਲਖ ਗਾਲਿ,
ਲਖ ਠਗੀਆਂ, ਪਹਿਨਾਮੀਆਂ, ਰਾਤਿ ਦਿਨਸੁ ਜੀਆ ਨਾਲਿ ।
ਤਗੁ ਕਪਾਹਹੁ ਕਤੀਐ, ਬਾਹਮਣੁ ਵਟੇ ਆਇ,
ਕੁਹਿ ਬਕਰਾ ਰਿੰਨੁ ਖਾਇਆ, ਸਭੁ ਕੋ ਆਖੈ 'ਪਾਇ' ।
ਹੋਇ ਪੁਰਾਣਾ, ਸੁਟੀਐ, ਭੀ ਫਿਰਿ ਪਾਈਐ ਹੋਰੁ ;
ਨਾਨਕ ਤਗੁ ਨ ਤੁਟਈ, ਜੇ ਤਗਿ ਹੋਵੈ ਜੋਰੁ ॥

† Asa di Var, M. 1, *Shlok* 15 (1).

ਦਇਆ ਕਪਾਹ, ਸੰਤੋਖੁ ਸੂਤੁ, ਜਤੁ ਗੰਢੀ, ਸਤੁ ਵਟੁ;
ਏਹੁ ਜਨੇਊ ਜੀਅ ਕਾ, ਹਈ ਤਾ ਪਾਂਡੇ ਘਤੁ ।
ਨਾ ਏਹੁ ਤੁਟੈ, ਨਾ ਮਲੁ ਲਗੈ, ਨਾ ਏਹੁ ਜਲੈ, ਨ ਜਾਇ।
ਧੰਨੁ ਸੁ ਮਾਣਸ, ਨਾਨਕਾ, ਜੋ ਗਲਿ ਚਲੇ ਪਾਇ ।

The above incident, and that at the village school, may appear strange in connection with a boy of the Master's age, but it must be remembered that the Master's life is not to be judged by ordinary human standards. While the modern rationalists might ascribe them to precocity of brain development, to a Sikh they are proof positive, if such a proof be ever needed, of the Master's Divine character. The hymns, which were sung by the Master on these occasions, are preserved in the Granth Sahib and their authenticity is unquestioned. There is inherent evidence in these *shabads* that they were addressed by the Master on each occasion to the person who was trying to lead him the way of the ordinary man of the world. The Master wore no thread and His Sikhs have worn none since then.

For some years after this, the Master seems to have been left to himself by his father. Every domestic incident, however, showed that the Master cared little for the things of this world. As a student, as a cowherd and as a young farmer, he was believed to have failed. In the important *yagyopwit* ceremony he had now mortified the Priest, as he had shut up the school teacher, some years before. Each incident that took place convinced Kalu that his son was not an ordinary boy, but he credited him with nothing more than a religious bent of mind. His fear, however, was that he might one day become an anchorite, and leave home and wander about in strange places. When the Master was approaching his eighteenth year, Kalu thaught of a plan to put his son to trade, which would allow him an opportunity for wandering as well as association with holy people. If his interest for trade could be roused, he might yet become an earning member of the family. He thus gave the Master some money and asked him to go out to a market town he desired to visit and buy such goods as would bring good profit. He should enter into a *Khara Sauda*, good bargain, the father told him. He was also provided with an escort, as he was so young, and would require help in his journey. Accompanied by Bala, a Jat servant, entrusted by Kalu with the care of the young would-be trader, the Master left home. A couple of days later, they came across a party of *Sadhus* (ascetics) near Chuharkana, and the Master came to know that the *Sadhus* had had no food for several days. He forthwith placed the whole of his capital at their feet. The good *Sadhus*, however, wanted food, not money. The Master then sent Bala to the market to bring as much provisions as the money could buy ; and they all enjoyed a liberal feast. The place where this feasting of the hungry *Sadhus* took place is the site of a big Gurdwara, which is called *Khara Sauda*, the Good Bargain.

When the Master returned home, after making the good bargain, he stopped in the grove outside the village, and Bala went home and informed Kalu what had happened. Kalu was much exasperated, came to where the Master was sitting, and slapped him in the face "Thou saidst, father, I should make a good bargain. What better bargain than the one I have made could there be?" The site where the man of the world slapped his Divine Son in the face is the site of a Gurdwara, called *Tambu Sahib.* Rai Bular heard of the incident and sent for both the father and the son. He paid the amount that had thus been lost to Kalu but was invested in a good bargain by his son, which Kalu received with considerable relutance. Thenceforward the Rai asked Kalu to have no direct dealings with his son. The Rai undertook to look to the Master's needs thereafter. It was agreed that the Master should be removed from the house of his father, at any rate for some time. The Rai, however, could not then be allowed to accommodate the Master in his own house, however much he desired to do so, for he was a Muhammadan, and in those days, and indeed till recently, the Hindus never associated with Muhammadans at the table. The matter was still under consideration, a few months later, when an incident took place, which may well be called the last straw for Kalu which broke the camel's back. One morning, the Master was returning home after his bath at the village tank, when he met a mendicant, with whom he had a short discourse. When leaving him, the Master handed over to him his brass jug and a gold ring which he was wearing. On his return home Kalu found this out, and turned the Master out of doors.

Turned out of home, with apparently no other place to go to, it being yet, it appears, too early for him to start his Mission, he was still in an unsettled condition, when Rai Bular, his noble disciple, came to his aid. The Rai sent for both, the father and the son, but now not with the object of inducing the former to take the latter back into his home, but to ask him to permit the Master to be sent to his sister, *Bibi* Nanki, who, it may be mentioned, was married some time before this incident to *Lala* Jai Ram, *Diwan* to *Nawab* Daulat Khan Lodhi of Sultanpur Lodhi. Kalu raised no objection to the proposal, and the Master, accompanied by Bala left Talwandi, the scene of his early life, in November 1487, of the Christian era, for an indefinite period. He reached Sultanpur five days after his start, and was affectionately welcomed by his sister and brother-in-law.

This early spiritual bent of mind and indifference to everything earthly may lead some to surmise the Master to have an *ascetic* turn of mind, but it may be pointed out that he never intended to renounce his connection with the world. He had a higher mission. He had come to save the world, and he was fully conscious of the mission he had come for. Notwithstanding his dislike of the ways of the world, and liking, almost affection, for the *faqirs*, he never actually followed them. His early habits were those of reticence, reserve, contemplation and constant solitude. An ordinary man of these habits, under favourable circumstances, and a little inducement, express or tacit, by some ascetic mendicant, would easily have become a mendicant himself. But the Master, though believed to be possessed of this powerful inclination, did not renounce the world, *because he was not to leave the world behind.*

It may here be pointed out that *Maulvi* Ghulam Muhammad, author of the *Siyar-ul-Mutakharin*, who has, in this instance, been quoted by Muhammad Latif, a Mussalman compiler of the "*History of the Punjab*," was probably under the influence of religious enthusiasm and sectarian feeling when he alleged that the Master was a pupil of Seid Hussain, and had passed his early life in the company of that Moslem "devotee." "Nanak was the son of a Grain Merchant," says Ghulam Muhammad, "of the khatri tribe, who, in his youth, was as remarkable for his good character as for the beauty of his person, and for his talents. Nor was he destitute of fortune. There was then, in those parts, a *dervish* of note, called Seid Hussain, a man of eloquence as well as of wealth, who, having no children of his own, and being struck with the beauty of the young Nanak, conceived a great regard for him, and charged himself with his education. As the young man was early introduced to the knowledge of the most esteemed writings of Islam and initiated into the principles of our (Moslem) most approved doctrines, he advanced so much in learning, and became so fond of his studies, that he made it a practice, in his leisure hours, to translate literally and make notes and extracts of our (Moslem) moral maxims. Those which made the deepest impression upon him were written in the idiom of the Punjab, his maternal language. At length he connected them into order, and put them into verse. By this time, he had so far shaken off those prejudices of Hinduism which he had imbibed with his milk, that he became quite another man. His collection became extensive, it took the form of a book, which he entitled Granth, and he became famous in the times of the Emperor Baber, from which time he was followed by multitudes of converts." The sentiments contained in the above quotation are a sufficient justification for its length, and one single inference which can be gathered out of it is the pertinacity with which the Master was claimed by his Muhammadan countrymen also. And this is quite consistent with the sentiments which were expressed by his Moslem followers at his funeral. But, apart from this, so far as facts are concerned, there is hardly any force in the position taken up by the *Maulvi*. He did not perhaps care to note that nowhere in his life do we find the Master as a scholar, except on the two occasions, already noted, when he was put by his father to the vernacular and Persian schools, and where too the period of his scholarship did not extend for more than a few days. Neither is it true that the Master ever left his village and home to study under any one's instruction elsewhere, nor could his orthodox Hindu parents entrust him to a Muhammadan "devotee" to take entire charge of his education, so as to be "early introduced to the knowledge of the most esteemed writings of Islam, and initiated into the principles of our (*Maulvi's*) most approved doctrines." The position taken up by the *Maulvi* that the Master "made it a practice in his leisure hours to translate literally and make notes and extracts of the moral maxims of Islam," wrote them in the idiom of the Punjab, and, connecting them into order and putting them into verse, "he entitled" the collection, that became extensive, as the Granth, is equally untenable. No sayings of the Master, as contained in the Granth Sahib, have been quoted to us, nor could any be found, to show that they were literally translated or even adapted from any maxims peculiar to Islam. On the contrary, we constantly come across his sayings which go against the popularly accepted doctrines of the Mohammadan religion. Nor is it true that the Master connected them into order, for his sayings were preserved for us, partly by the efforts of his successor, Guru Angad, who put those that he heard or found in scattered scraps into writing, and mostly by the noble work of Guru Arjan Dev, who, *and not Guru Nanak*, as the *Maulvi* says, compiled and entitled the Granth.

To show the utter absurdity of the *Maulvi's* assertion it may further be observed that Seid Hussain had not yet begun his life when the Master was already in the height of his glory. One Seid Hussain, we know, was a contemporary of the fifth Guru, by whom were rejected the Seid's sayings as unworthy of being included in the Granth, because they were *not consistent* with the Sikh doctrines. Another Seid Hussain of any importance has not yet been found to have ever existed.

Another note as to the teachership of Guru Nanak has somewhere been struck, which seems to have been generally repeated by most of the European writers, though without quoting their source, that Guru Nanak was a pupil of *Bhagat* Kabir of Benares. It seems likely that the Master did meet Bhagat Kabir at Benares during his travels, and had a discourse with him. But that was when the Master had already fairly advanced in his mission. There is no contemporary authority to justify ascribing to *Bhagat* Kabir the teachership of Guru Nanak. As has been shown above, the Master never left his native village up to the end of his eighteenth year, and then too he left it only for Sultanpore, where *alone* he remained for a period of more than ten years. His biographies do not show that he visited any third place, excepting, of course, the native village of his wife, during this long period, and it is also not shown where he received his lessons from *Bhagat* Kabir, who does not appear to have visited the Punjab.

III.

Business.

The short sketch of the Master's early life which has been given in the last chapter must have shown indications to the reader that Guru Nanak was an uncommon personality. Some superficial readers have vaguely asserted that he took to religious life as he was an utter failure in his secular dealings. This they seem to gather from the over-anxiety of *Mehta* Kalu on account of his son's "failure" in business. It is true that the Master, who had come with a special mission to perform and was not intended to materially prosper, in the world, did give unmistakable signs in his early life showing that he was not made to "succeed" in the world, in the sense in which his father wished him to do. But these men, in bringing this charge against the Master's capacity, seem to utterly lose sight of about 10 years of his life that he spent as *Modi* to the *Nawab* Daulat Khan Lodhi at Sultanpore, where the Nawab held extensive *jagirs*. It was shortly* after his arrival at his sister's, that his brother-in law Jairam, who was the Nawab's *Diwan*, in charge of his Sultanpore estates, secured, at his request, for him, the post of *Modi*, whose duties were to supply necessaries for the Nawab's household and retainers, at the contract rates, which post was then lying vacant. That he quite succeeded in this business will be apparent from what is to follow.

Muhammad Latif, in his *History of the Punjab*, says that Guru Nanak was put in charge of the charity house of the Nawab. But it is to be observed that a *modikhana* is not at all a charity house, nor were the Lodhis ever famous for their charity. The duties of a *modi* were almost those of a supply agent and Storekeeper of to-day. Money was, from time to time, advanced by Government to the *Modi* to purchase and supply, when needed, provisions to the Nawab. At the *modikhana*, the Master used to extend his helping hand to the poor, so much so that, after supplying his own family wants, out of his allowances and profits, he would give away a large part of his earnings in charity

* Only 8 days after his arrival, it is said, he entered upon his duties in the *Modikhana*.

to the needy. This led several times to a *bazar* rumour to the effect that the *modi* was running into bankruptcy and was squandering Government money. These rumours also reached the Nawab, and the accounts were checked. If Muhammad Latif's assertion were true, it would be hard, in the first place, for a man to keep exact accounts of a charity house, so as to put them before competent men to check them; and, in the next place, the Nawab would not have taken action on mere *bazar* rumour that the *modi* was freely distributing Government stores and money in charity to the Faqirs, because that would have been the very performance of his duties. We know for certain that several times and, among them, twice on account of the said *bazar* rumours, these accounts were checked. On one occasion, the Master was even kept in confinement, pending examination of accounts, in a room, which is now the site of a *Gurdwara* called *Kothri Sahib.* We also know that the result of the special audit on each occasion was that the Government of the Nawab was found to owe several hundreds of rupees to Guru Nanak, as the supplies actually taken out had exceeded the money advanced to him till then. Here too, Muhammad Latif's theory fails; for, had it been a charity house, the Nawab could not have been found owing anything to the *modi.*

When the Master had taken over charge of the *modikhana,* Bala, who was still staying with him, asked his permission to return home; but the Master told him to stay on and work with him at the *modikhana*. He told him, in words which could not be mistaken, that the business which he had then entered upon was not *his*; that it was simply a means to pass the days; and that *his real work* was still lying undone before him. Of his *real business* he had given a faint indication in the "True Bargain", already mentioned. The world was suffering from spiritual starvation, and he had come to feed all. Bread supplied to hungry *sadhus* was but a symbol. Thus Bala remained with him throughout the period which he spent in the *modikhana*.

Shortly after his appointment, Guru Nanak married, in June 1488, Sulakhni, daughter of Mul Chand, a resident of Batala, who was employed at Pakhoke Randhawa, in the Gurdaspur District. At Batala, house of Mul Chand has since given place to a beautiful *Gurdawara*, as the place of Guru Nanak's marriage.

At the time of his marriage, he was asked by Mardana* for some gift (*bakhshish*). Instead

---

* Mardana was by caste a *Mirasi*, members of which community play upon the harp and beat drum, on happy occasions, and act as family bards and keep family pedigrees. In the Punjab, these *Mirasis* are also generally employed by the Hindu and Muhammadan population on menial service of various kinds. Each *Mirasi* is attached to a group of families, in his village, who are called his *jajmans* (clients), because they support him and his family, in return for his services.

of giving him a pecuniary gift, the Master gifted him with the divine art of music. Ever afterwards, Mardana was reputed to be one of the best musicians. He also told Mardana in the course of his talk, that his real mission was a different one, for which time was not yet come, and that his present employment was only a stop-gap one.

Guru Nanak had two sons out of his marriage with *Mata* Sulakhni. The first, who was born in July, 1494, was named Sri Chand, and the second, born in February, 1497, was named Lakhmi Chand. On the thirteenth day after the birth of Sri Chand, when the Master returned home from his *modikhana*. for his meals, he found that preparations were being made for the ceremony of purifying the house, from the *sutak*, which, according to the Hindu belief, had attached to all articles in the house on account of the birth in it of a child. In consequence of this supposed pollution, which attached not only to everything in the house but also to every human being belonging to that family and even to that caste, no Brahman is allowed to partake of food or water from that house, or from the hands of the members of that family and caste, till the ceremony of purification is performed. About these preparations the Master seems to have remained ignorant, until his coming home; and, from what was already known of Him, it seems also natural and probable that he was not consulted beforehand. When he came home and saw the *Pundit* with his usual appliances, he enquired what was all that fuss about. The *Pundit* told him that, according to the *Shastras*, everything in the house became polluted by a birth or death therein, and they could only be purified by performing the ceremony which the *Shastras* had laid down for it. But hardly did the *Pundit* conceive that, in laying down this proposition, he was practically admitting that the house could never be pure. "If we do believe in the *sutak*", said the Master, "then there will ever and always be *sutak*. So many living creatures are in the cowdung* and other fuel; no grain of corn is without a living being; nay, the very water, which satiates all, contains living beings. How, then, can this impurity be kept off, when it is always present in our kitchens and food. The *sutak* then cannot be washed away but by the knowledge of God," (by which alone these absurd notions can be got rid of).† The *Pundit* was thus taken unawares and got puzzled. He mustered courage

* People in the Punjab burn dried cakes of cowdung, as fuel.

† Asa di *Var*, M. 1, *Shlok* 18 (1).

ਜੇਕਰਿ ਸੂਤਕਿ ਮੰਨੀਐ, ਸਭ ਤੈ ਸੂਤਕਿ ਹੋਇ ।
ਗੋਹੇ ਅਤੇ ਲਕੜੀ ਅੰਦਰਿ ਕੀੜਾ ਹੋਇ ।
ਜੇਤੇ ਦਾਣੇ ਅੰਨ ਕੇ ਜੀਆ ਬਾਝੁ ਨ ਕੋਇ ।
ਪਹਿਲਾ ਪਾਣੀ ਜੀਉ ਹੈ, ਜਿਤੁ ਹਰਿਆ ਸਭੁ ਕੋਇ ।
ਸੂਤਕੁ ਕਿਉ ਕਰ ਰਖੀਐ, ਸੂਤਕੁ ਪਵੈ ਰਸੋਇ।
ਨਾਨਕ ਸੂਤਕੁ ਏਵ ਨ ਉਤਰੈ, ਗਿਆਨੁ ਉਤਾਰੇ ਧੋਇ ॥

to ask the Master if all the *Vedas** and *Shastras* were mistaken in laying down this ceremony. and if, in his opinion, there was no *sutak*. The Master's reply to this question was in the affirmative. "Covetousness," he said, "was the *sutak* of the mind and lie of the tongue; casting a lustful eye at another's wife, beauty and riches, is that of the eyes, and of the ears is the hearing of false tales. With these impurities man goeth tied up to the city of *Yama* (hell)."† "All superstition is", he continued, "*sutak*, for it recogniseth other than the One. Birth and death are the order of God, by Whose Will is the coming and going (to and from this world). All eating and drinking is pure, for all food is sent by Him. No *sutak* sticks to those who have comprehended the Truth"‡ This ended the disputation, and the *Pundit* was gently asked to leave at once.

* The writer does not take the responsibility for the statement that *Vedas* do lay down the superstitious ceremony which the Hindus have been performing on such occasions. Whether they do or not, the Brahmans are often heard referring vaguely to *Vedas* and *Shastras* in support of what they enjoin upon others to perform

† Asa di *Var*, M. 1, *Shlok* 18 (2)

ਮਨ ਕਾ ਸੂਤਕੁ ਲੋਭੁ ਹੈ, ਜਿਹਵਾ ਸੂਤਕੁ ਕੂੜੁ ।
ਅਖੀ ਸੂਤਕੁ ਵੇਖਣਾ, ਪਰ ਤ੍ਰਿਅ, ਪਰ ਧਨ, ਰੂਪੁ ।
ਕੰਨੀ ਸੂਤਕੁ ਕੰਨਿ ਪੈ, ਲਾਇ ਤਬਾਰੀ ਖਾਹਿ ।
ਨਾਨਕ ਹੰਸਾ ਆਦਮੀ, ਬਧੇ ਜਮ ਪੁਰਿ ਜਾਹਿ ॥

‡ Asa di *Var*, M. 1, *Shlok* 18 (3).

ਸਭੋ ਸੂਤਕੁ ਭਰਮੁ ਹੈ, ਦੂਜੈ ਲੱਗੈ ਜਾਇ ।
ਜੰਮਣੁ ਮਰਣਾ ਹੁਕਮੁ ਹੈ, ਭਾਣੈ ਆਵੈ ਜਾਇ ।
ਖਾਣਾ ਪੀਣਾ ਪਵਿਤ੍ਰੁ ਹੈ, ਦਿਤੋਨੁ ਰਿਜਕੁ ਸੰਬਾਹਿ
ਨਾਨਕ ਜਿਨੀ ਗੁਰਮੁਖਿ ਬੁਝਿਆ, ਤਿਨਾ ਸੂਤਕੁ ਨਾਹਿ ॥

One day, the Master was weighing out provisions to the steward of the Nawab. The weight in his scale-pan was a five-seer one, and he had to count the number of times he was weighing out the article. When, in so counting, he reached the number thirteen (*tera*, which in Punjabi also means 'thine'), his mind at once travelled beyond the earthly thing that he was weighing, and was absorbed in the Almighty Father, calling *tera*, *tera*, *tera* (Thine, Thine, Thine), while mechanically he went on weighing out the provisions. His mind, transfixed on the Divine, would not stoop to earthly thing, and all subsequent *dharans* (weighments) went for the *thirteenth*. At this juncture, the attention of Bala, the servant, was attracted, and he at once advanced and caught his arm to stop him from weighing. The article was re-weighed, and lo, it was only 65 seers and no more.

At his home, he performed all the duties incidental to a married life. He looked after the expenses of his wife and family, and saw that all necessaries were supplied to them properly. No doubt, he did not lay by anything and did not hoard money ; and, on this account, his wife sometimes complained. Otherwise, as regards her necessaries and comforts, she had no cause to murmur. Whatever he could spare from his family expenses, which were of course very moderate, he spent in meeting the wants of others.

For about 10 years, Guru Nanak led a virtuous married life. By doing business he showed to the world that, if he had subsequently left the worldly transactions, it was not on account of his failure therein. He was capable of doing business and succeeding in life, as much as any virtuous man could be accredited with success. But his mission was a higher and nobler one. He could live in the world, earn a living and support a family, as he had done ; but he had come to save mankind from the dreadful traps of materialism. What is the " world " but the various entanglements, which hinder man's development and advancement towards ideal perfection ? Many reformers have been frightened by the 'world', and hence have become timid and cowardly cold and indifferent to reform. Matthew Arnold wrote the following beautiful sonnet on the " Triumphs of the World " over reformers, who have, from time to time, tried " to recast her new ":—

So far as I conceive the world's rebuke
To him address'd who would recast her new,
Not from herself her fame of strength she took,
But from their weakness who would work her rue,
'Behold', she cries, 'so many rages lull'd,
'So many fiery spirits quite cool'd down ;
'Look how so many valours, long undull'd,

" After short commerce with me fear my frown !

'Thoù too when thou against my crimes wouldst cry

'Let thy foreboded homage check thy tongue !'

The world speaks well ; yet might her foe reply :

" Are wills so weak ? then let not mine wait long :

' Hast thou so rare a poison ? let me be

' Keener to slay thee, lest though poison me ?

But the Master showed to the world that he was above the type of reformers who " fear her frown " after short commerce with her. He proved, in the course of about 10 years, that he was not afraid of the world's rebuke ; that He was never to render homage to her ; that *His will* was not weak ; and that He was strong enough to meet her face to face, and yet be out of her snares. Born with, and for, His mission, to save others from the world's dreadful jaws, to him that "rare poison" was harmless ; for, like the lotus leaf, he had not fixed his mind in the waters of the world. He was detached from, though in so close proximity to, her. Living in, and for, the world, he was to raise the latter to his own level, rather than fall a prey to her.

IV

THE MASTER'S MASTER.

No chronicles give the details how the Master spent His time at Sultanpur, but what can be gathered from the available material is that he used to get out of his bed long before dawn, washed at the B'een stream and remained absorbed in his Spiritual contemplations till late in the morning. He then attended to his work at the *Modikhana*, and remained there throughout the day except at noon, when he would go home for his meals. At the *Modikhana*, he was often found engaged in spiritual conferences with the *Sadhus*, who approached him there. It was here and during this period that Bhagirat of Mailsian, near Sultanpur, got his spiritual instruction from him and then recommended Man Sukh of Lahore for similar instruction. Both were duly blessed by the Master.

In the year 1497 of the Christian era, he went out one morning as usual before dawn to the B'een for his morning ablutions, attended by a servant ; and having undressed and handed over his clothes to the servant, he plunged into the water, at the place which since then is called *Sant Ghat,* and was seen no more. All efforts to recover the body proved futile, though no means which the resources of the Nawab himself could manage to be adopted were spared. The Bazar was full of wild gossip and many theories were invented and charges laid against him. The most common of them was one of bankruptcy. The news were also conveyed about these charges to the Nawab and full investigation was ordered. When, however, the accounts were checked, the Nawab was found to owe a considerable amount to the *Modi* and there was a large surplus stock. Thus most of the theories which the tongue of scandal could invent crumbled to dust. People then deplored the sad accident which had thus cut short such a popular life in the town and the greatest regret felt was that even the dead remains could not be found. Of all the population, it was only *Bibi* Nanki, who did not believe that her Divine brother was lost. She consoled her own husband and *Mata* Sulakhni, both of whom were extremely grieved, the latter being then in a delicate condition. She directed the servant to remain in attendance with the Master's clothes at the *Ghat* and wait his return and she herself remained in continuous prayer

On the other hand, the Master himself remained in continuous and full communion with God, unobserved by a human eye. It is here that His biographers have graphically described the Master's journey to, and attendance at, the Court of the Almighty Father, in obedience to the Command that had been received. The legend records that the Almighty Father gave Him a goblet, full of the Elixir of God's Name, which the Master drank, and the Voice of the Lord commanded him thus :

Thou art welcome, O Nanak, that hath absorbed thyself in the Name. Do go hence now and do the Work for which Thou wast born.

People of the *Kaliyuga* have adopted horrible practices and are extremely degraded in mind ;

They worship a variety of gods, have forsaken the Name, and are immersed in sin.

Go thou, spread Love and Devotion to the Name, and thus lighten the burdens of the Earth.

Go thou, and glorify the Name of God and destroy hypocrisy.

The Master thereupon prayed for Light and Succour, and, in answer to this, He was blessed with the First Principle of the creed by the Lord Himself, thus :

> *There is but One God, True is His Name, the Creator, the All-pervading, Devoid of fear and enmity, Immortal, Unborn, Self-existent ; Realise by the Master's Grace* '

And the Supreme Voice continued :

GO, NANAK, PREACH THIS AND DEPEND NOT ON WHAT IS CREATED.

WHOMSOEVER THOU SHALT BLESS WITH THY GRACE SHALL BE THE RECIPIENT OF MY GRACE. GO AND PREACH THY MISSION. THOU BE THE DIVINE MASTER.

Having thus been commanded, the Master redescended to the Earth and re-appeared at the *Sant Ghat* on the B'een. It was full three days after his disappearance.

The Master Himself has also referred to his attendance at the Divine Court in one of his songs :

I, the bard of the Lord, was summoned to the Court of the True and Supreme Master

He graced me by granting me the *Khilaat* of the Praise of the True Name,

He fed me with the Divine Nectar of the Name of the Great Truth.*

---

* *Var* Majh, M. 1, 27.

ਢਾਢੀ ਸਚੈ ਮਹਲ ਖਸਮ ਬੁਲਾਇਆ ।

ਸਚੀ ਸਿਫਤ ਸਲਾਹ ਕਪੜਾ ਪਾਇਆ ।

ਸਚਾ ਅੰਮ੍ਰਿਤ ਨਾਮ ਭੋਜਨ ਆਇਆ ।

Bhai Gurdas has also referred to it thus :

The Baba (Nanak) first obtained Grace at the Divine Court and *then* performed austerities :

....

....

He went to the Divine Court, and from there received the treasure of the Name and humility.

He from there saw, in his contemplation, that the entire world was in agony,

And that, without the Master, it was all dark,

Humanity, he saw, was crying in anguish :

He then adopted the garb of a monk, and started the *Udasi* order ; and issued out to reform the world and its people.*

---

* *Vars* of Bhai Gurdas, 1, 24.

ਪਹਲਾ ਬਾਬੇ ਪਾਇਆ ਬਖ਼ਸ ਦਰ, ਪਿਛੋਂ ਦੇ ਫਿਰ ਘਾਲ ਕਮਾਈ।

....

....

ਬਾਬਾ ਪੈਧਾ ਸਚ ਖੰਡ, ਨੌ ਨਿਧ ਨਾਮ ਗ੍ਰੀਬੀ ਪਾਈ।

ਬਾਬਾ ਦੇਖੇ ਧਿਆਨ ਧਰ, ਜਲਤੀ ਸਭ ਪ੍ਰਿਥਮੀ ਦਿਸ ਆਈ।

ਬਾਝਹੁ ਗੁਰੂ ਗੁਬਾਰ ਹੈ, ਹੈ ਹੈ ਕਰਦੀ ਸੁਣੀ ਲੁਕਾਈ।

ਬਾਬੇ ਭੇਖ ਬਣਾਇਆ, ਉਦਾਸੀ ਦੀ ਰੀਤ ਚਲਾਈ।

ਚੜ੍ਹਿਆ ਸੋਧਨ ਧਰਤ ਲੁਕਾਈ॥

When he appeared he was pleased to find the servant still present with his clothes, and having then clothed himself, he blessed the servant and proceeded to the *Modikhana*, where he distributed all the stores to the poor and the needy, and went out of the town once more and sat down in the graveyard and was absorbed in deep contemplation. When he recovered from his Trance, he uttered the keynote of his Mission, "There is no Hindu, there is no Mussalman."

The utterance of this paradox soon raised a commotion against him, and led many to conjecture that either he was possessed of an evil spirit or had turned insane. The news of his reappearance reached the Nawab, who lent ear to the gossip and was anxious to get his *Modi* cured of his supposed disease or evil spirit. He deputed *Mullas* and physicians for the treatment.

The *Mulla* came forward on this and began his incantations to dispossess the Master of the supposed evil spirit. He also began writing the incantation on a piece of paper with the object of tying the amulet round the Master's neck. The Master thereupon sang a couplet thus:

No room to gather fruit for him whose crop decayed,

Accursed life of him who selleth Name of
God.*

This, however, did not deter the Mullah from completing his charms and formulae. He was anxious to obtain his expected reward from the Nawab. Having finished his ceremonies, he addressed the supposed spirit, possessing the Master, by putting the usual question, "Who art thou."† The following was the reply that came :—

Some call me *bhut*, some call *baital*,
Some human being Nanak call.‡

On this, it was declared that no spirits had possessed him but that he was mad ; to which the Master replied in the same strain, as follows :

Aye, mad is Nanak afer Lord
He recogniseth none but Him

---

* *Var* Sarang, M. 1, *Shlok* 20 (1).

ਖੇਤੀ ਜਿਨ ਕੀ ਉਜੜੈ ਖਲਵਾੜੇ ਕਿਆ ਥਾਉ ।
ਧ੍ਰਿਗੁ ਤਿਨਾਂ ਕਾ ਜੀਵਿਆ, ਜਿ ਲਿਖਿ ਲਿਖਿ ਵੇਚਹਿ ਨਾਉ ॥

† The prevailing impression with these people is that, as long as a man is so possessed, it is the spirit that acts and speaks in him, and not he himself. Therefore, the question is put in this form, as being addressed directly to the spirit. It is believed that if there is in reality any evil spirit, it is bound to disclose itself to the adept who puts such a question.

‡ Rag Maru, M. 1, Sh. 7 (1).

ਕੋਈ ਆਖੈ ਭੂਤਨਾ, ਕੋ ਕਹੈ ਬੇਤਾਲਾ ।
ਕੋਈ ਆਖੈ ਆਦਮੀ ਨਾਨਕ ਵੇਚਾਰਾ ।

He mad alone, who fears God,
And recogniseth none but Him.

He mad alone who recketh none but One,
Abideth in Will Supreme, relieth not in wit;

He mad alone who loveth One,
Himself deemeth low, others high,*

The *Byd* (Physician) now stepped forward to diagnose the ailment from which the Master was believed to be suffering. He felt the Master's pulse, and he found the Master's heart beating high. He began prescribing a medicine, but the Master addressed him thus:

Called thou art, O *Byd*, to cure;
Feeleth thou my pulse;
Simple thou art, O *Byd* my dear,
Knoweth thou not the pain in heart.

---

* Rag Maru, M. 1, Sh. 7 (2), (3) (4).

ਭਇਆ ਦਿਵਾਨਾ ਸਾਹੁ ਕਾ ਨਾਨਕ ਬਉਰਾਨਾ,

ਹਉ ਹਰਿ ਬਿਨੁ ਅਵਰੁ ਨ ਜਾਨਾ।

ਤਉ ਦਿਵਾਨਾ ਜਾਣੀਐ ਜਾ ਭੈ ਦੇਵਾਨਾ ਹੋਇ।

ਏਕੀ ਸਾਹਿਬ ਬਾਹਰਾ ਦੂਜਾ ਅਵਰੁ ਨ ਜਾਣੈ ਕੋਇ।

ਤਉ ਦੇਵਾਨਾ ਜਾਣੀਐ ਜਾਂ ਏਕਾ ਕਾਰ ਕਮਾਇ।

ਹੁਕਮੁ ਪਛਾਣੈ ਖਸਮ ਕਾ, ਦੂਜੀ ਅਵਰ ਸਿਆਣਪ ਕਾਇ।

ਤਉਂ ਦੇਵਾਨਾ ਜਾਣੀਐ ਜਉ ਸਾਹਿਬੁ ਧਰੇ ਪਿਆਰੁ।

ਮੰਦਾ ਜਾਣੈ ਆਪ ਕਉ, ਅਵਰੁ ਭਲਾ ਸੰਸਾਰੁ ॥

Go thy home, dearest *Byd*,
  Take from me no sigh,
I am steeped in Love of God,
  For whom prescribeth medicine thou.
Able physician thou be, O *Byd*,
  Shouldst thou diagnose disease,
And then find a potion which
  Removeth cause of pain.
Where pain is, Cure there be;
  Byd cometh to prescribe;
My body crieth, my spirit demandeth,
  Byd yet prescribeth not.
Go thy way, *Byd*;
  Saints alone know my pain;
Lord hath granted pain to me;
  He alone shall relieve it too.*

Upon this, the *Mulla*, the *Kazi*, the Physician and others declared that the *Modi* was neither possessed of spirits, nor was he mad or otherwise diseased, that he had develop-

---

* *Vide* Bhai Bala's *Janamsakhi*. In it this story of physician is stated as having occurred long before this occasion. The first two lines also occur in *Var* Malar, M. 1, *Shlok* 3 (1).

ਵੈਦੁ ਬੁਲਾਇਆ ਵੈਦਗੀ; ਪਕੜਿ ਢੰਢੋਲੇ ਬਾਂਹ;
ਭੋਲਾ ਵੈਦ ਨ ਜਾਣਈ ਕਰਕ ਕਲੇਜੇ ਮਾਹਿ ॥
ਜਾਹਿ ਵੈਦ ਘਰ ਆਪਣੈ; ਮੇਰੀ ਆਹਿ ਨ ਲੇਹੁ ।
ਹਮ ਰਤੇ ਸਹੁ ਆਪਣੇ ਤੂ ਕਿਸ ਦਾਰੂ ਦੇਹੁ ?
ਬੈਦਾ ਬੈਦ ਸੁਜਾਨ ਤੂ ਪਹਲਾ ਰੋਗ ਪਛਾਣ ;
ਐਸਾ ਦਾਰੂ ਲੋੜ ਲਹੁ ਜਿਸ ਵੰਞੇ ਰੋਗਾਂ ਘਾਣ ।
ਦੁਖ ਲਗੇ ਦਾਰੂ ਘਣਾ ਬੈਦ ਖਲੋਇਆ ਆਇ;
ਕਾਇਆ ਰੋਵੈ, ਹੰਸ ਪੁਕਾਰੇ, ਵੈਦ ਨ ਦਾਰੂ ਲਾਇ ।
ਜਾਇ ਬੈਦ ਘਰ ਆਪਣੇ ਜਾਣੇ ਕੋਇ ਮਕੋਇ ।
ਜਿਨ ਕਰਤੇ ਦੁਖ ਲਾਇਆ, ਨਾਨਕ ਲਾਹੇ ਸੋਇ ॥

ed Love of God and indifference to things earthly, and that he must therefore be left to shake off his spiritual trance himself. They held a counsel with the Nawab, who then proposed to the Master that if he was really devoted to One God and recognised no distinction between Hindu and Muhammadan, as his words implied, he might accompany them to the *Masiid*, there to pray to the One God, the God of all universe, in their company. They also, he said, acknowledged that "there was no God but God." "Yea, I shall pray with ye, if ye but pray to God," the Master replied, and he accompanied them to the *Masjid*. All began praying in their fashion, but the Master joined them not. When they finished, the Nawab questioned the Master why he had broken his word and had refrained from praying to the common God of the Hindu and Mussalman and of all others. "But who was praying to God that I might have joined, O Nawab." "I was doing so and others as well," the Nawab replied. "Nay," said the Master,

Thou struckst thy forehead on the earth,
Thy mind did travel in the sky;
Well, listen, Daulat Khan Afghan
To Kabul horses wert to buy."*

---

* *Bhai* Bala's *Janamsakhi*.

ਮੱਥਾ ਠੋਕੇ ਜ਼ਿਮੀ ਪਰ, ਦਿਲ ਉਠੇ ਅਸਮਾਨ,
ਘੋੜੇ ਕਾਬਲ ਖ਼ਰੀਦ ਕਰੇ, ਦੌਲਤ ਖਾਂਨ ਪਠਾਨ ॥

The Nawab was much confused, but he mustered courage to say that there were so many others and among them the noble *Kazi*, to which the Master rejoined that the mind of the *Kazi* was at the time of the prayer following his colt, which he had noticed loosened in his courtyard, when he had left home that morning, and he was thinking if any of his servants had secured the animal or not and whether it had not fallen into the deep pit, he had in his yard. Both hung down their heads in shame, upon which the Master delivered the first of his sermons, after his renunciation. In it the Master put an entirely new meaning on Islam. He pulled down the vanities of the Muhammadans and taught them how they can be real Moslems, acceptable at the Lord's Court.

" It is difficult," said the Master, "to be a real Mussalman. Possess the necessary qualities, before ye call yourselves Moslem. First of all, Love your faith, and leave off vanity and pride of riches. Be humble but firm, and shake off dread of death and of life. Submit to God with patience, believe in Him and sacrifice self unto Him. Be merciful to all living beings; then alone you can call yourselves Mussalman.*

---

* *Var* Majh, M. 1, *Shlok* 8 (1).

ਮੁਸਲਮਾਣੁ ਕਹਾਵਣੁ ਮੁਸਕਲੁ ਜਾਂ ਹੋਇ ਤਾਂ ਮੁਸਲਮਾਣੁ ਕਹਾਵੈ ।
ਅਵਲਿ ਅਉਲਿ ਦੀਨੁ ਕਰਿ ਮਿਠਾ, ਮੁਸਕਲ ਮਾਨਾ ਮਾਲੁ ਮੁਸਾਵੈ ।
ਹੋਇ ਮੁਸਲਿਮੁ ਦੀਨ ਮੁਹਾਣੈ। ਮਰਣ ਜੀਵਣ ਕਾ ਭਰਮੁ ਚੁਕਾਵੈ ।
ਰਬ ਕੀ ਰਜਾਇ ਮੰਨੇ ਸਿਰ ਊਪਰਿ ਕਰਤਾ ਮੰਨੇ ਆਪੁ ਗਵਾਵੈ ।
ਤਉ ਨਾਨਕ ਸਰਬ ਜੀਆ ਮਿਹਰੰਮਤਿ ਹੋਇ ਤ ਮੁਸਲਮਾਣੁ ਕਹਾਵੈ ॥

Compassion should be your Masjid ; sincerity your prayer-carpet; and honesty your *Al Qoran*. Let modesty be your circumcision, and amiability your fasting, which befit a Mussalman. Let good deeds be your *Kaaba*, truth the Prophet's *Kalma* and charity your prayer. Acquire meekness for your rosary and thus be honoured before God.* What is due to others is like pork to one (Mussalman) and beef to the other (Hindu) and remember that the prophet too will claim ye only if ye will not eat what is so forbidden. Mere talk cannot take ye to paradise. Truth and sincerity alone will lead to your emancipation. Whatever is unlawful for ye does not become lawful by being spiced. So too, by these false ways of yours, you will have but false things ; (in other words, truth will not be acquired by falsity, although seasoned with appearances).† There are five prayers

---

* *Var* Majh, M. 1, *Shlok* 7 (1).

ਮਿਹਰ ਮਸੀਤਿ, ਸਿਦਕੁ ਮੁਸੱਲਾ, ਹਕੁ ਹਲਾਲੁ ਕੁਰਾਣੁ ।
ਸ਼ਰਮ ਸੁੰਨੱਤ ਸੀਲੁ ਰੋਜਾ, ਹੋਹੁ ਮੁਸਲਮਾਣੁ ।
ਕਰਣੀ ਕਾਬਾ, ਸਚੁ ਪੀਰੁ ਕਲਮਾ, ਕਰਮ ਨਿਵਾਜ ।
ਤਸਬੀ ਸ਼ਾਂਤਿ ਸੁਭਾਵਸੀ, ਨਾਨਕ ਰਖੈ ਲਾਜ ॥

† *Var* Majh, M. 1, *Shlok* 7 (2).

ਹਕੁ ਪਰਾਇਆ ਨਾਨਕਾ ਉਸੁ ਸੂਅਰ ਉਸੁ ਗਾਇ ।
ਗੁਰ ਪੀਰੁ ਹਾਮਾ ਤਾਂ ਭਰੇ ਜਾਂ ਮੁਰਦਾਰੁ ਨ ਖਾਇ ।
ਗਲੀ ਭਿਸ਼ਤਿ ਨ ਜਾਈਐ ਛੁਟੈ ਸਚੁ ਕਮਾਇ ।
ਮਾਰਣ ਪਾਹਿ ਹਰਾਮ ਮਹਿ, ਹੋਇ ਹਲਾਲਿ ਨ ਜਾਇ ।
ਨਾਨਕ ਗਲੀ ਕੂੜੀਈ, ਕੂੜੋ ਪਲੈ ਪਾਇ ॥

for five different times and with as many different names. Let then " truth " be your first prayer ; " lawful acquisition," the second ; " charity," the third ; " sincerity of mind," the fourth ; and " praise of God " the fifth. Let good actions be your *Kalma* : and then alone will you be Mussalman. Otherwise, remember that, on account of the falsity of ways, only false things are acquired by people who deal in false things."*

So saying, the Master left the Masjid and was followed by a large number of people. But the Nawab wanted to ask his wish with regard to the money that was due to him from the State. He, however, needed it no longer and advised the Nawab to spend it in meeting the wants of the poor.

After this, the Master paid a visit to his sister, *Bibi* Nanki, and to his wife and son, and then again left the town. It was with difficulty that he could prevail upon his wife to remain at home, while he *had* to go abroad. His wife was strongly opposed to his leaving home. But his sister, *Bibi* Nanki, did not press him

---

* *Var* Majh M. 1, *Shlok* 7 (3).

ਪੰਜਿ ਨਿਵਾਜਾਂ ਵਖਤ ਪੰਜਿ, ਪੰਜਾਂ ਪੰਜੇ ਨਾਉਂ ।
ਪਹਿਲਾ ਸਚੁ ਹਲਾਲੁ ਦੁਇ, ਤੀਜੀ ਖੈਰ ਖੁਦਾਇ,
ਚਉਥੀ ਨੀਅਤਿ ਰਾਸਿ ਮਨੁ, ਪੰਜਵੀ ਸਿਫਤਿ ਸਨਾਇ ।
ਕਰਣੀ ਕਲਮਾ ਆਖਿਕੈ, ਮੁਸਲਮਾਣੁ ਸਦਾਇ ।
ਨਾਨਕ ਜੇਤੇ ਕੂੜਿਆਰ, ਕੂੜੈ ਕੂੜੀ ਪਾਇ ॥

much, for she fully understood her brother, from his very childhood, and was proud of him. The fact that *Bibi* Nanki was the only one of his relatives, who from the outset, instead of opposing him in his mission, encouraged him and even assisted him, in her own way, is remarkable, and testifies to her devotion to him. She asked if she shall be favoured with his *darshans* occasionally, and the Master told her that he shall be with her whenever she thaught of him. To *Mata* Sulakhni, he explained that he had received the Divine Call and will not be able to tarry long with her, at any rate till his Mission was performed. It is but natural that she should be nervous in view of being left alone. She was also at the time in a delicate state of health, and the Master agreed to stay in the vicinity till her confinement was over. He counselled her to have perfect faith in the Lord, Whose Commands he had but to obey. After her recovery he advised her to go to and stay with her parents till he returned and settled down once more. *Mata* Sulakhni acquiesced but not without much reluctance. The Master consoled her and went back to the graveyard.

V.

Renunciation.

The news of the Master's Renunciation. and of what followed it, spread rapidly and soon reached Talwandi. *Mehta* Kalu sent the family bard, Mardana, to Sultanpur to verify the rumour and to persuade the Master, if need be, to abandon his idea of *Faqiri*. Mardana was instructed to strain every argument to induce him to come back home. He was to be reminded of all his relations, and his particular attention drawn to the requirements of his wife and family, who would be unprotected and unprovided for after he had gone. Mardana was instructed to appeal to the Master's heart, which was known to play the foremost part in his constitution.

Mul Chand, father of the Master's wife. *Mata* Sulakhni, was full of indignation when he received the news. He came down to Sultanpur personally, and, having learnt the details of the Renunciation and what followed it from his daughter, met the Master in the graveyard. Such, however, was his resentment when he saw the Master that he indulged in unceasing raillery and banter, which the Master heard with perfect equanimity, and, out of his regard for the father of his wife, answered not. When his fury was thus expended, Mul Chand went back to the town, and later returned to the Master, accompanied by a *Pundit*, Shiama by name, to argue with the Master somewhat more calmly. Shiama addressed the Master respectfully but represented his Renunciation as a childish game, calculated to lower his family in the eyes of the public. The burthen of Shiama's argument was that the Master may abandon the dirty surroundings of the graveyard and return home and there engage himself in philosophic contemplation of the relations between *Jiwa* and *Ishwara*, and work up to the attainment of eternal bliss. On this the Master sang thus :

> Human soul, an innocent babe, dwelleth in the castle of sand ; subject it is to the evil cravings :

> There is the mystery of two mothers (Matter and Ignorance) and two fathers (*Jiwa* and *Ishwara*), which needeth solution, O Pundit

Listen, O Pundit, and explain to me
How may I meet the Lord of my Soul.*

Mul Chand, whose fury was already exhausted, intervened and remarked why he had married and begotten a family if these were his ideas, upon which the Master sang the second stanza of the hymn :

Fire existeth within the green tree, and
water runneth alongside it ;

The sun and the moon (*i. e.*, the Light) are
within, and yet the Soul knoweth it not.†

Upon this, Shiama reminded him that, if all was within, he could engage in spiritual contemplations while living at home and doing

---

*Rag Basant M. 1.

ਰਾਜਾ ਬਾਲਕੁ, ਨਗਰੀ ਕਾਚੀ,
ਦੁਸ਼ਟਾਂ ਨਾਲਿ ਪਿਆਰੋ ।
ਦੁਇ ਮਾਇ, ਦੁਇ ਬਾਪਾ ਪੜੀਅਹਿ,
ਪੰਡਿਤ ਕਰਹੁ ਬਿਚਾਰੋ ॥ ੧ ॥
ਸੁਆਮੀ ਪੰਡਿਤਾ, ਤੁਮ ਦੇਹੁ ਮਤੀ,
ਕਿਨ ਬਿਧਿ ਪਾਵਉ ਪ੍ਰਾਨ ਪਤੀ ॥
੧ ॥ ਰਹਾਉ ॥

† *Ibid.*

ਭੀਤਰਿ ਅਗਨਿ ਬਨਾਸਪਤਿ ਮਉਲੀ,
ਸਾਗਰ ਪਿੰਡੈ ਪਾਇਆ ।
ਚੰਦੁ ਸੂਰਜੁ ਦੁਇ ਘਰ ਹੀ ਭੀਤਰਿ ।
ਐਸਾ ਗਿਆਨੁ ਨਾ ਆਇਆ ॥੨॥

his daily business, to which the Master replied in the third stanza:

> Knowledge that God pervadeth within cometh only if, unattached to Matter, one may use it for good;
>
> Knowledge of His Attributes cometh only when riches of contentment are collected within.†

Mul Chand got impatient during this discourse and could not resist remarking that he was a *sirari* (mono-maniac) and, without listening to what others say, goes on talking in riddles. Upon this remark, the Master concluded his song thus:

> Listeneth not and heedeth not he who abideth permanently with those (Matter and Ignorance);
>
> And thus moveth between two extremes, saith Nanak, the S'lave.†

---

* *Ibid.*

ਰਾਮ ਰਵੰਤਾ ਜਾਣੀਐ ।
ਇਕ ਮਾਈ ਭੋਗੁ ਕਰੇਇ ॥
ਤਾਕੇ ਲਖਣ ਜਾਣੀਅਹਿ ।
ਖਿਮਾ ਧਨੁ ਸੰਗ੍ਰਹੇਇ ॥ ੩ ॥

† *Ibid.*

ਕਹਿਆ ਸੁਣਹਿ ਨ ਖਾਇਆ ਮਾਨਹਿ ।
ਤਿਨ੍ਹਾ ਹੀ ਸੇਤੀ ਵਾਸਾ ।
ਪ੍ਰਣਵਤਿ ਨਾਨਕ, ਦਾਸਨ ਦਾਸਾ ।
ਖਿਨ ਤੋਲਾ ਖਿਨੁ ਮਾਸਾ ॥ ੪ ॥

Shiama bowed to the Master and was blessed with Grace and both left wiser than they had come.

Mardana had also reached Sultanpur in the meanwhile, and received a cordial welcome from the Master. With him the Master had to discuss nothing. A single look of the Master was enough to disarm him of all the earnestness with which he had been sent to reclaim the Master for the world. He himself became a convert and disciple and determined to spend the rest of his life in the Master's service, in spite of the Master warning him that he may have to suffer hunger and privations in his company. The Master, the great Apostle of the doctrine of Brotherhood and Equality of man, conferred on him the title of *Bhai*, Brother, and it was thus that the first Brother in Sikhism was a man of Islamic origin taken from a lowly caste. The Master thus demonstrated at the outset that neither birth nor caste, neither riches nor titles, neither estates nor worldly offices, were needed for entry into the Brotherhood in God, for which devotion and purification of the soul were alone necessary. Faith, unflinching faith, was all that was essential. Mardana, in whose person the Master's spirit was already working in the shape of Music, was not found wanting in Faith and Devotion, and being supplied with a rebeck, had the honour of remaining with the Master throughout his life. He was the first disciple, who followed the Master after his Renunciation, and was blessed with the title of *Bhaï*.

Bala's name is also, in some of the later chronicles of the Master, associated with that of Mardana, as being the Master's companion during His travels, but a careful examination of the available material shows that the statement cannot be accepted as correct. Bala was first engaged by the Master's father to accompany him when he was sent out, at about the age of eighteen, as a young merchant ; and was again sent by his father to Sultanpur, and there he was retained to help in the *Modikhana* business, when this job had been secured. Bala seems to have continued in the Master's service so long as he was engaged in this business, but left him soon after the *Modikhana* was resigned. The *Janamsakhis* are all agreed that, though the rumour about the Master's Renunciation had already reached Talwandi, the details were conveyed there by Bala. There are a number of versions of the *Janamsakhi*, which start as if the story of the Master's life was narrated to Guru Angad Dev by Bala which was thus recorded for the first time, and it is in these chronicles in which Bala is mentioned as having accompanied the Master in his migrations. These *Janamsakhis*, however, are comparatively recent productions, in which considerable interpolations were introduced by the Hindalis

Bhai Santokh Singh, who composed his monumental works on the Lives of the Sikh Gurus about the beginning of the nineteenth century of the Christian era, has exposed these interpolations but seems to have adopted the story of Bala reciting the history of Guru Nanak Dev to the second Guru and consequently also the statement regarding Bala having gone with the Master on his travels. The oldest *Janamsakhi*, so far as is at present ascertained, is the one, of which one of the manuscript copies was secured by the British, when they first occupied Delhi, and has since then remained in deposit at the India Office in London. It starts with the simple narration of the Master's biography in a form which at once carries conviction that it must be treated as one of the earliest records of the Master's life. Bhai Gur Das, the Sikh Savant, under the fifth Guru, who compiled the Granth Sahib, has also left some very brief description of the Master's work in his *Vars* or Ballads. The authenticity of this latter composition and the period when it was composed have never been doubted. In these earliest records Bala does not appear to have accompanied the Master during his extensive travels. Even in the later *Janamsakhis*, where Bala's name is added to that of Mardana, the latter is recorded very often to have put questions to the Master whenever he had failed to comprehend matters, but Bala does nowhere appear to have done so. It thus seems tolerably certain that Bala's connection with the Master was purely that of a business agent and terminated when the business ended. It is not possible to believe that, having spent a number of years with the Master, he had not imbibed the spirit of the Master's creed, but he would have been quite an unnecessary encumbrance during the travels and was sent back to his home in Talwandi soon after the Renunciation. Mardana's musical attainments made him almost indispensable, for holy music is one of the necessary accompaniments of the Church founded by the Master. In both the oldest records, so far known, we frequently find references to Mardana playing upon the *Rabab* (rebeck), while the Master sang his inspired songs. Bhai Gur Das distinctly mentions that Mardana was alone with the Master when he went to Mecca.

Three months after the Renunciation, while the Master was still staying in the graveyard at Sultanpur, *Mata* Sulakhni gave birth to her second son, who was named Lakhmi Das. Bhagirath and Mansukh, who had often met him before at the *Modikhana* also visited him here, and when informed that the Master contemplated going out to preach his Mission, prayed for further instruction, and it was here that they were now given the First Principles of the Creed, and were permitted to take down in writing the hymns which the Master used to sing. He instructed them to rise quarter of the night before daybreak, wash themselves with clean water, and sing hymns of the Lord that had been sung by the Master. They should concentrate their minds on the *Sat Nam*, realise God's Presence, and end their morning service with a prayer, beseeching the Lord of All to give them strength to withstand the blandishments of the Matter. The same programme was to be repeated at sunset. Whenever they needed help they must pray. If they performed these duties, Sat Guru would always succour them.

It is not possible to know exactly how long the Master stayed thus at the graveyard at Sultanpur, but eventually, before he decided to leave, he came home to visit His sister, *Bibi* Nanki, to take leave of her. She readily agreed but prayed that she may not be kept away from his *Darshan* for long, and the Master told her that he would visit her whenever her desire to see him was intense. She gave some money to Mardana to keep against need, for in certain places people may not be hospitable enough, but the Master, when he came to know of it, had the amount returned and told Mardana not to rely upon such flimsy support. Reliance was to be placed on God alone, who could satisfy all cravings and needs and fed all living beings everywhere. He would not let him starve. Mardana was satisfied, and, accompanied by him, the Master left Sultanpur.

VI.

THE PROPHESY.

It is extremely difficult to write a true and connected account of the Master's travels, at this distance of time. The *Janamsakhis* give such a disconnected and mixed description of them that a superficial reading of them often misleads. The oldest authentic record, still available in its original form, is contained in the ballads (*Vars*) of Bhai Gur Das, who composed them in the time of Guru Arjan Dev, about fifty years after the Master's ascension. The earlier record which was prepared under the orders and supervision of the Second Guru, immediately after the Master's ascension, is not unfortunately available in its original form. The ballads sung by Bhai Gur Das give a very meagre and scrappy account and lack in chronological exactness. There are also several reasons why the chronology of the Master's travels, as given in the *Walaitwali* or *Hafizabadi Janamsakhi*, which seems to have been written in the time of the Sixth Guru, many years after Bhai Gur Das, cannot be accepted in its entirety. In the first place, no dates are mentioned in it, and, in the next place, we have the intrinsic evidence in it that the author did not pay that regard to the sequence of events which one would expect from a modern historian Some of the later writers, among them Bhai Santokh Singh, who composed his monumental works about the beginning, and Bhai Gyan Singh, who wrote in almost the closing years, of the last century, have tried to formulate a connected account, but in doing so they seem to have also drawn on conjecture and unfortunately have not given us the sources of their information or the reasons for their framing the itinerary as they have done.

The chronology therefore apart, so far as the incidents recorded go, we can safely rely on the earlier records, at any rate where they are fully supported by the Master's own word, as preserved in the Granth Sahib, and are generally in consonance with the Master's character and personality, as revealed in his songs. The dates of some of the incidents can also be ascertained by reference to contemporary historical events, to which the Master has alluded in his hymns In some other cases.

it is possible to find evidence of a different nature to fix their period, but when all is said and done, it must be added that there will still be some scope for surmise, based perhaps on geographical position of the places visited by the Master. An attempt will be made to trace the Master's route, so far as it is possible to do so, on the basis of the available materials, but in almost all cases the incidents themselves will be tested by the Master's own word.

When the Master left Sultanpur, he seems to have passed through the present town of Goindwal, and for some time to have halted on the banks of the Lake, since then converted into the Tank of the Waters of Immortality, which has given its name to the present town of Amritsar. A visitor to the Golden Temple at Amritsar will be readily shown the place called *Dukhbhanjni Sahib*, midway along the eastern bank of the Lake, where the Jujuba tree, under which the Master stayed, is still preserved and worshipped as *Ber Sahib* A dip in this hallowed part of the Lake of Immortality is believed, as the name *Dukhbhanjni* implies, to remove all pains. Proceeding further north-west from there, the Master came up to Syadpur near where the present town of Amenabad is situate, and went straight to the house of one Lalo, a carpenter both by caste and profession. Lalo was preparing wooden pegs, when the Voice roused him, "Lalo, what art thou doing?" Lalo looked up. His eyes met the Master's eyes and he bowed. The question was a significant one. It was meant not only for Lalo, on whom it had a magical effect, but, through Lalo, it was addressed individually to all human beings—"What art thou doing?" Lalo understood it, and he bowed. Shall the world understand it? How many know themselves what they are doing? "Mending wooden pegs?" Is that their business?

O man! thou hast come for gain:

What trash art thou engaged in?

Mind, the night is about to end:*

The Master stayed with Lalo for a few days, and Mardana got leave to pay a visit to his home at Talwandi before going any further, for previously he had not left home with the intention of not returning soon. While Mardana was away, the Master used to spend the day out in the country, where he frequently sat on the pebbles, now the site of the shrine called *Rori Sahib*, and return to Lalo's house in the evening, when He would teach His host,

---

*ਪ੍ਰਾਨੀ, ਤੂ ਆਇਆ ਲਾਹਾ ਲੈਣ
ਲਗਾ ਕਿਤੁ ਕੁਫਕੜੇ, ਮੁਕਦੀ ਚਲੀ ਰੈਣ ।

how to utilize his time to his best "advantage", both for here and hereafter. But Mardana returned to Him very soon, and with him brought an humble and earnest request from Rai Bular for at least one visit of the Master to him in his old age. This request of His old friend and disciple the Master could not refuse. But it is said that Lalo did not like his so early departure from him, and even proposed to accompany Him wherever He went, but the Master held out a hope to him that He would soon return and remain with him for some time more.

At Talwandi, the Master had lot of trouble. His parents and other relations all assembled to induce Him to stay at home, and it was with great difficulty that He could get leave of them. All sorts of dainties, silk clothes, horses and other articles of comfort, were named by his uncle, *Mehta* Lalu, which could be supplied to him at home; he was to have a free option to follow any profession—agriculture, business, trade or service,—or no profession at all; but the Master called all of them "poor pleasures" of this world, and told them, in words which could not be mistaken, that He had a higher and nobler mission to perform, and that a Higher Being had the control of his movements. When an appeal was made to him in the name of His relatives—mother, father, uncle, wife, children, and friends of his youth, the Master replied as follows :—

" Forgiveness is my mother, and contentment
my father ;
" Truth is my uncle, and with the help of
these I have controlled my mind.
" Hear, O Lalu, this admonition,
" What are those relations who bind one to
this world ?
" Devotion, my brother, is with me, and
True Love is my son ;
" Endurance is my daughter, and in the company of these I enjoy myself ;
" Meekness is friend to me, and purpose
my retinue ;
" This is all my family with whom I ever
reside.
" One God is my Master who has created me,
" He who forsaketh Him and seeketh another
" shall suffer pain, saith Nanak."*

---

* Rag Ramkulli M. 1, *vide* Bala's Janamsakhi.

ਖਿਮਾ ਹਮਾਰੀ ਮਾਤਾ ਕਹੀਏ. ਸੰਤੋਖ ਹਮਾਰਾ ਪਿਤਾ,
ਸੱਤ ਹਮਾਰਾ ਚਾਚਾ ਕਹੀਏ, ਜਿਨ ਸੰਗ ਮਨੂਆ ਜਿੱਤਾ ।
ਸੁਣ, ਲਾਲੂ, ਗੁਣ ਐਸਾ,
ਸਗਲੇ ਲੋਕ ਬੰਧਨ ਕੇ ਬਾਂਧੇ, ਸੋ ਗੁਨ ਕਹੀਏ ਕੈਸਾ ?
ਭਾਉ ਭਾਈ ਸੰਗ ਹਮਾਰੇ ਪ੍ਰੇਮ ਪੂਤ ਸੋ ਸਾਚਾ,
ਧੀ ਹਮਾਰੀ ਧੀਰਜ ਬਣੀ ਐਸੇ ਸੰਗ ਹਮ ਰਾਚਾ,
ਸਾਂਤ ਹਮਾਰੇ ਸੰਗ ਸਹੇਲੀ, ਮਤਿ ਹਮਾਰੀ ਚੇਲੀ ।
ਇਹ ਕੁਟੰਬ ਹਮਾਰਾ ਕਹੀਏ ਸਾਸ ਸਾਸ ਸੰਗ ਖੇਲੀ ।
ਇੰਕੰਕਾਰ ਹਮਾਰਾ ਖ਼ਾਂਵੰਦ, ਜਿਨ ਹਮ ਬਨਤ ਬਨਾਏ,
ਉਸ ਕੋ ਛਾਡ ਅਵਰ ਕੋ ਲਾਗੇ, ਨਾਨਕ ਸੋ ਦੁਖ ਪਾਏ ॥

Thus, said the Master, he could stay with them no longer. Regarding their last complaint as to " what would the people say about Him, that He had deserted His parents and so on," He said :—

" From these materialists of Kaliyuga, how may I save my honour ?
" If I speak, they would say, " he chatters much "
" If I be silent, they would say " he is fool" !
" If I sit (at home), they would say, " he is a drone."
" If I go away, they say, he has run away and brought discredit to his family."
" If I be humble, they say he humiliates himself on account of fear."
" In no way can I be safe from the people of this world, where then may I pass my time without anxiety ?
" Here (in this world) and there (in the next), the Creator alone will save my honour, saith Nanak."*

---

*Shabd M. 1, *vide* Bala's Janamsakhi.

ਏਸ ਕਲੀਉਂ ਪੰਜ ਭੀਤੀਉਂ, ਕਿਉਂਕਰ ਰੱਖਾਂ ਪੱਤ ?
ਜਾ ਬੋਲਾਂ, ਤਾਂ ਆਖੀਏ, ‘ਬੜ ਬੜ ਕਰੇ ਬਹੁਤ" ।
ਚੁਪ ਕਰਾਂ, ਤਾਂ ਆਖੀਏ ‘ ਇਸ ਘਟ ਨਾਹੀ ਮੱਤ" ।
ਜੇ ਬਹਿ ਰਹਾਂ ਤਾਂ ਆਖੀਏ, "ਬੈਠਾ ਸੱਥਰ ਘੱਤ" ।
ਉਠ ਚਲਾਂ, ਤਾਂ ਆਖਦੇ, ‘ ਛਾਰ ਗਿਆ ਸਿਰ ਘੱਤ" ।
ਜੇਕਰ ਨਿਵਾਂ, ਤਾਂ ਆਖੀਏ. "ਡਰਦਾ ਕਰੇ ਨਗੱਤ" ।
ਕਾਈ ਗਲੀ ਨਾ ਮੇਵਨੀ, ਕਿਤ ਵਲ ਕਢਾਂ ਝੱਤ ।
ਏਥੇ, ਓਥੇ, ਨਾਨਕਾ, ਕਰਤਾ ਰਖੇ ਪੱਤ ॥

Rai Bular was highly gratified by the Master's visit. At the first meeting he attempted to bow down to Him, but the Master prevented his doing so and said: "Let this not be". The Master embraced Rai Bular instead, and both of them spent considerable time together. The master tarried at Talwandi many days, during which he sometimes slept at home and sometimes at the house of Rai Bular, while his days he spent in the jungle. Rai Bular was instructed fully in the knowledge of the Divine and how to attain it through *Bhakti*, while he spent sufficient time to explain to His father and mother that He had to obey the call of the Lord and go out to preach the *Name*. His mother was the first of his parents to be blessed with understanding, and, before his departure from home, he had the satisfaction to know that both of them had considerably softened and were fairly on their way to be later the Recipients of Grace. They as well as Rai Bular much desired that He should stay with them longer but they would no longer stand in His way.

When the Master was leaving Talwandi, the Rai requested Him to bid him some service, to which the Master replied thus:

> One recommendation would I make to thee: Have faith in the Lord.
>
> Where thy own might is of no avail, with folded hands contemplate on Him.

Such a true Guide, O Rai ! nowhere else can be found :

Do as pleaseth Him :

Tact and orders will not avail, Let them be tried !

The learned *Sheikhs* and the occultists shall all be called to accoun.

(Even) the Ten Incarnations (of Vishnu) came and ruled the world ;

But in the end they crumbled to dust and gained nothing.

The great and powerful warriors and heroes,

Saith Nanak, I saw all crumbling to dust.*

---

* Rag. Sarang Mohalla 1. *Vide* Bala's *Janamsakhi* :

ਹਿਕ ਫੁਰਮਾਇਸ਼ ਆਖੀਐ, ਜੇ ਮਨੋ ਸਾਂਈ।
ਜਿਸ ਤੇ ਜੋਰ ਨ ਚਲਈ, ਕਰ ਜੋਰ ਧਿਆਂਈ॥
ਐਸਾ ਸਤਿਗੁਰ, ਰਾਏ ਜੀ, ਕਿਸੈ ਹਥ ਨ ਆਵੈ।
ਸਾਈ ਕਾਰ ਕਮਾਵਣੀ, ਜੋ ਤਿਸ ਕੇ ਭਾਵੈ॥
ਹਿਕਮਤ ਹੁਕਮ ਨ ਚਲਈ, ਕੋਈ ਕਰ ਦੇਖੇ।
ਸ਼ੇਖ ਮੁਸਾਇਖ ਸਿਧ ਸਾਧ, ਸਭ ਲਈਏ ਲੇਖੇ॥
ਦਸ ਅਵਤਾਰੀ ਆਇਆ, ਜਗ ਹੁਕਮ ਚਲਾਇਆ।
ਅੰਤ ਕਾਲ ਧਰਤੀ ਪਏ, ਕੁਝ ਹਥ ਨਾ ਆਇਆ॥
ਵਡੇ ਵਡੇ ਮਹਾ ਬਲੀ, ਜੋਧੇ ਅਰ ਸੂਰੇ।
ਕਹ ਨਾਨਕ ਸਭ ਦੇਖਿਆ, ਸਭ ਧਰਤੀ ਪਏ॥

From Talwandi, the Master visited Lahore where he saw Mansukh and Jawahar Mal, and had a conference with Seid Ahmad Mir Tuqi, who was the *murshid*, spiritual preceptor, of *Sultan* Sikandar Lodhi of Delhi. He convinced the Syed that, in the eyes of God, all men, whether belonging to the Mussalman social system or Hindu castes, were equal, and it was an offence against God's own creation to persecute any one on account of his religious beliefs. Merit was gained only by right thinking, right living and devotion to God.

Here the Master learnt that *Faqir* Hamza Ghous had started the *chilla* austerities, at Sialkot, to destroy the town, on account of the offence given to him by one Ganga, *Khatri*, by breaking his promise to offer his eldest born son to the *Faqir* as a disciple. The Master at once repaired to Sialkot and sat under a Jujuba tree (*Beri*)* and sent word to Hamza Ghous to permit a talk on the subject of his austerities. Hamza Ghous, however, was shut up in a domed hut, the doors of which were securely fastened and sealed. Hamza Ghous could not break his *chilla* : so he replied from inside. He could not break his vow by opening the door and consequently could not come out. He must complete his *chilla* to destroy the whole town The Master looked with compassion towards the domed closet, in which Hamza was

* *Ziziphus Jujuba*

confined, and the dome burst open at the top. Thus baffled and alarmed, Hamza came out and, after a brief talk, he was convinced of his error and of the mischievousness and futility of his unjust indignation. The town was not inhabited solely by people who were vile breakers of their promises. There were lot of God-fearing people living in it and the Master told the *Faqir* that the sinful were to be reclaimed for the Kingdom of God by Love and not by threatening them with destruction. By way of practical demonstration, the Master directed Mardana to go to the town and buy " Truth and Falsehood " worth two pice from there. After a while Mardana returned with a piece of paper on which was inscribed the following line :

" DEATH THE TRUTH – LIFE THE FALSEHOOD."

Hamza, however, would not believe that the man who wrote the line realised the meaning of it or practised the principle underlying it in his life. The man, who was Mula by name, was then called and was exhaustively questioned by Hamza as to his mode of life and the principles which were implied in the maxim that had been written by him on the piece of paper. The *Faqir* was perfectly satisfied as a result of this examination and raised his *chilla*. The Jujuba tree is in existence and is known as the Baba's *Ber*, where a big Gurdwara commemorates the event, while Hamza's domed closet is standing not far from it with the burst out top still admitting light from above.

On his return to Syedpur, the Master stayed again with Lalo carpenter, this time for a pretty lengthy period. People now came to know of his high caste by Birth and began objecting to His staying with a *shudra*. Those who heard of His heterodox teachings also began calling him a *heretic* (*Kurahya*, wayward), and Mardana was everywhere hissed and hooted as heretic's musician.

About this time, an incident took place which brought the matters to a head. One Malik Bhago was the Dewan of the Pathan magnate, who ruled this district. He was an unscrupulous oppressor, but occasionally feasted people of all castes at *Brahmbhoj*, God's feast. One such feast was held when the Master was staying there. The Brahman, sent out to extend invitation to all residents of the town, came to Lalo's house and invited the Master also to the *Brahmbhoj*. The Master, however, excused himself by saying that he was a *Faqir* who desired not to come. Thereupon the Brahman rudely remarked that for this he was called heretic and that if he did not attend Malik Bhago would be indignant. The Master. however, heeded him not. Next day, when the *Brahmbhoj* was finished, the Malik enquired if all had come and had been feasted, and the Brahman told him that " the heretic Tappa" had not. Thereupon the Master was called and when he refused to go, he was brought to Malik Bhago by five men, who were deputed to fetch Him there by force. When the Malik insisted for an explanation why his invitation had not been accepted and the Master's humble reply that He was of no significance in the town to which he did not belong, was not accepted, the Master asked him to bring some dainties prepared by him, and also sent Lalo to fetch the remnants of coarse food he had at his house. The Master squeezed both of them, one in each hand, and while milk flowed out of the coarse bread of Lalo, blood trickled down the Malik's dainties. The Master then explained that Lalo had his food by sheer honest labour, while the Malik feasted people with dainties bought of cruel exactions from the poor and helpless. The Malik was thus put to utter shame and the Master left unmolested. The incident, however, did not fail to cause a serious breach in the population. While fair-minded people saw the force of the Master's fearless argument and some of them became also His followers, others, inspired in many cases by the Malik's satellites, began to invent explanations of the incident by saying that the Master was possessed of magical powers or had otherwise played a trick or sleight of hand. At any rate, a strong faction grew up against the Master and his followers and made it difficult for the latter to pursue their normal life in peace.

Amid all these persecutions, however, was heard the bold and undaunted voice of the Master :

> "MARDANA, FEAR NOT : THE WORLD IS FOOLISH AND WILL TURN TO THEE AFTER GROVELLING IN THE DUST FOR AGES !"

Prophetic and forcible as these words were, they could not but have a most salutary effect upon their hearer. *Mardana never waivered after this, till his death.*

It was here that, on one occasion, Lalo mentioned to the Master the various persecutions to which the population was being subjected by the Afghan Rulers and their satellites, and asked whether this condition would last for ever. The Master was extremely touched by the sufferings of the people, which were described to Him, and addressed two stanzas to Lalo, which are found in *Rag* Tilang of the Granth Sahib. In the first stanza, the Afghan advent into India is described as a bridegroom's party, who demanded the hand of the bride (wealth of India) by force, persecution and blood-shed, and, in the second, the coming retribution is prophesied. Literally translated the text runs thus :

I.

As the Word cometh to me from the Lord,
  I impart knowledge thereof, O Lalo !
From Kabul, the bridegroom hath brought
  a party of Sins ;

By force demandeth "gift" of the Bride,
O Lalo !
Modesty and righteousness have vanished,
Falsehood holds the chief authority,
O Lalo !
Kazi and Brahman are abandoned,
Satan offitiates at the marriage ceremony
O Lalo !
Mossalman women read the books, and
In agony call upon God, O Lalo !
The Hindu caste women also !
Follow the same line (crying to the Lord),
O Lalo !
In blood are composed the marriag songs,
saith Nanak,
In gory fluid of human veins are the marriage raiments dyed, O Lalo !*

---

*Rag Tilang, M. 1, (1).

ਜੈਸੀ ਮੈ ਆਵੈ ਖਸਮ ਕੀ ਬਾਣੀ,
ਤੈਸੜਾ ਕਰੀ ਗਿਆਨ, ਵੇ ਲਾਲੋ ॥
ਪਾਪ ਕੀ ਜੰਞ ਲੈ ਕਾਬਲਹੁ ਧਾਇਆ,
ਜੋਰੀ ਮੰਗੈ ਦਾਨੁ, ਵੇ ਲਾਲੋ ।
ਸਰਮੁ ਧਰਮੁ ਦੁਇ ਛਪਿ ਖਲੋਏ,
ਕੂੜੁ ਫਿਰੈ ਪਰਧਾਨੁ, ਵੇ ਲਾਲੋ ।
ਕਾਜੀਆ ਬਾਮਣਾ ਦੀ ਗਲ ਥਕੀ,
ਅਗਦੁ ਪੜੈ ਸੈਤਾਨੁ, ਵੇ ਲਾਲੋ ।
ਮੁਸਲਮਾਨੀਆਂ ਪੜਹਿ ਕਤੇਬਾਂ,
ਕਸ਼ਟ ਮਹਿ ਕਰਹਿ ਖੁਦਾਇ, ਵੇ ਲਾਲੋ ।
ਜਾਤਿ ਸਨਾਤੀ, ਹੋਰਿ ਹਿੰਦਵਾਣੀਆਂ,
ਏਹਿ ਭੀ ਲੇਖੇ ਲਾਇ, ਵੇ ਲਾਲੋ ।
ਖੂਨ ਕੇ ਸੋਹਿਲੇ ਗਾਵੀਅਹਿ, ਨਾਨਕ,
ਰਤੁ ਕਾ ਕੁੰਗੂ ਪਾਇ, ਵੇ ਲਾਲੋ ।

II.

Nanak singeth praises of the Lord !

Speaketh he of the Event on this earth
of flesh :

He who created the multi-coloured universe

Looketh on from His Detachment.

He is True, True is His Retribution,
Right shall be His Verdict of Justice :

The "Body" shall be rent into pieces,
The Hindustan shall be conquered by
the Deaf :*

In Seventy-eight shall they come, in
ninety-seven shall they go.

There shall then arise the Disciple of Man !

---

*" Babar was hard of hearing. He conquered Bajaur, in the Trans Indus territory, in 1519 of the Christian era, and then crossed the Indus and claimed the Punjab as his inheritance in virtue of his descent from Timur, says Vincent Smith. The first entry of Babar in the Punjab with the declaration of his claim to this country took place in 1521 of the Christian era, corresponding to 1578 of Bikramajit's era. Between that year and 1524 when he sacked Syedpur he came thrice, but these three invasions are described by Smith in the nature of reconnaissances, and his invasion of 1524 as serious.

> Words of Truth hath Nanak said ;
> Truth he speaketh ; the Hour of Truth
> is come."*

The oldest *Janamsakhi*, so far known, records that the Master met and reformed Sajjan, a thug in southern Punjab, before going on his First Udasi which was to the East, and it was to him that the First *Manji* was entrusted. Bhai Santokh Singh in his *Nanak Parkash* has identified Sajjan's residence near Talamba, in the modern District of Multan, but he mentions the incident to have taken place after the conclusion of all the four principal trips which the Master had taken. Whenever the incident took place, it is certainly worth mentioning as showing the sort of people the Master was out to reclaim for the Lord's Kingdom.

---

* Rag Tilang, M. 1 (2).

ਸਾਹਿਬ ਕੇ ਗੁਣ ਨਾਨਕੁ ਗਾਵੈ,
ਮਾਸ ਪੁਰੀ ਵਿਚਿ ਆਖੁ ਮਸੋਲਾ।
ਜਿਨਿ ਉਪਾਈ ਰੰਗਿ ਰਵਾਈ,
ਬੈਠਾ ਵੇਖੈ ਵਖਿ ਇਕੇਲਾ।
ਸਚਾ ਸੋ ਸਾਹਿਬੁ, ਸਚ ਤਪਾਵਸੁ,
ਸਚੜਾ ਨਿਆਉ ਕਰੇ ਗੁ ਮਸੋਲਾ।
ਕਾਇਆ ਕਪੜੁ ਟੁਕੁ ਟੁਕੁ ਹੋਸੀ,
ਹਿੰਦੁਸਤਾਨੁ ਸਮਾਲਸੀ ਬੋਲਾ।
ਆਵਨਿ ਅਠਤਰੈ, ਜਾਨਿ ਸਤਾਨਵੈ,
ਹੋਰੁ ਭੀ ਉਠਸੀ ਮਰਦ ਕਾ ਚੇਲਾ।
ਸਚ ਕੀ ਬਾਣੀ ਨਾਨਕੁ ਆਖੈ,
ਸਚੁ ਸੁਣਾਇਸੀ ਸਚ ਕੀ ਬੇਲਾ।

Sajjan kept a Moslem mosque and a Hindu *Thakardwara*, side by side, apparently for the weary travellers to rest and worship, in a lonely jungle pathway. The way-farers, however, always found their fatal end during the night that they were thus tempted to rest at Sajjan's *Dera*, and there lay the bones of the most of them in the pit, constructed in the innermost recesses of the estate. Ordinarily Sajjan would be found on his prayer carpet, with his long rosary and pious appearance, in front of the Mosque. The Master, accompanied by Mardana, was his guest one night. Sajjan, without knowing them, served them with utmost devotion. He saw the sparkle of a million jewels on the Master's forehead, and took him to be extremely rich, though with simple externals.* So he said to his followers Late at night, Sajjan asked the Master to retire for rest : it was late and he must be tired. "Let us sing a song to the Almighty Father before going to bed, O Sajjan." "Yea, do so, and let a hermit like me also listen," said the Thug "Take up thy Rebeck, Mardana, Start the tune, for the Song cometh." Mardana played the tune and the Master sang :

> Brilliant is the white bronze, but extremely black is its touch,
>
> Counterfeit it remains, wash it a hundred times, if you will.

---

* Pooran Singh's description.

Sajjan (meaning friend) is he that may accompany one on his departure herefrom ;

Where accounts are demanded, he may be found present to help.

Houses and mansions, well painted on the outside,

Are of no use, when demolished, if devoid of substance within.

Pure white are the plumes worn by heron, stayeth he by the side of holy waters ;
Pure he is not, for he swalloweth fish and frogs alive.

Huge is the *Mimosa* tree, Flights of parrots are drawn to it.

Useless, however, are its fruit : such are its attributes.

Blind man carrieth the burden ; the path is long and mountainous ;

He hath no sight to feel, how may he mount and reach destination :

Of what avail shall be the services, hospitalities, and other wily acts (chicaneries):

Do thou contemplate on the Name, saith Nanak, whereby thou mayst escape thy bonds.*

Such was the heavenly music sung by the Master that Sajjan was overwhelmed with remorse He was washed with the Divine Song. He fell down on the Master's feet and cried out, "Save me, even me, O Divine One. Do thou forgive my innumerable sins, of thy own unlimited mercy." "Do thou now speak out the truth, O Sajjan. Hast thou committed

---

* Rag Suhi, M. 1, Gh. 6, (3).

ਉਜਲੁ ਕਹਿਆ ਚਿਲਕਣਾ, ਘੋਟਮ ਕਾਲੜੀ ਮਸੁ ।
ਧੋਤਿਆ ਜੂਠਿ ਨ ਉਤਰੈ, ਜੇ ਸਉ ਧੋਵਾਂ ਤਿਸੁ ॥੧॥
ਸਜਣ ਸੇਈ ਨਾਲਿ ਮੈਂ, ਚਲਦਿਆਂ ਨਾਲਿ ਚਲੰਨਿ ।
ਜਿਥੈ ਲੇਖਾ ਮੰਗੀਐ, ਤਿਥੈ ਖੜੇ ਦਿਸੰਨਿ ॥ ਰਹਾਉ॥
ਕੋਠੇ ਮੰਡਪ ਮਾੜੀਆ ਪਾਸਹੁ ਚਿਤਵੀਆਹਾ ।
ਢਠੀਆਂ ਕਮਿ ਨ ਆਵਨੀ, ਵਿਚਹੁ ਸਖਣੀਆਹਾ ॥੨॥
ਬਗਾ, ਬਗੇ ਕਪੜੇ, ਤੀਰਥ ਮੰਝਿ ਵਸੰਨਿ ।
ਘੁਟਿ ਘੁਟਿ ਜੀਆ ਖਾਵਣੇ, ਬਗੇ ਨਾ ਕਹੀਅਨਿ ॥੩॥
ਸਿਮਲ ਰੁਖੁ ਸਰੀਰੁ ਮੈਂ ਮੈਜਨਿ ਦੇਖਿ ਭੁਲੰਨਿ ।
ਸੇ ਫਲ ਕਮਿ ਨ ਆਵਨੀ, ਤੇ ਗੁਣ ਮੈ ਤਨਿ ਹੰਨ ॥੪॥
ਅੰਧੁਲੈ ਭਾਰਿ ਉਠਾਇਆ, ਡੂਗਰ ਵਾਟ ਬਹੁਤੁ ।
ਅਖੀ ਲੋੜੀ ਨਾ ਲਹਾ, ਹਉ ਚੜਿ ਲੰਘਾ ਕਿਤੁ ॥੫॥
ਚਾਕਰੀਆ ਚੰਗਿਆਈਆ, ਅਵਰ ਸਿਆਣਪ ਕਿਤੁ ।
ਨਾਨਕ ਨਾਮੁ ਸਮਾਲਿ ਤੂੰ ਬਧਾ ਛੁਟਹਿ ਜਿਤੁ ॥੬॥

murders? Confess all thy crimes and abstain from them any more: Thus alone will thy repentance bear fruit." Sajjan confessed his numerous crimes, gave away in charity all that he had hoarded, and became an absolute pauper. He was instructed in the Name of Lord the Merciful, and, here, the *Janamsakhi* adds, the first *Dharamsal* was established.

VII.

The First Udasi.

The First *Udasi* or migration, which was to the East, seems to have commenced in or about the year 1501 of the Christian era. During this journey the Master visited, among others, Kurukhshetra, Karnal, Panipat, Hardwar, Delhi, Brindaban, Nanakmatta in the Pilibhit District, Ajudhia, Lucknow, Benares, Patna, Gaya, Raj Mahal, Maldev, Dacca, Dhanpur, Kamrup, Dhubri, Lushari and Nanga Hills in Assam, Chittagong, Sondwip Islands, and Jagan Nath (Puri) ; and returned through the Vindhya Mountains, Central India and Rajputana. In most of these places, Gurdwaras still mark the places which the Master had blessed with his feet. Some distance away from Nanakmatta, which was then called Gorakhmatta, where the Master had a somewhat lengthy contest with the Jogis, and about 20 miles into the forest from Pilibhit, the place which the Master had sanctified by his stay is still marked out by the Soap-nut tree, of which one branch, under which the Master then tarried, still produces sweet fruit, while its other branches bear their usual bitter and pungent nuts.

It was the great Fair of the Sun Eclipse, which was being held at the ancient battlefield of Kurukhshetra, where famous Hindu Temples still existed, when the Master visited the place. Thousands of Hindus collect here on the occasion of an eclipse every year, to purify themselves in the holy waters of the Lake from the contamination which is believed to attach not only to all human beings but also to the entire creation, animate and inanimate, on account of the attack made upon the Sun-god by the demons Rahu and Ketu, which resulted in the Eclipse. Most valuable gifts are made by the Hindus to the Brahmans to appease the terrible and offended demons and thus to secure the release of the beneficent Sun-god from their grip. The Master saw this and deplored the superstitious beliefs of the ignorant, and the deceitful practices of the 'learned', who, instead of trying to dispel the prevailing delusions, deliberately feasted upon the credulity of the illiterate people. He felt the Divine call within, that here was the Work to be done. The people, however, were so much engrossed in their self-purification and alms-giving, and the learned were so much busy in collecting the gifts presented to them, that it became a problem to attract attention. The Master sat down in a prominent place on the bank of the lake, when Mardana began his music and the Master began his song of the Lord. The people, however were in no mood to listen to the song. ,About this time, a nobleman, who is described by Bhai Gian Singh Giani as ex-Raja Juggat Rai, son of Raja Amrit Rai of Hansi, arrived, having in the way killed a buck, when passing through the forest, the carcase of which, however,was well wrapped up to hide it from human gaze. He sat down, along with his mother, close to where the Master was singing.and the party were so much impressed that the Rani-mother narrated her story how she and her son had been deprived of their estate by their enemies and asked for the Master's blessings for the restoration of the young ex-Raja to his State. The Master atonce saw that the Lord had Himself disclosed the way to him, and he directed the Rani and her son to feast the poor in the assemblage, and, when told that they had not the means to do so, the Master told the Rani to cook the meat of the buck that their companions were carrying for them and,as *Khshatris*, offer the same as a feast to the poor. They saw the danger but finding how the Master had divined the contents of the bundle, they immediately opened it, cut up the meat, and, getting a big earthen *matka*, began cooking it.

The news of the sacrilege, however, soon spread throughout the huge concourse of people like wild fire, and, indignant at the act of pollution that had been committed, the more bigotted fanatics of them ran, in their frenzy, with their formidable clubs and bludgeons and other arms in their hands, to where the Master was sitting. Although the crowd was furious at what they had learnt, they stopped on seeing the Master calm and unperturbed, and began questioning Him as to what was being cooked. Those who, however, had themselves seen the meat being cooked said it was no use questioning on the matter, and the Master, thereupon, said to them in a voice which immediately calmed them down that if they desired to strike down innocent people as an act of merit on an occasion for which they had collected there, no one was going to resist them and they might fulfil their object atonce, but if they wanted to know and understand things they should calm themselves and sit down to have a talk. He invited the learned and holy among the c owd to lead the discussion. People thereupon hung down their arms, and one Pundit Nanu Chandra, who was one of the most learned amongst them, led the conversation. In the course of this discourse, the Master first broke down their prejudices against meat diet, and said to them that they could under no circumstances avoid it, try as best as they might. It were the fools, he said, who quarrel over this or that object of diet; it were only the ignorant who run mad at the sight of meat. "Of flesh ye are born, in flesh ye are nurtured, and of flesh ye are made. *Gyan* and *Dhyan* ye know not, and yet ye, O Pundits, call yourselves learned. What is this prejudice about meat, when ye accept gifts of all sorts from meat-eaters. All sorts of sins are committed and go un-noticed and un-punished ! and yet meat must be strictly prohibited. Nay, no harm, if meat is used in secret ! It must not be used in the public ! Is this your morality, O Brahmans ? Have you not read that, in ancient times, meat formed an element of the *samagree* used in important *Yagyas* ? If all those have gone to hell, and all those who use it now are bound for hell, how can you, who accept gifts from them, go to heaven.* You ask me what caste I am and

---

*Shlok M. 1.

ਮਾਸੁ ਮਾਸੁ ਕਰਿ ਮੂਰਖੁ ਝਗੜੇ,
ਗਿਆਨੁ ਧਿਆਨੁ ਨਹੀ ਜਾਣੈ ।
ਕਉਣੁ ਮਾਸੁ, ਕਉਣੁ ਸਾਗੁ ਕਹਾਵੈ,
ਕਿਸੁ ਮਹਿ ਪਾਪ ਸਮਾਣੈ ॥
ਗੈਂਡਾ ਮਾਰਿ ਹੋਮ ਜਗ ਕੀਏ,
ਦੇਵਤਿਆਂ ਕੀ ਬਾਣੈ ।
ਮਾਸੁ ਛੋਡਿ ਬੈਸਿ ਨਕੁ ਪਕੜਹਿ,
ਰਾਤੀ ਮਾਣਸ ਖਾਣੈ ।
ਫੜੁ ਕਰਿ ਲੋਕਾਂ ਨੋ ਦਿਖਲਾਵਹਿ,
ਗਿਆਨੁ ਧਿਆਨੁ ਨਹੀ ਸੂਝੈ ।

P, T. O.

what my name ? Why harp upon caste when all are under the protection of the same Lord ? Call yourselves good and high, but bear in mind you will be really so if ye are honoured in the eyes of the Almighty Father.* You say, it is an inauspicious occasion, when the Sun-god is in the grip of the Demons, and people are praying for the release of the god, for any one to indulge in such food ? In spite of all your ablutions and almsgiving and almstaking, the god is subjected to this seizure year after year, and you have not been able to procure your god's immunity from

---

(In continuation of Footnote from last page).

ਨਾਨਕ ਅੰਧੇ ਸਿਉ ਕਿਆ ਕਹੀਐ,
ਕਹੈ ਨ ਕਹਿਆ ਬੂਝੈ ॥
... ...
... ...
ਮਾਸਹੁ ਨਿਮੇ ਮਾਸਹੁ ਜੰਮੇ,
ਹਮ ਮਾਸੈ ਕੇ ਭਾਂਡੇ ।
ਗਿਆਨੁ ਧਿਆਨੁ ਕਛੁ ਸੂਝੈ ਨਾਹੀ,
ਚਤੁਰ ਕਹਾਵੈ ਪਾਂਡੇ ॥
... ...
... ...

*Var Sri Rag. M. 1, *Shlok* 3 (1).

ਫਕੜ ਜਾਤੀ ਫਕੜੁ ਨਾਉਂ,
ਸਭਨਾਂ ਜੀਆਂ ਇਕਾ ਛਾਉਂ ।
ਆਪਹੁ ਜੇ ਕੋ ਭਲਾ ਕਹਾਏ,
ਨਾਨਕ, ਤਾਂ ਪਰੁ ਜਾਪੈ, ਜਾਂ ਪਤਿ ਲੇਖੈ ਪਾਏ ॥

any further attacks. You say that these alms are really for the benefit of one's deceased ancestors. It is non-sense. Poor ancestors remain as unsatisfied as they were when they left their earthly bodies. These articles, gifted in their names to the Brahman, remain here and are enjoyed by the Brahman before our own eyes. So many devices, fair and foul, are employed to collect and amass the wealth of this world, and you assure the simpletons that on occasions, when nature repeats her phenomena, a gift in the name of the ancestors reaches them. Vain is all this assurance and hope. Supposing it were true that the ancestors will get what has thus been sent, how will such ancestors fare if the article gifted here happens to have been acquired by foul means and is recognized by some other deceased person, also living in the same higher or lower regions, to whom it legitimately belonged. The giver's ancestor would then be seized as a swindler, and the agent, through whom the article has been sent, shall be hauled up as an abbettor. The latter's hands shall then be ordered to be cut. Don't be foolish, O people, the ancestors must reap as they themselves had sown here. They do not depend upon your charity after they have left their bodies here. It is only what you yourselves give away in charity to those who deserve it here, out of your lawful earnings, which will benefit your souls hereafter. Leave off these vainglories and worship the Lord of all gods and demons and behave honestly to your fellow-beings. O fools !*

The tradition says that after this discourse, when the lid of the *matka* was raised, it was found to contain rice and milk and all people present enjoyed the holy feast. After this, individual instruction was given to all those who, impressed with what they had seen and heard, approached the Master. Many were such who were initiated in the Faith and Name of All-Merciful Father. The place where the Master thus taught is the site of a Gurdwara which was established to carry on the Master's mission after he left it.

In Brindaban, the Master noticed the evil effects, on young men and young women, of the performances of Krishna *leela*, as they were in vogue there. Bhai Santokh Singh has described the practice as follows :

> Darkness prevailed all round ; none with pure heart could be found ; all were bound up in earthly cravings : None

---

*Asa di *Var*, M. 1, *Shlok* 17 (1).

ਜੇ ਮੋਹਾਕਾ ਘਰੁ ਮੁਹੇ, ਘਰ ਮੁਹਿ ਪਿਤ੍ਰੀ ਦੇਇ;
ਅਗੈ ਵਸਤੁ ਸਿਵਾਣੀਐ, ਪਿਤ੍ਰੀ ਚੋਰ ਕਰੇਇ;
ਵਢੀਅਹਿ ਹਥ ਦਲਾਲ ਕੇ ਮੁਸਫ਼ੀ ਏਹ ਕਰੇਇ;
ਨਾਨਕ ਅਗੈ ਸੋ ਮਿਲੈ, ਜਿ ਖਟੇ, ਘਾਲੇ, ਦੇਇ ॥

could thus be redeemed. All were surrounded with lust, anger, avarice, vanity and earthly attachments. Many were the deceptions practised during the day, when they posed as holy men, while all along they were coveting the rights of others. At night, while they adopted the roll of Krishna and Radha, they committed all sorts of sins. Boys as well as girls, thus attired, danced while others enjoyed the performances and viewed them with evil intent and thus excited their lust. They then satisfied their lust with both boys and girls, without any compunction : And all this in the name of Religion.

The Master saw one of these performances, and his heart was moved. He asked Mardana to start the tune, for the Song had come. Mardana played the tune, and the Master sang :

> The same sun, the same moon, and the same stars shine today as shone in the earlier *yugas* ;
>
> The same earth remains spread out and the same air rushes forth in space;
>
> Leave off Craving for Life !

It is *Kaliyuga* now, because the human soul, born now, ephemeral and mothlike, is steeped in ignorance and sin.*

Otherwise, have heard not *Kaliyuga* coming to a particular country, nor seated in a specified place of pilgrimage,

Nor is it where the giver giveth away in charity, nor has it a castle for its abode.†

Benefactors get not the fruit of their benefactions, those engaged in austerities obtain no solace :

Those engaged in realising the Name are called evil names : These are the attributes of *Kaliyuga*.‡

---

* Ram Kali M. 1, *Asht-padi.*

ਸੋਈ ਚੰਦੁ ਚੜਹਿ, ਸੇ ਤਾਰੇ, ਸੋਈ ਦਿਨੀਅਰ ਤਪਤ ਰਹੈ ।

ਸਾ ਧਰਤੀ, ਸੋ ਪਉਣ ਝੁਲਾਰੇ, ਜੁਗ ਜੀਅ ਖੇਲੇ ਥਾਵ ਕੈਸੇ ॥੧॥

ਜੀਵਨ ਤਲਬ ਨਿਵਾਰ ।

ਹੋਵੈ ਪਰਵਾਣਾ, ਕਰਹਿ ਧਿਙਾਣਾ, ਕਲਿ ਲਖਣ ਵੀਚਾਰ ॥੧॥
ਰਹਾਉ ॥

† *Ibid.*

ਕਿਤੈ ਦੇਸਿ ਨ ਆਇਆ ਸੁਣੀਐ, ਤੀਰਥ ਪਾਸਿ ਨ ਬੈਠਾ ।

ਦਾਤਾ ਦਾਨੁ ਕਰੇ, ਤਹ ਨਾਹੀ, ਮਹਿਲ ਉਸਾਰਿ ਨ ਬੈਠਾ ॥੨॥

‡ *Ibid.*

ਜੇ ਕੋ ਸਤੁ ਕਰੇ, ਸੋ ਛੀਜੈ, ਤਪ ਘਰ ਤਪ ਨ ਹੋਈ ।

ਜੇ ਕੋ ਨਾਉ ਲਏ, ਬਦਨਾਵੀ, ਕਲਿ ਕੇ ਲਖਣ ਏਈ ॥੩॥

Noble men have anxiety, afraid they are of their servants.
Should they have a fall ; they die at the hands of their servants :*
Such are the attributes of *Kaliyuga.*
No more are the austerities of the earlier *yugas* of any avail : One could gain merit, should the Lord grant him His Grace.†
The Kazi has become black-hearted, when adjusting legal disputes.
The dictates of the Atharva Veda, sung by Brahma, are now of no avail . He may be reached by the process of good deeds and *Harikirtan* alone.‡
Of what avail is worship without acceptance conduct without Truth, sacred thread without chastity ;
Bathe and wash, anoint thyself with *tilak* : Pure thou shalt not be without purity of thoughts.§

---

* *Ibid.*
ਜਿਸੁ ਸਿਕਦਾਰੀ, ਤਿਸਹਿ ਖੁਆਰੀ, ਚਾਕਰ ਕੇਹੇ ਡਰਣਾ ।
ਜਾ ਸਿਕਦਾਰੈ ਪਵੈ ਜੰਜੀਰੀ, ਤਾ ਚਾਕਰ ਹਥੋਂ ਮਰਣਾ ॥੪॥

† *Ibid.*
ਆਖੁ ਗੁਣਾ ਕਲਿ ਆਈਐ ।
ਤਿਹੁ ਜੁਗ ਕੇਰਾ ਰਿਹਾ ਤਪਾਵਸੁ, ਜੇ ਗੁਣ ਦੇਹਿ ਤ ਪਾਈਐ ॥ ਰਹਾਉ ॥

‡ *Ibid.*
ਕਲਿ ਕਲਿ ਵਾਲੀ ਸਰਾ ਨਿਬੇੜੀ, ਕਾਜ਼ੀ ਕ੍ਰਿਸ਼ਨਾ ਹੋਆ ।
ਬਾਣੀ ਬ੍ਰਹਮਾ ਬੇਦੁ ਅਥਰਬਣੁ ਕਰਣੀ ਕੀਰਤਿ ਲਹਿਆ ।

§ *Ibid.*
ਪਤਿ ਵਿਣੁ ਪੂਜਾ, ਸਤ ਵਿਣੁ ਸੰਜਮੁ, ਜਤ ਵਿਣੁ ਕਾਹੇ ਜਨੇਊ ।
ਨਾਵਹੁ, ਧੋਵਹੁ ਤਿਲਕ ਚੜਾਵਹੁ ਸੁਚ ਵਿਣੁ ਸੋਚ ਨ ਹੋਈ ।੬॥

In *Kaliyuga*, the Books and the Koran are being administered,
The Fundit's *Shastras* and *Purans* are ignored ;
Rahman hath become the name of the Lord : It is, however, the same Creator, saith Nanak.*
Should one attain the honour of the Lord's Name, no higher destiny than this can there be.
Possessing the Object at home, should one go abegging, no greater degradation can be thought of, saith Nanak.†

All listened spell-bound to the Divine song, and the Master then started a second tune :

The followers play and the preceptors dance, shake their feet and roll their heads :
Dust‡ riseth and getteth deposited on their heads : People look on, laugh and return home :

---

* *Ibid.*

ਕਲਿ ਪਰਵਾਣੁ, ਕਤੇਬ ਕੁਰਾਣੁ,
ਪੋਥੀ ਪੰਡਿਤ ਰਹੇ ਪੁਰਾਣੁ।
ਨਾਨਕ, ਨਾਉ ਭਇਆ ਰਹਮਾਣੁ,
ਕਰਿ ਕਰਤਾ ਤੂੰ ਏਕੋ ਜਾਣੁ ॥ ੭ ॥

† *Ibid.*

ਨਾਨਕ, ਨਾਮੁ ਮਿਲੈ ਵਡਿਆਈ,
ਏਦੂ ਊਪਰਿ ਕਰਮੁ ਨਹੀ।
ਜੇ ਘਰਿ ਹੋਦੈ ਮੰਗਣਿ ਜਾਈਐ,
ਫਿਰਿ ਓਲਾਮਾ ਮਿਲੈ ਤਹੀ ॥ ੮ ॥

‡ In India, they did not use to have proper stages for the performance of dramas. Therefore, whenever they acted, they did so on bare ground, and hence the dust.

For the sake of food they beat time, and
Dash themselves on the ground, when
 dancing :
The milk-maids sing, the Krishnas sing,
 Sitas and Ramas royal sing :
But mind, Formless is the Fearless One,
True is His name ;
He is the Creator of All.*

In the same strain the song went on at some length, in which the Master indicated to them that dancing and jumping were recreations of the mind ; that each danced as had been appointed for him as his part in the drama, but that those that laughed and danced now shall bewail their fate hereafter : they cannot thus escape death or be possessed of supernatural powers. These acts do not indicate their love of God, nor make them God-fearing. Fear and Love of God must co-exist in an earnest heart. The chief Manager, or the Pundit as he is called, then tried to explain to the Master the Divine character of Sri Krishna and Sri Ram Chandra,

* Asa di *Var*, *shlok* 5 (2).

ਵਾਇਨ ਚੇਲੇ, ਨਚਨ ਗੁਰ,
ਪੈਰ ਹਲਾਇਨ, ਫੇਰਨ ਸਿਰ ।
ਉਡ ਉਡ ਰਾਵਾ ਝਾਟੈ ਪਾਇ,
ਵੇਖੈ ਲੋਕ ਹਸੈ ਘਰ ਜਾਇ ।
ਰੋਟੀਆਂ ਕਾਰਨ ਪੂਰੇ ਤਾਲ,
ਆਪ ਪਛਾੜਹਿ ਧਰਤੀ ਨਾਲ ।
ਗਾਵਨ ਗੋਪੀਆਂ ਗਾਵਨ ਕਾਨ ।
ਗਾਵਨ ਸੀਤਾ, ਰਾਜੇ ਰਾਮ ।
ਨਿਰਭਉ ਨਿਰੰਕਾਰ ਸਚ ਨਾਮ ।
ਜਾਕਾ ਕੀਆ ਸਗਲ ਜਹਾਨ ॥

whose lives were the subject matters of the plays, and he opined that in exhibiting their lives in the open all sightseers developed a love and respect for the gods. On this the Master sang thus :

How can Thy greatness be sung, O Lord ?
Thou pervadest and givest light to all.

Thou hast created air and established the whole earth in space and hast arranged water and fire.

The Ten-headed* one (Ravan), blinded by passion, got beheaded. How art Thou Great because of the killing of Ravan ?

Thou, having created the living beings, hast retained their destinies in Thy own hands ; what greatness could be achieved by the killing of Kali ?†

Whose husband shouldst Thou be called' and who Thy wife ? Thou art present in all.

Brahma, the giver of blessings, with all his family and descendants, went out to investigate Thy Universe ;

---

*Ravan, Raja of Lanka, is said to have got ten heads on his neck. He was killed by Rama, who is therefore believed to have been an incarnation of God The point here is that God is the Creator of all the elements, then why sing of Him as killer of Ravan, who was in fact blinded by his passion and had thus lost his life. Is He great *because* Rama killed Ravan ?

† Kali was a large dreadful cobra, believed to have been killed by Krishna.

But could not find its limits. What greatness then in slaying Kans.*

Thou created the *ratans* (gems) ; others were led astray to think that *they* obtained them by churning the ocean.†

Nanak says, how couldst Thou be concealed by hiding ? yet they divide Thee in several parts.‡

---

*Kans, maternal uncle of Krishna, was a cruel heartless monarch, who was killed by his nephew.

† It is believed that Vishnu churned the ocean and got 14 *ratans* out of them,

‡ Rag Asa, M. 1, Sh. 2 (7).

ਕਿਆ ਉਪਮਾ ਤੇਰੀ ਆਖੀ ਜਾਇ ?
ਤੂ ਸਰਬੇ ਮਹਿ ਰਹਿਆ ਲਿਵ ਲਾਇ ।
ਪਉਨ ਉਪਾਇ ਧਰੀ ਸਭ ਧਰਤੀ,
ਜਲ ਅਗਨੀ ਕਾ ਬੰਧ ਕੀਆ ।
ਅੰਧੁਲੇ ਦਹਿਸਿਰ ਮੂੰਡ ਕਟਾਇਆ,
ਰਾਵਣ ਮਾਰ ਕਿਆ ਵਡਾ ਭਇਆ ?
ਜੀਉ ਉਪਾਇ ਜੁਗਤ ਹਥ ਕੀਨੀ,
ਕਾਲੀ ਨਥ ਕਿਆ ਵਡਾ ਭਇਆ ?
ਕਿਸ ਤੂ ਪੁਰਖ ਜੋਰੂ ਕਉਣ ਕਹੀਐ,
ਸਰਬ ਨਿਰੰਤਰ ਰਵ ਰਹਿਆ ।
ਨਾਲ ਕੁਟੰਬ ਸਾਥੁ ਵਰ ਦਾਤਾ,
ਬ੍ਰਹਮਾ ਭਾਲਨ ਸ੍ਰਿਸਟ ਗਇਆ ।
ਆਗੇ ਅੰਤ ਨ ਪਾਇਓ ਤਾਕਾ,
ਕੰਸ ਛੇਦ ਕਿਆ ਵਡਾ ਭਇਆ ?
ਰਤਨ ਉਪਾਇ, ਧਰੇ ਖੀਰ ਮਥਿਆ,
ਹੋਰ ਭਖਲਾਇ, ਜਿ ਅਸੀ ਕੀਆ ।
ਕਹੇ ਨਾਨਕ ਛਪ ਕਿਉ ਛਪਿਆ,
ਏਕੀ ਏਕੀ ਵੰਡ ਦੀਆ ।

Then followed the following *shabd* as to how should one dance to the Lord of the Universe:

Praise Him in full chime!
All other dancing is a vain pleasure.

Let veneration be the instrument and devo tion the tambourine,

To win joy and everlasting Aspiration,
Perform this devotion and this service:
And keep time in such dancing.

Let truth and contentment be the two cymbals,

And felicity the musical instrument of the feet,
Let thy melody be distinguished by absence of love for the second one:

And keep time in such dancing.

Let thy turning round be fear of God,

Ever and always, while sitting and while rising,

Let thy reclining (in dance) be the humility:
And keep time in such dancing.

Let such disciples be initiated into the assembly,

As love to hear God's True Name from the Guru :
Nanak says again and again,
Keep time in such dancing.*

---

* **Rag Asa, M. 1. Sh. 2 (5).**

ਪੂਰੇ ਤਾਲ ਜਾਨੈ ਸਾਲਾਹਿ !
ਹੋਰ ਨਚਣਾ ਖੁਸੀਆਂ ਮਨ ਮਾਹਿ ।

ਵਾਜਾ ਪਤ, ਪਖਾਵਜ ਭਾਉ,
ਹੋਇ ਅਨੰਦ ਸਦਾ ਮਨ ਚਾਉ ।

ਏਹਾ ਭਗਤ ਏਹਾ ਤਪਤਾਉ:
ਇਤ ਰੰਗ ਨਾਚਹੁ ਰਖ ਰਖ ਪਾਉ।

ਸਤਿ ਸੰਤੋਖੁ, ਵਜਹਿ ਦੁਇ ਤਾਲ,
ਪੈਰੀ ਵਾਜਾ ਸਦਾ ਨਿਹਾਲ,

ਰਾਗ ਨਾਦ ਨਹੀ ਦੂਜਾ ਭਾਉ:
ਇਤ ਰੰਗ ਨਾਚਉ ਰਖ ਰਖ ਪਾਉ

ਭਉ ਫੇਰੀ ਹੋਵੈ ਮਨ ਚੀਤ,
ਬੈਹਦਿਆ ਉਠਦਿਆਂ ਨੀਤਾ ਨੀਤ;

ਲੋਟਣ ਲੇਟ ਜਾਣੇ ਤਨ ਸੁਆਹ:
ਇਤ ਰੰਗ ਨਾਚਉ ਰਖ ਰਖ ਪਾਂਉ ।

ਸਿਖ ਸਭਾ ਦੀਖਿਆ ਕਾ ਭਾਉ,
ਗੁਰਮੁਖ ਸੁਣਨਾ ਸਾਚਾ ਨਾਉ ।

ਨਾਨਕ, ਆਖੇ ਵੇਰਾ ਵੇਰ:
ਇਤ ਰੰਗ ਨਾਚਉ ਰਖ ਰਖ ਪੈਰ ।

Many were the people who followed the Master, and a *Manji*, now called Dharmsal Mai Than, was established at the place, where the Master sat and sang.

During his visit to Hardwar, the Master had discussions with *Byragis* and *Sannyasins*, who, though ascetic monks, always quarrelled over the privilege of precedence in bathing at the Ganges, on occasions of festivals. These orders, originally meant for philosophic studies and spiritual development, had long ceased to serve their original purposes, and had degenerated into mere formalism. Their mutual jealousies had become proverbial, and their disputes were often sanguinary. Devoid of either learning or loving sacrifice in the service of the Lord, these mendicants, for they were nothing more than that, were subject to exactly the same vices and passions as troubled men of the world; in their case perhaps their licentiousness assumed the garb of religion and was all the more baneful in its results. The Master exposed their doings most unequivocally, and many were there who hung their heads in shame.

> "Ye colour your clothes to adopt the garb of your Order, and ye seem to wear a surplice of worn out cloth and a good sound bag to receive alms in. Ye go abegging from door to door, without being humble, and ye assume the roll of teachers of the world. Thus ye, O blind fellows, lose all honour and respect.

> Lost in absurd superstition, ye comprehend not the Word and thereby gamble away your souls for a mere trifle. Women ye have abandoned, and, subdued by passion, ye attach yourselves with other people's wives. Mind ye, O people, blessed is he, who dwelleth at the feet of the Lord in Love, be he a householder, a Sannyasin, or a Yogi."*

Rohela clan of the Afghans had mostly settled down in the sub-montaine tracts towards the north of the Ganges, now known as Rohelkhand, and it was here that, uncontrolled by the Central Government, they practised Slave trade in its worst possible form. No traveller or wayfarer was safe through this province, and all stood the grave risk of being captured and sold away as slaves. The Master visited the country, but before entering it asked Mardana to keep away for a few days, at any rate till he was recalled. Mardana obeyed and the Master entered the country, and sat prominently on a high mound. A Rohela horseman

---

* **Rag Maru M. 1, Asht., Shlok 7 (2).**

ਘੋਲੀ ਗੇਰੂ ਰੰਗ ਚੜ੍ਹਾਇਆ, ਵਸਤ ਭੇਖ ਭੇਖਾਰੀ।
ਕਾਪੜ ਫਾੜਿ ਬਨਾਈ ਖਿੰਥਾ, ਝੋਲੀ ਮਾਇਆਧਾਰੀ।
ਘਰ ਘਰ ਮਾਂਗੈ ਜਗ ਪ੍ਰਬੋਧੈ, ਮਨ ਅੰਧੈ ਪੱਤਿ ਹਾਰੀ।
ਭਰਮ ਭੁਲਾਣਾ ਸਬਦੁ ਨ ਚੀਨੈ, ਜੂਐ ਬਾਜੀ ਹਾਰੀ।
ਇਸਤ੍ਰੀ ਤਜ ਕਰ ਕਾਮ ਵਧਾਇਆ, ਚਿਤ ਲਾਇਆ ਪਰਨਾਰੀ।
ਧਨ ਗਿਰਹੀ ਸਨਿਆਸੀ ਜੋਗੀ, ਜਿ ਹਰਿ ਚਰਣੀ ਚਿਤੁ ਲਾਇ।

passed that way, captured the Master and deemed himself most fortunate for the acquisition of that day, for he believed that a handsome, strong, and attractive person, as the Master was, and of his age, must fetch a very high price as a slave. He next day offered Him for sale in the market, and a Rohela Chief purchased him in exchange for two Iraq horses. This Rohela Chief held a sort of religious sanctity in the clan and wielded considerable influence and power. He held the title of *Mir*. He ordered the Master to fetch fresh well water for his morning ablutions, but the Master came back with the news that there was no water in any of the wells and springs in the vicinity. It was an unpleasant surprise for the *Mir*, but when the fact became known in the town it caused consternation everywhere. All the wells and springs, which were full of water only the night before, had suddenly dried up. Of all the inhabitants of the locality, only the Master appeared unperturbed. The Master was sent round in the evening to search for water and fetch it from wells and springs more distant than those that had been found dried up in the vicinity, but not a drop could be had anywhere, and the Master returned without it long after it was dark. The *Mir* saw the Master coming back in the dark, surrounded with a lustrous aureola, and was further struck with amazement when he saw that the vessel, which the Master was carrying on his head for water, touched the head not. The *Mir*, who was of the Sufi faith and understood something of Spiritualism, immediately fell down on his knees, and prayed for mercy. "Use thy immense powers and influence, O *Mir*, to relieve the drought," said the Master. "I have powers over and influence with my own kind," the *Mir* replied, "they obey me and reck not what I do. Be merciful, O Great and Holy One." "Why then art thou misguiding the people, who follow thee in perfect innocence, by thy hypocrisies. How shalt thou obtain contentment thyself." "Satan permits me not to cast off this mask. I am surrounded by base influences. Do Thou save me now," prayed the *Mir*. "Satan is within thee, O man, blame not a power foreign to thee for what thou art. Thy own mind is thy foe, and thy own deeds constitute thy fall. Thou poseth what thou art not. Thou art thyself acting a Satan. Thy own evil passions are moving thee to sinful deeds. Hadst thou realised, understood and performed the duties, which thy position lay on thee, thou wouldst have found power within thee to subdue all influences of thy surroundings, which thou wouldst now condemn. Thou wouldst then not have smothered thy own spirit. Verily thy own mind has been thine enemy. Thou hast been capturing innocent men and reducing them into slavery. Thou hast been buying and selling them like cattle. Thou hast been torturing people both in body and spirit. Those that have ever approached thee for light and guidance, thou hast sent back more ignorant and more rapacious, only to misuse them to support thy impositions and hypocrisies. Those who have received God's Grace and ever live in Him and His Name, thou hast reduced to slavery and tortured and imprisoned. Thou hast forged thy own chains, O man. Endless pain thus awaits thee. It is thy misdeeds that have reflected on the people living in thy vicinity, and thou hast given them stones for their hearts, and made them dacoits and worst criminals. Heavy is thy burden, O man."

"Forgive me, O Holy One," again prayed the *Mir*, "Do tell me how may I be saved."

The Master replied thus :

'Thou hast set the house on fire, and art asleep within. Remove thy assumed ignorance, O man. Open the doors of thy jails, wherein innocent men are imprisoned ; Return all thou hast gained by evil means ; Release all slaves from bondage ; and declare there shall be no more slavery wherever thy influence extends."

The *Mir* obeyed, and amongst the prisoners thus released was one *Bhai* Hara, who immediately recognized his liberator and fell down on His Feet, saying

> Praise to Thee, O Lord, that Thou hast been so Merciful.
>
> I fall on the Feet of Him Who is so Forgiving and Gracious, Nanak.

It was now that the *Mir* and others came to know who the Divine Slave was. They had already heard of his name. All slaves in the locality were freed, and *Bhai* Ganesha Singh states that the Master established a *Manji* there. It requires some investigation, however, to locate the exact place.

At Benares, the holy *Kashi* of the learned Pundits, the Master had a very busy time. Here he had to face all the superstitious and ignorant practices of Hindu Society, and side by side he had to contend with their most learned men. It was here that he found the untouchability of the lower castes in its worst features. He however declared :

> Evil conscience is the *Dumni* ;
> Want of mercy the *kasain* ;
> Backbiting the sweepress ;
> And anger the *Chandal* :
> These are ever abiding with thee ;
> What use is thy drawing boundary lines of
> thy purified cooking floor ?

On the other hand :

> Adopt Truth as thy conduct ;
> Noble deeds as thy purified floor ;
> Remembrance of God's Name as thy bath :

For they are the blessed ones hereafter,
Who give not way to sins.*

As regards, their assumed purity of lives, the Master declared :

Thy mind is impure,
Thy body is impure,
Thy tongue is impure,
Thy mouth is impure,
By telling a lie, O man ;
How canst thou be pure ?†

To one, Chattar Das, a Pundit of great renown, the Master addressed a hymn on idol-worship, as follows :

Thou worshippest Saligram (Idol) ?
Thou counteth the rosary made of *Tulsi* beads ?
Yea, do worship, O Brahman, by taking on the rosary of pure deeds.
Abide in the Holy Name of the All-pervading,

---

* *Var* Sri Rag, *shlok*, M. 1, 20 (1).

ਕਬੁਧ ਡੂਮਣੀ ਕੁਦਇਆ ਕਸਾਇਣ,
ਪਰਨਿੰਦਾ ਘਟ ਚੂਹੜੀ ਮੁਠੀ ਕ੍ਰੋਧ ਚੰਡਾਲਿ ।

ਕਾਰੀ ਕਢੀ ਕਿਆ ਥੀਐ ਜਾ ਚਾਰੇ ਬੈਠੀਆਂ ਨਾਲ ।
ਸਚੁ ਸੰਜਮ ਕਰਨੀ ਕਾਰਾ ਨਾਵਣ ਨਾਉ ਜਪੇਈ ।
ਨਾਨਕ ਅਗੇ ਉਤਮ ਸੇਈ ਜੇ ਪਾਪਾਂ ਪੰਧਿ ਨ ਦੇਈ ।

† Rag Goojri, M. 1, Sh. 1, (2).

ਮਨ ਜੂਠਾ, ਤਨ ਜੂਠਾ ਹੈ
ਜੇਹਵਾ ਜੂਠੀ ਹੋਇ,
ਮੁਖ ਜੂਠੇ ਝੂਠ ਬੋਲਣਾ,
ਕਿਉਕਰ ਸੁਚਾ ਹੋਇ,

And ask Him, the Gracious, for Mercy :
For this shall supply thy sails to hereafter.
Why art thou irrigating barren soil ?
Thou art thus losing thy opportunity in life :
Why art thou applying *gach* (plaster of Paris) to a wall of mud ?
It shall but tumble down.
Weed out lust and anger from thy body, O brother ;
As thou weedest, happiness shall come unto thee,
Labour is never lost.
Let thy mind drive the Irrigation wheel
With which thou mayst water thy soul with Nectar.
Yea, Soak each bed of thy soil well with Ambrosia,
So will the Gardener own thee.
From heron thou shalt improve into swan,
Shouldst thou think of the All-Merciful ;
May He be gracious unto thee, prayeth Nanak, the slave of His slaves.*

---

*Rag Basant Hindol, M. 1, Gh 2 (9).

ਸਾਲਗ੍ਰਾਮ, ਬ੍ਰਿਪ ਪੂਜਿ ਮਨਾਵਹੁ,
ਸੁਕ੍ਰਿਤ ਤੁਲਸੀ ਮਾਲਾ ।
ਰਾਮ ਨਾਮੁ ਜਪਿ ਬੇੜਾ ਬਾਧਹੁ,
ਦਇਆ ਕਰਹੁ ਦਇਆਲਾ ॥ ੧ ॥
ਕਾਹ ਕਲਰਾ ਸਿੰਚਹੁ,
ਜਨਮ ਗਵਾਵਹੁ ।
ਕਾਚੀ ਢਹਗਿ ਦਿਵਾਲ,
ਕਾਹੇ ਗਚੁ ਲਾਵਹੁ ॥ ਰਹਾਉ ॥

P. T. O.

Questioned whether the bathing and worshipping of the images of gods were of absolutely no advantage, the Master told him, " Yea, Wash thy mind rather than bathe images of stone; Rub thy soul of all its filth, that it may be a fit vessel for salvation."*

Questioned whether all the learning and knowledge imparted at *Kashi* by hosts of Pundits and sages was of no avail and what other knowledge can be of help in attaining salvation, the Master addressed 54 stanzas of Dakhni O'ankar, in Rag Ramkalli, for which the

---

(In continuation of footnote from last page.)

ਕਾਮ ਕ੍ਰੋਧੁ ਦੁਇ ਕਰਹੁ ਬਸੋਲੇ,
ਗੋਡਹੁ ਧਰਤੀ ਭਾਈ ।
ਜਿਉ ਗੋਡਹੁ ਤਿਉ ਤੁਮ ਸੁਖੁ ਪਾਵਹੁ,
ਕਿਰਤ ਨ ਮੇਟਿਆ ਜਾਈ ॥ ੨ ॥
ਕਰ ਹਰਿਹਟ ਮਾਲ ਟਿੰਡ ਪਰੋਵਹੁ,
ਤਿਸ ਭੀਤਰਿ ਮਨ ਜੋਵਹੁ ।
ਅੰਮ੍ਰਿਤੁ ਸਿੰਚਹੁ ਭਰਹੁ ਕਿਆਰੇ,
ਤਉ ਮਾਲੀ ਕੇ ਹੋਵਹੁ ॥ ੩ ॥
ਬਗੁਲੇ ਤੇ ਫੁਨਿ ਹੰਸੁਲਾ ਹੋਵੈ,
ਜੇ ਤੂੰ ਕਰਹਿ ਦਇਆਲਾ ।
ਪ੍ਰਣਵਿਤਿ ਨਾਨਕ, ਦਾਸਨ ਦਾਸ,
ਦਇਆ ਕਰਹੁ ਦਇਆਲਾ ॥ ੪ ॥

* Sri Rag. M. 1, Asht, Sh. 5 (1).

ਬਾਹਿਰ ਦੇਵ ਪਖਾਲੀਅਹਿ,
ਜੇ ਮਨਿ ਧੋਵਹਿ ਕੋਇ ।
ਜੂਠ ਲਹੈ ਜੀਉ ਮਾਜੀਐ,
ਮੋਖ ਪਿਆਲਾ ਹੋਇ ।

reader is referred to the original in Granth Sahib.

Here the Master had several other discourses with representatives of the various ascetic and learned orders of many denominations, and the place where all this took place became the seat of a *Manji*, where a fairly commodious Gurdwara now stands, with a well of sweet water, the only such well in the town, the water of all others being brackish.

At Dhanpur, about 4 miles from Dacca, in East Bengal, the Master stayed outside the City but Mardana went in to ask for bread. The story is a long one which Puran Singh has beautifully condensed thus:

> Nur Shah, a woman of black magic, exercised strange powers over all that locality. She fascinated and subordinated many by her spells, compelling them to dance to her tunes. She owned the whole country around, and many a mystic and many a celibate and *yogi* had fallen into her snare. Mardana went into the city to get some bread for himself, and he fell a victim to the machinations of the slaves of Nur Shah, and could not return to the Guru. They fed him, worshipped him, but "made him a lamb." They put him under their spell, and he drank without water and he ate without bread. Mardana was thus imprisoned in the spell of black magic of Nur Shah, and could not return to the

> Guru. Guru Nanak went to search for his Mardana, and found a lost disciple in Nur Shah also. She came at last and renounced her magic at the feet of the Guru. All her slaves were set free and she obtained her freedom in the Song of *Nam*.

A Gurdwara in commemoration of the event, where Noor Shah was installed by the Master on a *Manji* to preach the Name, with which she herself had been blessed, still exists.

At the Juggen-nath temple of Lord Krishna, in Puri, the priests performed *Arti* worship every evening in front of the god's image, enshrined there. They had a large golden salver, enchased with pearls, and fitted in the centre with a lamp made of the same precious metal, in which burnt a number of wicks, fed with ghee for oil. The High priest held the candelabrum in his hands and flourished it in front of the Image of Krishna, while he and others offered burning incense, rice, flowers, sweets, safron water and other fragrant dainties to the god. All along, a number of priests fanned the god with beautiful *Chowries*, and all, priests and worshippers, sang song in praise of the god, with the accompaniment of musical instruments.

The Master entered the temple at one of these services, but sat down aside, paying no heed to the worship in which others were engaged standing. After finishing the *Arti*, the priests, who were indignant at the Master's conduct, asked him for an explanation for showing disrespect to the Great God of the Universe. "Nay, yours was not the *Arti* to the Lord of the Universe, O Pundit. I was in fact performing *Arti* to Him. I am doing so ever and anon, night and day, here as well as there." The High priest was further incensed and called the Master a liar and an atheist, on account of his holding aloof when the holy service of the Lord was going on. "Where is thy *Arti*, O Pilgrim?" The Master, thereupon, sang to them the following *Arti*:

The firmament is Thy salver, O Lord; the orbs of the stars, the pearls enchased in it; the sun and moon are Thy lamps.

The whole perfume is Thy incense; the wind fans Thee; the whole vegetable kingdom are thy flowers, O Lord of Light!

How fine is the *Arti*! O Destroyer of fear;
Unbeaten strains of ecstasy sound for trumpets.

Thou hast a thousand eyes, yet not one eye; Thou hast a thousand forms, yet not one form;

Thou hast a thousand stainless feet yet not one foot;

Thou hast a thousand organs of smell, yet not one organ:

I marvel at this play of Thine!

The Light, which is in every thing, is Thine, O Lord of Light!

From its brilliancy everything is brilliant
By the Guru's teaching the Light becometh manifest.
That which pleaseth Thee is Thy *real Arti.*
O God! my mind is fascinated with the essence of Thy lotus feet,
Night and day I thirst for it.
Give the water of Thy favour to the *sarang*, Nanak, so that he may rest contented in Thy Name.*

---

* Rag Dhanasri, M. 1, Arti, Sh. 9.

ਗਗਨ ਮੈ ਥਾਲ; ਰਵਿ ਚੰਦ ਦੀਪਕ ਬਨੇ;
ਤਾਰਕਾ ਮੰਡਲਾ ਜਨਕ ਮੋਤੀ।

ਧੂਪ ਮਲਿਆਨ ਲੌ, ਪਵਨ ਚਵਰੋ ਕਰੇ;
ਸਗਲ ਬਨ ਰਾਇ ਫੂਲੰਤ ਜੋਤੀ।

ਕੈਸੀ ਆਰਤੀ ਹੋਇ, ਭਵ ਖੰਡਨਾ! ਤੇਰੀ ਆਰਤੀ।
ਅਨਹਤਾ ਸਬਦ ਵਾਜੰਤ ਭੇਰੀ।

ਸਹੱਸ ਤਵ ਨੈਨ, ਨਨ ਨੈਨ ਹੈ ਤੋਹਿ ਕੋ;
ਸਹੱਸ ਮੂਰਤ, ਨਨਾ ਏਕ ਤੋਹੀ।

ਸਹੱਸ ਪਦ ਬਿਮਲ, ਨਨ ਏਕ ਪਦ; ਗੰਧ ਬਿਨ,
ਸਹੱਸ ਤਵ ਗੰਧ, ਇਵ ਚਲਤ ਮੋਹੀ।

ਸਭ ਮੈ ਜੋਤ ਜੋਤ ਹੈ ਸੋਇ,
ਤਿਸਕੇ ਚਾਨਨ ਸਭ ਮਹਿ ਚਾਨਨੁ ਹੋਇ।

ਗੁਰ ਸਾਖੀ ਜੋਤ ਪ੍ਰਗਟ ਹੋਇ।
ਜੋ ਤਿਸ ਭਾਵੈ ਸੋ ਆਰਤੀ ਹੋਇ।

ਹਰ ਚਰਨ ਕਮਲ ਮਕਰੰਦ ਲੋਭਤ,
ਮਨੁ ਅਨਦਿਨੋ ਮੋਹਿ ਆਹੀ ਪਿਆਸਾ।

ਕਿਰਪਾ ਜਲਦੇ ਨਾਨਕ ਸਾਰੰਗ ਕਉ।
ਹੋਇ ਜਾਂਤੇ ਤੇਰੈ ਨਾਇ ਵਾਸਾ॥

When passing through the Vindhya mountains on his return journey, Mardana was again captured, now by certain cannibals, but the Master found another lost disciple in Kauda, the Chief of the tribe, who was similarly entrusted with the mission of reclaiming others of his tribe.

VIII.

THE SECOND UDASI.

The Second Udasi or journey which was to the South commenced in about 1506, of the Christian era, and included Sirsa, Bikaneer, Ajmere, Pushkar, Abu, Ujjain, Bider, Pangal, Anainapur, Godapa, Madras, Nagapatam, and Ceylon. The return journey was taken *via* Rameshwaram along the Malabar Coast, when the Master passed through Sargarh Peeth, where he had a talk with the successor of Shankeracharya, Sudamapuri, Dwarka, Kathiawad, Sindh, Satghara (in the modern District of Montgomery), Talwandi and Lahore. This tour ended in about the year 1510.

The visit to Ceylon was very fruitful. Mansukh of Lahore, who had received his initiation and instruction from the Master at Sultanpur, some years before, was a wealthy merchant who carried on trade of considerable importance in Ceylon. He had occasions to spend part of his time in that country. On one occasion, after his initiation by the Master, he spent several months there at a stretch. His pious life, coupled with rejection of all known practices of worship, and adoption of recitation of a strange *mantram*, attracted considerable notice, and the matter was reported to the Raja, whose name is mentioned in the *Janamsakhis* as Shiv Nabh. Raja Shiv Nabh sent for him, and, as much by his fearless attitude as by the answers he gave to all questions put to him by the Raja, Mansukh was able to make a deep impression on him regarding the Master's personality and teachings. At the request of the Raja, Mansukh thereafter spent considerable time with the Raja during the period he stayed in Ceylon, and instructed him about the Master's Creed. The Raja's imagination was so much roused that when Mansukh prepared to leave for home, the Raja asked him if he could accompany him to the Punjab to see the Master. His heart pined to lay itself at the Master's feet. Mansukh, however, advised him to desist from that course for the time being, as it would upset all his administration. He was also not sure where the Master might then be, and he assured the Raja that if his desire to meet the Master became sufficiently intense, the Master, during his journeys, would be himself attracted to Ceylon. The Raja, thereupon, mostly engaged himself in singing the Master's songs, which he had learnt from Mansukh, and the more he did so, it gave him internal satisfaction and his heart pined to meet the Master. The matter became known all round and many were the *Sadhus* who came to the Raja and posed to be the Master he was in search of. They adopted the name of Nanak, but, in each case, a brief contact exposed the imposition, for the Raja could find no consolation in spite of his serving them faithfully. These impostors had thus made Raja Shiv Nabh very cautious and he always thereafter tested those who were reported to him as having come to his capital to have an interview with the Raja. It was a hard test that he prescribed. Presents of dainties, silver and gold, as well as comfortable beds and handsome damsels played considerable part and no wonder that none of the impostors could withstand these temptations.

The Raja was in this somewhat sceptic mood about the visitors to him, and was almost despairing, when it was reported to him that an *Udasi*, accompanied by a musician, had arrived, and stayed in an old abandoned and dried up garden, where the trees were showing signs of life and had become green. The Raja, however, wanted to apply his usual tests before exposing himself to further ridicule by his people and he sent all sorts of dainties and silks as presents, through beautiful damsels. The Master, who was engaged in his contemplations, accepted no presents and looked at none of the women who had brought them. It is said that all sorts of blandishments were employed by these women to seduce him. They sang lascivious songs but the Master was not moved.

Eventually the Raja came himself and after showing the usual respects, he enquired of the Master who he was, whether he followed the practices of the *Yogis*, *Sanyasins* or monks of some other order. The Master sang his song, while Mardana played the tune, thus :

> What is thy Name, O Lord, and what Thy caste ?
> When Thou callest me Within, I ask Thee in perfect communion.
> In Thy pure Name is the exercise of my *Yoga* ;
> In Love for Thy ever-True Personality lieth the cessation of life and death.
> Bath in Thy Divine Knowledge is my Brahmanism, and worship of Thy Divine Attributes my communalism.
> Thou art One, One Thy Name, Thy Spirit alone pervadeth the universe.
> I am the Trader at Thy Shop alone, O, the Capitalist Master of all.
> I weigh Thy Immeasureable Name in the scales of my material tongue.
> Thou, my True Master, hath ended the doubts regarding here and hereafter, my soul liveth now in certainty : This he alone understandeth who liveth in communion with Thee alone,
> Who liveth in the Word, removeth doubt, and, day and night, remaineth ever in Thy Service

In the sublimest of human senses lieth the soul, and within it liveth my Unapproachable Guru.

Under His Instruction, whether at home or abroad, hath Nanak become an *Udasi*.*

---

*Rag Maru, M. 1.

ਜੋਗੀ ਜੁਗਤਿ ਨਾਮੁ ਨਿਰਮਾਇਲੁ,
ਤਾਂਕੈ ਮੈਲੁ ਨ ਰਾਤੀ ।
ਪ੍ਰੀਤਮੁ ਨਾਥੁ ਸਦਾ ਸਚੁ ਸੰਗੇ,
ਜਨਮ ਮਰਨ ਗਤਿ ਬੀਤੀ ॥੧॥
ਗੁਸਾਈ, ਤੇਰਾ ਕਹਾ ਨਾਮੁ, ਕੈਸੇ ਜਾਤੀ ।
ਜਾ ਤਉ ਭੀਤਰਿ ਮਹਲਿ ਬੁਲਾਵਹਿ,
ਪੂਛਉ ਬਾਤ ਨਿਰੰਤੀ ॥ ਰਹਾਉ ॥
ਬ੍ਰਹਮਣ ਬ੍ਰਹਮੁ ਗਿਆਨ ਇਸਨਾਨੀ,
ਹਰਿ ਗੁਣ ਪੂਜੇ ਪਾਤੀ ।
ਏਕੋ ਨਾਮੁ ਏਕੁ ਨਾਰਾਇਣੁ,
ਤ੍ਰਿਭਵਣ ਏਕਾ ਜੋਤੀ ॥ ੨ ॥
ਜਿਹਬਾ ਡੰਡੀ, ਇਹੁ ਘਟੁ ਛਾਬਾ,
ਤੋਲਹੁ ਨਾਮੁ ਅਜਾਚੀ ।
ਏਕੋ ਹਾਟੁ ਸਾਹੁ ਸਭਨਾ ਸਿਰਿ,
ਵਣਜਾਰੇ ਇਕ ਭਾਤੀ ॥੩॥
ਦੋਵੈ ਸਿਰੇ ਸਤਿਗੁਰੂ ਨਿਬੇੜੇ,
ਸੋ ਬੂਝੈ ਜਿਸ ਏਕ ਲਿਵ ਲਾਗੀ,
ਜੀਅਹੁ ਰਹੈ ਨਿਭਰਾਤੀ ।
ਸਬਦੁ ਵਸਾਏ ਭਰਮੁ ਚੁਕਾਏ,
ਸਦਾ ਸੇਵਕੁ ਦਿਨੁ ਰਾਤੀ ॥੪॥
ਊਪਰ ਗਗਨੁ, ਗਗਨ ਪਰਿ ਗੋਰਖੁ,
ਤਾਕਾ ਅਗਮ ਗੁਰੂ ਪੁਨਿ ਵਾਸੀ ।
ਗੁਰ ਬਚਨੀ ਬਾਹਰਿ ਘਰੁ ਏਕੋ,
ਨਾਨਕੁ ਭਇਆ ਉਦਾਸੀ ॥ ੫ ॥

The Song, and particularly its ending, assured the Raja that the Master he had been waiting for all these years had come and he laid his Self prostrate at his feet and wept. The Master consoled him and gave him further instruction. A *Dharmsal* was constructed, where Raja Shiv Nabh himself became the Rev. Brother. It is said that the composition, *Pran Sangli*, of which only fragments are now extant, was sung there. It was recorded by Saida but was handed over to Raja Shiv Nabh, with instructions that if some Sikh came from the Punjab, he should be allowed to take a copy. The composition, so far as it can be had, describes the method of spiritual development of the human soul. It is, however, not included in the Granth Sahib. From historical point of view, this visit requires further investigation.

It is necessary to mention here that Bhai Santokh Singh, author of the Nanak Parkạsh, records this visit to Ceylon prior even to the First Udasi, which was to the east. It was a hurried tour, he says, which was undertaken because the yearnings of Raja Shiv Nabh, after he had been instructed by Mansukh, had become so intense that he spent days and nights in spiritual reveries and forsook all affairs of State. Bhai Santokh Singh, however, has referred to no authority for it, and, in the older available records, this visit is recorded as part of the second Udasi.

It was on his return from this Udasi that the Master passed through Lahore, and was invited to the *Shradh* feast by Duni Chand, a wealthy Khatri of the town, whose house in Chohatta Mufti Bakar, near Wazir Khan's Mosque, inside the Delhi Gate, is since the site of a Gurdwara. The Master accepted the invitation and reached the place after the *Shradh* ceremonies were concluded and the Brahmans had been duly feasted. Duni Chand received the Master with due respect and when he offered to serve the food to him, the Master enquired of him what the feast was all about. Duni Chand said that the feast had been given by him in the memory of, and to satisfy the soul of, his deceased father. "Has thy father then been fed and satiated," the Master asked? Duni Chand said that the Pundits and Brahmans had blessed the feast as having done so. The Master looked above into space and smiled. "Listen, Duni Chand: The priests and Brahmans have been fed; but thy father hath received nothing. Thy father has had no food since three days. He is hungry as a wolf, and is not satisfied yet." He then directed Duni Chand to proceed five *kos* towards the north where he shall find a hungry wolf lying prostrate, and shall then also see his father, who will tell him all. Duni Chand went out immediately, and, at about the place indicated, he found a wolf lying near some bushes, and the etherial body of his father, wholly disengaged from that of the wolf, at first arising in the form of mist, formed itself and stood out visibly to Duni Chand. The latter held communion with him there for some time and learnt that his father had received no satisfaction whatsoever. He then learnt that his father's spirit had been wandering all these years in hunger, which had not been satisfied when he was in human body on this earth, and that, by the Grace of the Master, who was then sitting at his house, he had been disengaged from those bonds in which he had been suffering pain. The spirit then blessed Duni Chand and directed him to go and receive instruction from the Master and live up to those instructions, and melted away in space. Duni Chand returned home and described to the Master what he had seen and learnt. The Master gave Duni Chand a needle and said, "Duni Chand, keep it with thee, and I shall get it back from thee hereafter." Duni Chand and his wife, however, said that it could not go with them after death; how could they return it there. Well, Duni Chand, what use are thy millions to thee then. Thou hast seen thy father's plight now, and ought to take a lesson. The Master then instructed Duni Chand in the Name and how to live in the world and in what manner to use his wealth. It is said that fifteen *pauris* of the Asa-Di-Var were sung to him by the Master by way of instruction. The entire life of Duni Chand was now switched on to the Spiritual development of his soul. He gave away most of what he had in charity and meeting the wants of others, built one *dharamsal* at his house and another where he had met the etherial body of his father. Both are still in existense.

The Master, thereupon, went round and eventually selected a spot on the right Bank of the Ravi river, opposite to Pakhoke Randhawa, where his wife and sons were living with his father-in-law, about sixty miles to the north of Lahore, and settled down there. One Karori Khatri of Lahore adopted the Faith and offered to construct a Chak on the spot, which, when done, was called Kartarpur, *i.e.*, the Colony of God the Creator. This became the first holy place of the Sikhs of the Master, and it was here that the practice of Divine music every morning was established. The Master stayed here for about two years before setting out on his Third Udasi which was into the Himmalayan mountains. During this period the Master was informed that his wife and sons were not quite comfortable at the house of his father-in-law, Mul Chand, who considered them an unnecessary encumbrance, and, at the request of his wife, the Master permitted them to settle down in the holy colony of Kartarpur.

IX.

THE THIRD UDASI.

The Third Trip was commenced in about the year 1514, and was taken into the Himmalayan mountains. It is difficult to say which route the Master adopted when he went up, but it is certain that he visited Mansarowar Lake, where he had discourses with the Yogis, who held considerable power in those regions. having practically undermined the Budhistic practices there beyond recognition. From there the Master climbed up the higher mountains and passed into Tibbet and is also believed to have visited China before taking his return journey home, across the Kailash mountains and through Ladakh, Kashmere, Riasi and Jammu. The journey occupied between two and three years.

It seems of interest to mention here that when a Punjab University Trip to the Mansarowar Lake was taken a few years ago, the party included Professor Kashmira Singh, then of the Khalsa College at Amritsar. On the authority of Professor Kashmira Singh, Bhai Vir Singh ji, Editor of Santokh Singh's Nanak Parkash, has recorded, in a footnote at page 691 of the Second Volume, that in the Four Cave Temples on the Mansarowar Lake the images of Guru Nanak are also worshipped among others. It is these temples which are the main objects of pilgrimage by the Tibbetan Budhists on one side and Indian Sadhus on the other. Another Sikh, *Bhai* Didar Singh, has also been travelling in these higher mountains, and supports the view that many indications of an unmistakable character are found everywhere in these hills showing the lasting influence which the Master's visit left on the worship and practices of the various Hill tribes. There is a class of people living in Tibbet and other Himmalayan countries, who have substituted or added the Mantra, *Om, Ahum Bhadra Guru Parm Sidhi Ham*, for or to the usual Budhist Mantra, *Om, Mani Padmi Ham*, and it is these men in whose temples the image of Guru Nanak is given a prominent place. When questioned, these people explain that the *Bhadra Guru* or the Great Master, whom they worship, had appeared in the Punjab, had turned the Mecca, had sweetened the *reetha* (soap-nut) fruit, had defeated the Yogis, had appeared in Ten Forms, and had founded the Great *Tirath* at Amritsar.

These people have been often seen making pilgrimage at Rowal Sar, in Mandi State, and at Amritsar, by the process of *Dandwat.* Sardar Tirath Singh Gharjakhia, a Tahsildar in the Kashmere State Service, who has for many years been in Ladakh and Leh, supports this information and states that he also met several Chinese pilgrims, bound for Amritsar, who told him that Guru Nanak visited their country and established a temple at Nanking and that since then numerous Chinese have worshipped him. The matter, however, requires further investigation.*

At Mattan, in Kashmere, the Master had a short discourse with Pundit Brahm Das, whose Library was said to be two camel-loads. To the Pundit, the Master explained the futility of all study, if it failed to bring contentment within. By such extensive studies, as the Pundit had engaged in, he had stored

* Since the above was written, the present writer had an opportunity to visit the Kullu Valley, and met a Lahouli Budhist at Manali, in October 1928. The gentleman stated his age to be 68, and he was constantly counting his rosary, with the accompaniment of some silent recitations. It was with some difficulty that the writer was able to get a reply from him as to which *Mantra* he recited with his rosary. He said that he recited both of the *Mantras* which have been mentioned in the above text. Questioned as to what he understood by them he said that one was the *Mantra* of the Wahiguru and the other of the Shivji. Further questioned what he understood the Wahiguru to be, he remarked somewhat surprisingly that his questioner did not know it when the Wahiguru's Temple was at Amritsar and was so well known. He said he had been regularly making his pilgrimage at that temple every year, except for the last six, when he could not go on account of old age.

his brain with the thaughts of numerous authors, but, in that crowd of knowledge; he had lost his soul.

> Read and Read Cart-loads ;
> Read and read contents of numerous shelves;
>
> Read and read boat-loads ;
> Read and read contents of all cellars ;
>
> Read and read for years and years ;
> Read and read through months and months ;
>
> Read and read throughout life ;
> Read and read every breath of thy life ;
>
> Vain, vain all is, born in ego,
> Except for One Word, which alone shall avail thee, saith Nanak.*

---

*Asa di Var, Shlok M. 1.

ਪੜਿ ਪੜਿ ਗਡੀ ਲਦੀਅਹਿ ਪੜਿ ਪੜਿ ਭਰੀਅਹਿ ਸਾਥ ।

ਪੜਿ ਪੜਿ ਬੇੜੀ ਪਾਈਐ ਪੜਿ ਪੜਿ ਗਡੀਅਹਿ ਖਾਤ ।

ਪੜੀਅਹਿ ਜੇਤੇ ਬਰਸ ਬਰਸ, ਪੜੀਅਹਿ ਜੇਤੇ ਮਾਸ ।

ਪੜੀਐ ਜੇਤੀ ਆਰਜਾ, ਪੜੀਅਹਿ ਜੇਤੇ ਸਾਸ ।

ਨਾਨਕ ਲੇਖੈ ਇਕ ਗਲ ਹੋਰ ਹਉਮੈ ਝਖਣਾ ਝਾਖ ॥

Thou needest to unlearn what thou hast learnt, O Pundit; cease from over-great desire for knowledge, for "the more thou learnest of the book lore, the more distracted thou becomest.* It is the colossal ignorance of thy extensive knowledge which prevents thee from knowing the Truth. Thou must be reborn as a babe, before thou canst regain thy soul, lost in the wilderness of books." Pundit Brahm Das, whose egotistic knowledge had at first led him to object to the Master wearing skin clothes, while he was apparently engaged as a teacher of Religion, saw the scales falling off his spiritual eyes and prayed for the knowledge of the One Word which he had lacked. Nay, go to thy preceptor, waiting for thee in the ruins beyond, said the Master; and the Pundit wended his way in the direction indicated. He came upon some big ruins* and found a beautiful and magnificently attired damsel, laden with silks and jewels, standing amongst them. She beckoned him to come near, and when the Pundit approached her, she struck him on the head with her shoes and bade him turn back from where he had come. Throughout all his studies and engagements, the Pundit had been

* Var Asa. M. 1, Sh. 9, (2).

ਲਿਖਿ ਲਿਖਿ ਪੜਿਆ ਤੇਤਾ ਕੜਿਆ

* Reference probably is to the magnificent ruins of Martand situate at a distance of about 3 miles from Mattan.

really the worshipper of matter, wealth, decorations and external appearances, and these now gave him the answer that he had made himself a loathsome beast of burden. On his return, the Master found him cleansed of his ego, and told him thus :

There is but One path, and but one door ;
And Guru is the only step leading unto thy soul :
Beautiful is the Lord of Nanak :
In the True Name all happiness is .*

The Pundit saw the Celestial vision, and was installed on the *Manji* to share the bliss he had obtained with others.†

---

*Var Mallhar, Shlok M. 1.

ਏਕੋ ਪਾਧਰੁ ਏਕੁ ਦਰੁ, ਗੁਰ ਪਉੜੀ ਨਿਜ ਥਾਨੁ ।
ਰੂੜਉ ਠਾਕੁਰੁ ਨਾਨਕਾ, ਸਭਿ ਸੁਖੁ ਸਾਚਉ ਨਾਮ ॥

† The remnants of a Platform in the centre of the lower tank of the Twin Springs at Mattan indicates the spot where the Master had sat, while some ruins of the pillars of the causeway leading up to the platform from the left side of the Spring are also visible. In 1908, when the present writer first visited Kashmere, he saw one of the seven Gurdwaras, which had been built on three sides of the twin Springs, still standing and he read a sermon from the Granth Sahib to the assembled audience in that Gurdwara. That Gurdwara, however, has also gone in ruins, and a new one seems to have recently been constructed, not on that site but along the south-western corner of the lower Spring. It is difficult to say who is responsible for this act of vandalism.

X

The Fourth Udasi.

The Fourth journey was taken by the Master towards the West. It commenced in 1518 or 1519, and occupied three or four years. During this journey, the Master passed through Sindh for the second time, and took boat at Dwarka in Kathiawad, for Mecca. During this voyage and further journeys through Muhammadan countries, the Master is stated to have worn the usual blue garments of a *Haji*, carried a prayer carpet and a book under his arm, and was, like other Mussalman pilgrims, provided with a water jug (*kuza*) and an *Assa* (staff). After visiting Mecca and Medina, the Master travelled northwards through Jerusalem, Damascus and Alleppo, and turning to the south-east, stayed for some time at Baghdad. Syed Muhammad Latif, in his History of the Punjab, states that "it "appears that he visited Stamboul, a story being "related of his interview with the Sultan of "Turkey, who was noted for his cupidity and "his extreme oppression of his subjects. "Nanak's admonitions had a great effect on "the Sultan, who is said to have bestowed his "horded treasures on the *Faqirs* and the needy, "and to have discontinued his tyranny over his "people." Syed Muhammad Latif's remark seems to be based on a composition entitled *Nasihatnama*, which is said to have been addressed by the Master to a King, Karoon by name, but the authenticity of this composition cannot be established. Karoon, or, to be more precise in western terminology, Croesus, was not the name or title of the Ruler of any country during the Master's period. *Bhai* Mani Singh, who wrote his *Janamsakhi* of the Master early in the eighteenth century and *Bhai* Gyan Singh, who wrote his History of the Sikh Gurus in the end of the nineteenth century, of the Christian era, have said that the name of the King to whom *Nasihatnama* was addressed, was Sultan Hamid Karoon, and while *Bhai* Mani Singh says he was Sultan of Turkey, *Bhai* Gyan Singh describes him as Sultan of Egypt and adds that the Sikh soldiers, who took part in the Soudan Expedition against Mahdi, in 1886, actually saw a platform towards the south of the town of Kaikai, which was stated to be the place where the Master had met the Sultan, and that the Sikh soldiers held a congregation and sacrament there. While not denying the possibility of the Master having visited Stamboul, Egypt or Soudan, and, without questioning the statement made by *Bhai* Gyan Singh regarding the congregation held by the Sikh soldiers at the Platform, which was said to be the site sanctified by the

Master's feet, it is impossible to accept the statement regarding his meeting a King, Sultan Hamid Karoon by name, either in Turkey or Egypt or elsewhere. During the period of the Master's western Trip, Sultan Salim I (1512 to 1520) and his son, Suleiman (1520 to 1566), successively ruled in Turkey, while Baghdad was part of the Persian Empire of Shah Ishmael Safwi, the founder of the Safwi Dynasty of Persia (1499, to 1524), who had conquered the Province of Baghdad in the years 1503 to 1507. Nor had Egypt an independent King after 1516-17, when it was conquered and annexed to the Turkish Empire by Sultan Salim I. The names of the last few independent rulers of Egypt, which then included Soudan, were as follows :

En-Nasir Abu Sa'adat Muhammad, 1495—1499.

Kansooh Khamsa Meeyah, 1499 (11 days only).

Edli-Dhabir Abu-u-Nasr Kansooh, 1499-1500 (5 months).

El-Ashraf Kansooh Janbalat, 1500 (6 months).

El-Malik El-Adil Tooman Bey, 1500 to 1501.

Kansooh El-Ghouree-El-Malik El-Ashraf, 1501-1516.

The last of these was killed in battle by the Turks in 1517, since when the country was ruled, or rather misruled, as the historians say, by the Turks, through a Pasha or Governor called Sheikh-ul-Bald, and twenty-three Beys or Military Sub-Governors. With the conquest of Egypt, Arabia which till then was subject to the Egyptian rule also passed to the Turks, and the Shereef of Mecca handed over the keys of the City and proffered his allegiance to Sultan Salim I, in the year 1517. Medina, which once used to be the seat of the Caliphs, was since then held by the Turks "with a firm hand", as the historians have particularly remarked ; and this fact also seems to dispose of the suggestion in the *Janamsakhi*, going in the name of Bala, that Hamid Karoon was the name of the ruler of Medina, when the Master visited it and addressed him the composition named *Nasihatnama.* This composition is not contained in the Granth Sahib, and the language and style of it fully betray its spurious nature. It is impossible to believe that the Master could have used the vulgar language, as the word *harámi* (meaning bastard) undoubtedly is, which finds place in it, when addressing a man of even a humbler position than that of a Sultan.

When the Master reached Mecca, dressed as a *Haji*, he lied down with his feet towards the *Ka'aba*. The Maulvis and pilgrims saw this and were much disturbed. They began to swear at him, and one of them, Jiwan by name, struck him a kick and remarked, " Who the *Kafir* art thou that is sleeping with his feet at the house of God ?" "Pray be not furious," replied the Master, "I have come from afar. "I was tired and weary, and have but thrown "myself here. KINDLY TURN MY FEET TO "WHERE THE HOUSE OF GOD IS NOT." One Rukn-ud-Din immediately took hold of the Master's feet to turn them away, and an electric current passed through his body. His heart began to beat rapidly, and he turned the feet of the Master in different directions. But, Lo! The *Ka'aba* also went round and round. Rationalists have explained this into an allegorical way of stating that, in the discussion which followed, those that were present on the occasion began to realize that the House of God, who is All-Pervading, was on all sides and not only in the *Ka'aba*. The Islamic traditions, however, support the possibility of the *Ka'aba* moving from its place.

This led to further enquiries by the various people about the Master's antecedents, and when they learnt that he had come from Hindustan, some of them questioned him whether he was a Hindu or Mussalman. The Master replied that he was neither, but that his body was made of five elements and a Mysterious Power was playing within him. "Well, which of the two, Hindu or Mussalman was better," cleverly asked another. "Both of them," said the Master, "shall cry without "good deeds, and shall obtain no satisfaction "hereafter. *Kussumbha* dyes fade away and "shall not remain fast when washed. Hindus "and Muhammadans revile each other. Where "is the room for Ram, as God is named by "Hindus, or Rahim, as He is called by the "Moslems, to stay amongst them ? The world "is thus following the ways of Satan."*

Several Indian Muhammadan Faqirs happened to be on a pilgrimage to the *Ka'aba* in those days, and amongst them were Makhdum Rukn-ud-Din, Jallal the Second of Uch, Sheikh Ibrahim, Farid the Second of Pakpattan, and Sheikh Dastgir. Makhdum Rukn-ud-Din led the principal discourse with the Master, though Sheikh Ibrahim, referred to in the *Janamsakhis* as *Pir Patallia*† also put several questions. The Discourse is preserved still as *Mecca-di-gosht*, but, as it is not incorporated in the Granth Sahib, it cannot be said how much of it is genuine, and what must be treated as interpolations.

---

* *Vars* of Bhai Gurdas Ji, 1 (33)

ਪੁਛਣ ਗਲ ਈਮਾਨ ਦੀ ਕਾਜ਼ੀ ਮੁਲਾਂ ਇਕੱਠੇ ਹੋਈ,
ਵਡਾ ਸਾਂਗ ਵਰਤਾਇਆ ਲਖ ਨ ਸੱਕੈ ਕੁਦਰਤਿ ਕੋਈ।
ਪੁਛਣ ਖੋਲ ਕਿਤਾਬ ਨੂੰ ਵਡਾ ਹਿੰਦੂ ਕਿ ਮੁਸਲਮਾਨੋਈ ?
ਬਾਬਾ ਆਖੈ ਹਾਜੀਆਂ, ਸ਼ੁਭ ਅਮਲਾਂ ਬਾਝੋਂ ਦੋਵੇ ਰੋਈ,
ਹਿੰਦੂ ਮੁਸਲਮਾਨ ਦੋਇ ਦਰਗਹਿ ਅੰਦਰ ਲੈਨ ਨ ਢੋਈ।
ਕੱਚਾ ਰੰਗ ਕੁਸੁੰਭ ਕਾ ਪਾਣੀ ਧੋਤੇ ਥਿਰ ਨ ਰਹੋਈ।
ਕਰਨ ਬਖੀਲੀ ਆਪ ਵਿਚ, ਰਾਮ ਰਹੀਮ ਕਥਾਇ ਖਲੋਈ?
ਰਾਹ ਸੈਤਾਨੀ ਦੁਨੀਆਂ ਗੋਈ॥

† Corrupt form of *Pir* Pattania i. e., the *Pir* of Pak Pattan.

Makhdum Rukn-ud-Din asked the Master what would happen to those who, though indulgent in sins, listened not to what the sacred books said and rendered no prayers to the Almighty Father. The Master replied thus :

> Listen, O man to the words of Truth, which Nanak saith :
>
> God will call upon thee for an explanation, when the record of thy deeds is examined.
>
> Rebels shall be put up for retribution, if the account shewed a debit balance ;
> The arch-angel Israel shall be deputed for punishment :
>
> No way out shall then be found ; for narrow is the path through which one has to pass :
>
> Falsehood shall then end, saith Nanak, and Truth alone shall then prevail.*

---

* Shlok M. 1.

ਨਾਨਕੁ ਆਖੈ ਰੇ ਮਨਾ ਸੁਣੀਐ ਸਿਖ ਸਹੀ ।
ਲੇਖਾ ਰਬ ਮੰਗੇਸੀਆਂ. ਬੈਠਾ ਕਢਿ ਵਹੀ ।
ਤਲਬਾਂ ਪਉਸਨਿ ਆਕੀਆਂ. ਬਾਕੀ ਜਿਨਾ ਰਹੀ ।
ਅਜਰਾਈਲੁ . ਫਰੇਸ਼ਤਾ, ਹੋਸੀ ਆਇ ਤਈ ।
ਆਵਣ ਜਾਣ ਨ ਸੁਝਈ, ਭੀੜੀ ਗਲੀ ਫਹੀ ।
ਕੂੜ ਨਿਖੁਟੇ ਨਾਨਕਾ. ਓੜਕਿ ਸਚ ਰਹੀ ॥

It is said that before leaving Mecca, the Master left one of his sandals in the *Ka'aba*, as a souvenir, but that it was brought back to India by Makhdum Rukn-ud-Din, and is still preserved as a sacred relic at the Shrine of Uch, in the territories of the present Nawab of Bahawalpur.

At Baghdad, the Master stayed at the graveyard outside the town, and Mardana as usual was with him. Early in the morning before dawn, Mardana, as usual, played upon the *Rabab*, and the Master sang his song about the infiniteness of God and His Creation wherein occurred the expression, "There are numerous *patals*, earths, and innumerable *akashs*, skies," when some Muhammadan who was listening to it and understood its purport went and reported the blasphemy of the utterance, inasmuch as the Koran had mentioned seven earths and seven skies only, to the *Sajjadanashin* of the shrine of Peer Dastgir Abdul Kadir Jilani. The Dastgir Pir directed the offender to be stoned to death, and numerous people of the town immediately armed themselves with stones and rushed out. In the meanwhile the Master's morning prayers had concluded, and at the end the Master shouted out his greetings of *Sat Kartar*, in a voice full of Divine Electricity, which immediately disarmed the people. On this, one of the Peers, Bahlol by name, came forward and had a discourse with the Master on the subject of the Morning Song. The Peer was accompanied by his son, and such was the effect of the Master's answers, which it may be mentioned were never argumentative, that first the son and then the father confessed their conversion and admitted the truth of the maxim that Almighty God's creation was not confined to seven earths and seven skies, but was composed of millions and millions of planets and universes. The Master stayed in Baghdad for four months and held many conversations with the Peers and other holy men of the place. Before his departure from there he was presented with a robe as a token of respect and submission, on which some verses in Arabic characters were inscribed. This *Chola* or Robe is still preserved at Dera Baba Nanak. Bhai Santokh Singh mentions a similar robe, with inscriptions on it in five different characters, having descended on the Master from the Heavens in Abbysinia.

Swami Anandacharya, now said to be settled in Norway, in his work, entitled "Snow Birds," records that, during his travels, he found an inscription, dated the year 912 *hejri*, in the outskirts of Baghdad, in the Arabic language, which, translated, read thus :

> HERE SPAKE THE HINDU GURU NANAK TO FAKIR BAHLOL ; AND, FOR THESE SIXTY WINTERS, SINCE THE GURU LEFT

IRAN, THE SOUL OF BAHLOL HAS RESTED ON THE MASTER'S WORD, LIKE A BEE POISED ON A DAWN-LIT HONEY-ROSE.*

---

* Following is the composition of Sri Ananda Acharya, in the work mentioned above, Canto XC, page 182.

"ON READING AN ARABIC INSCRIPTION IN A SHRINE OUTSIDE THE TOWN OF BAGHDAD. DATED 912 HEJRA.

"Upon this simple slab of granite didst thou sit, discoursing of fraternal love and holy light, O Guru Nanak, Prince among India's holy sons!

"What song from the source of the Seven Waters thou didst sing to charm the soul of Iran!

"What peace from Himalaya's lonely caves and forests thou didst carry to the vine-groves and rose-gardens of Baghdad!

"What light from Badrinath's snowy peak thou didst bear to illumine the heart of Bahlol, thy saintly Persian disciple?

"Eight fortnights Bahlol hearkened to thy words on Life and the Path and Spring Eternal, while the moon waxed and waned in the pomegranate grove beside the grassy desert of the dead.

"And after thou hast left him to return to thy beloved Bharat's land, the fakir, it is said, would speak to none nor listen to the voice of man or angel;

"His fame spread far and wide and the Shah came to pay him homage but the holy man would take no earthly treasures nor hear the praise of kings and courtiers.

"Thus lived he—lonely, devoted, thoughtful—for sixty winters, sitting before the stone whereon thy sacred feet had rested;

"And ere he left this House of Ignorance he wrote these words on the stone: "Here spake the Hindu Guru Nanak to Fakir Bahlol, and for these sixty winters since the Guru left Iran, the soul of Bahlol has rested on the Master's word—like a bee poised on a dawnlit honey-rose."

It has been suggested that Bahlol, referred to in it was probably the *sajjadanashin* of Bahlol Dana, who was a Fakir of considerable renown. The matter certainly is worthy of further investigation.

During the recent Great War, when the British and Indian armies conquered Baghdad, they discovered this place where the Master had his Discourse with Bahlol. It lies to the west of the town and between the old graveyard to the north and the present Baghdad-Samara railway line to the south. The present writer's brother, Dr. Kirpal Singh, then a Captain in the Indian Medical Service, also saw it during the War, and he, in his letter to the present writer, dated the 15th October ,1918, described it as follows :—

> It is really a very humble looking building and known to very few people except the local Sikhs. To some Arabs it is known as well by the name of tomb of Bahlol. You enter the building by a small door, on which something is written in Arabic, not visible to a casual visitor. Even with attention it is difficult to read. I could not read it and hence could not copy it I have taken a photograph of the outside which I shall forward to you in due course. Entering the building, you come to a brick paved passage going to your right

straight into the room (with a verandah) wherein you find the tomb and the Raised Platform. In the courtyard there are a few trees, mostly pomegranates. The room in which there are the platform and the tomb, has two doors, one of which is open whilst the other is barred. As you enter the room, you come face to face with the platform which roughly is about 2 to $2\frac{1}{2}$ ft. high, and about 3′ by 4′ in dimensions. It is now covered with handkerchiefs of various colours presented by the Sikhs. In the centre close to the wall you find a picture of Sri Guru Nanak, presented by some energetic Sikh, above which you find the slab with the writing which I reproduce in this letter for you.* The name of the man in charge is Sayed Yusuf.'"

The site plan of the Memorial is given below:—

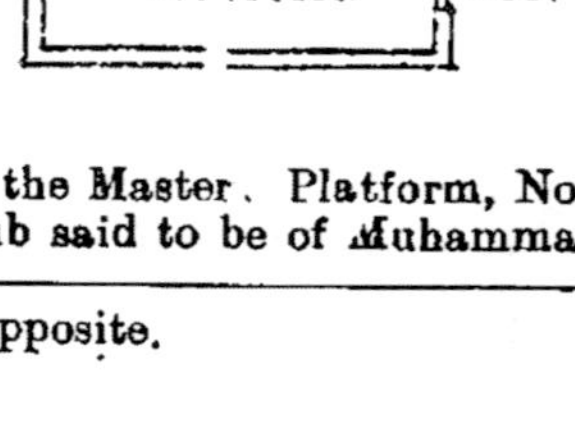

Note.—No. 1 is the Master. Platform, No. 2 is Bahlol's tomb and No. 3 is the tomb said to be of Muhammad Pasha Arnaoot.

*See the plate opposite.

To face page 156.

Inscription in Turkish language at Baghdad

Photo by Dr. Kirpal Singh.

A free translation of this inscription, which is in the Turkish language, is as follows :

> Murad saw the demolished building of Hazrat Rab-i-Majid, Baba Nanak, Fakir Aulia, and rebuilt it with his own hands, so that historic memorial may continue from generation to generation, and His *murid-i-s'eed* (the blessed disciple) may obtain heavenly bliss.—Year 917 H.

It is obvious that this inscription is not the same which Swami Anandacharya saw and translated in his 'Snow Birds', and it is possible that the inscription deciphered by the Swami is the old and ancient Arabic inscription which the writer's brother noticed outside the outer door of the building, but which he found no longer decipherable. The inscription of which the photograph is reproduced seems to be a later one which some descendant in faith of Bahlol seems to have put up on reconstructing the building, but he has not mentioned the year of the reconstruction.

The year under this inscription may be 917, or it may, it is said by one who is competent to read it and has given the above translation, be also read as 927. The latter reading seems to coincide with the chronology adopted in this biography. In this light, the Master visited Baghdad in the year 1520-21 of the Christian era. The reading of the year by Swami

Anandacharya, in the old inscription, which is either now lost or become undecipherable, seems erroneous.

From Baghdad, the Master seems to have returned, through Baku (where some Gurmukhi inscriptions on old delapidated temples, obviously giving the pedigrees of certain *Udasi* Sikh priests of the Temples, have been discovered, and formed the subject of a paper by Lala Parma Nand, before the Punjab Historical Society, some years ago), Persia, Turkestan, Kabul and Peshawar. A Gurdwara in Kabul, and another at the Water Springs at Askara, nine miles from Kabul, towards Jallalabad, are still associated with the Master's name.

Hassan Abdal is a town on the main road from Peshawar to Lahore, about thirty miles to the north-west of the modern town of Rawalpindi. A Dervesh of some spiritual pretensions, named Bawa Wali, of Kandhar, was staying at the top of a hill overlooking the town. There was a beautiful spring of fresh water at the place where the Dervesh lived, and no good water could be had at the foot of the hill. The Master, accompanied by Mardana, stayed at the bottom of the mountain and Mardana went up to bring water from the spring. As Mardana was going to dip his jug in the spring, Bawa Wali asked him who he was. Mardana told him as much, and, as well as he could, who his Master was and asked the Dervesh to come down and meet him also. He had described the Master as a Prophet. Bawa Wali was offended at this description, and told Mardana that his Master ought not to send for water from other people's abodes, if he was a prophet, and he repelled him without water. Mardana climbed down and told the Master what had happened. The Master, however, sent him back saying that he ought to approach the Wali with humility and not arrogance, and tell him that a humble creature of God wanted water as a gift of God. Wali, however, was not moved. Mardana returned again with empty vessel. The Master, thereupon, lifted a small stone from near where he was sitting and quietly commenced making his ablutions. A stream of water had rushed out from underneath the stone. Bawa Wali found that his spring had simultaneously dried up. Baffled and offended, he hurled a huge rock down on Master's head. The Master, *datan* in hand, was cleaning his teeth, when he saw the mountain's precipitous advance. He quietly raised his right free arm in defence. The rock touched his hand and stood still. An impression of his hand was left on the side of the rock, which it still bears, and is known as *Punja Sahib*, or the Holy Palm, and is an object of great reverence for the Sikhs. The flow of water also increased immensely and continues to this day.

The Dervesh saw this and came down. He met the Master, asked to be forgiven, when the Master gave him an insight into the way in which God's gifts might be used. Jealousy, the Master declared, smothered one's soul; and the mood of rebellion closed up the channels through which the human soul obtained heavenly airs. The Dervesh bowed to the Master, and obtained blessings from him. A magnificent Gurdwara rose up in time at the site of the Holy Palm, *Punja Sahib*, which also gave the second name to the town itself.

XI.

Fall of the Afghan Empire.

On return from the west, the Master took up his residence at the holy Settlement of Kartarpur, which he had founded after his southern trip. From here he occasionally went out on short journeys, during one of which, he happened to be in the vicinity of Syedpur when Baber sacked it. Both the Master and his bard, Mardana, were captured by Baber's soldiery as slaves, and while the Master was employed as a cooly to carry a burden for one of the Commanders, Mardana was employed as a groom for the horses of another. One day when carrying a bundle on his head, he met his disciple Mardana, now serving his new master as a groom and leading a horse. They walked together a little way, and then there passed by a small company of women, slaves of the conquerors, weeping and wailing aloud in misery. Mardana questioned the Master why such untold sufferings had been inflicted on the population, and why God could not stop this misery. "Take thy rebeck and play a tune, Mardana," said the Master," for the Song hath come". " I am holding the horse, my Satguruji, and, if I play the tune, it will get loose and I shall have to suffer punishment, at the hands of the Turk," replied Mardana. " Say Glory to God, and let go the bridle. Play thy tune, the horse will follow." Mardana obeyed ; the horse followed of itself, while the Master sang to the rebeck his famous lament, contained in the Granth Sahib :

I.

Khurasan he ruleth and Hindustan he hath invaded.

No blame to Thee, Who Ordaineth,
The Mughal hath come for retribution.

So much suffering hath been inflicted ; people are crying in agony. Hath Thou not felt ?

To Thee, O Lord the Creator, all are alike.

Should a potentate kill a potentate, no grievance need be felt.

The potentate, a lion, hath, however, fallen on the herd of cattle ; thou shalt hold him to answer, O Lord.

The hounds have ruined the jewels (innocent lives), and none heedeth the dead.

Thou hath brought the Nemesis : this is Thy greatness.

He who assumeth greatness and ordereth as pleaseth him

Is a mere worm to Thee, O Lord! He reapeth as he hath sown.

Glorified, however, shall he be who liveth in death (of self), and forgetteth not the Name, saith Nanak.*

---

* Asa M. I.

ਖੁਰਾਸਾਨ ਖਸਮਾਨਾ ਕੀਆ
ਹਿੰਦੁਸਤਾਨ ਡਰਾਇਆ ।
ਆਪੈ ਦੋਸੁ ਨ ਦੇਈ, ਕਰਤਾ,
ਜਮੁ ਕਰਿ ਮੁਗਲ ਚੜਾਇਆ ।
ਏਤੀ ਮਾਰ ਪਈ, ਕੁਰਲਾਣੇ
ਤੈਂ ਕੀ ਦਰਦੁ ਨ ਆਇਆ ॥ ੧ ॥
ਕਰਤਾ ਤੂੰ ਸਭਨਾ ਕਾ ਸੋਈ ।
ਜੇ ਸਕਤਾ ਸਕਤੈ ਕਉ ਮਾਰੇ,
ਤਾ ਮਨਿ ਰੋਸੁ ਨ ਹੋਈ ॥ ੧ ॥ ਰਹਾਉ ॥
ਸਕਤਾ ਸੀਹੁ ਮਾਰੇ ਪੈ ਵਗੈ,
ਖਸਮੈ ਸਾ ਪੁਰਸਾਈ ।
ਰਤਨ ਵਿਗਾੜਿ ਵਿਗੋਏ ਕੁਤੀਂ,
ਮੁਇਆਂ ਸਾਰ ਨ ਕਾਈ ।
ਆਪੇ ਜੋੜਿ ਵਿਛੋੜੇ ਆਪੇ,
ਵੇਖ ਤੇਰੀ ਵਡਿਆਈ ॥ ੨ ॥
ਜੇ ਕੋ ਨਾਉ ਧਰਾਏ ਵੱਡਾ,
ਸਾਦ ਕਰੇ ਮਨਿ ਭਾਣੇ ।
ਖਸਮੈ ਨਦਰੀ ਕੀੜਾ ਆਵੈ,
ਜੇਤੇ ਚੁਗੈ ਦਾਣੇ ।
ਮਰਿ ਮਰਿ ਜੀਵੈ ਤਾ ਕਿਛੁ ਪਾਏ,
ਨਾਨਕ ਨਾਮ ਵਖਾਣ ॥ ੩॥

II

Heads, adorned with plaited locks,
Vermillion painted where tresses part,
Are being shaven with daggers of steel;
Dust covereth them today ;
Used were they to live in Castles,
Find they not a seat in open.

Thy Command, O Lord, Thy Command !
Thou, The Primeval, the Immeasurable, looketh on
The altered mantels, under Thy Command.

Once the brides were married,
Adorned by swains their own ;
Carried were they in palanquins,
Ivory decorated all ;
Worshipped were they,
Robed in garments rich :
A lac (of rupees) was offered on their admission into new homes,
A lac when they walked ;
Coco-nuts and dates they ate,
Comfortable beds they enjoyed :

These are now being carried in chains,
 Torn off are their pearl-necklaces.
Enemies are now their beauty and wealth,
 Cherished that were herefore ;
Soldiers under command
 Carry them in disgrace to-day.
By Thy Will, O Lord, came the honour,
 By Thy Will cometh the Retribution.
Of future had they thaught,
 Why should punishment have come :
Kings had lost the Ideal,
 Had indulged in pleasantries untold ;
Baber's cohorts are rolling over,
 None can have a meal.
Some are eating Time ;
 Some have lost their worship ;
Hindu ladies can find no kitchen floor,
 Nor can they find rest ;
None had remembered *Ram*,
 Khuda they are not now permitted to recite.
Some return home,
 Enquire about their lost ones ;
Some, as ordained,
 Suffer mute pain ;

All happeneth as He Willeth,
Man is but helpless, saith Nanak.*

---

* Rag Asa, Ashtpadi, M. 1. Gl. 3 (11).

ਜਿਨ ਸਿਰ ਸੋਹਨ ਪਟੀਆਂ,
ਮਾਂਗੀ ਪਾਇ ਸੰਧੂਰਿ ।
ਸੁ ਸਿਰ ਕਾਤੀ ਮੁਨੀਅਨ,
ਗਲਿ ਵਿਚ ਆਵਹਿ ਧੂੜਿ ।
ਮੁਹੱਲਾਂ ਅੰਦਰ ਹੋਂਦੀਆਂ,
ਹੁਨਿ ਬਹਿਨ ਨਾ ਮਿਲੇ ਹਦੂਰ ॥
ਆਦੇਸ, ਬਾਬਾ, ਆਦੇਸੁ,
ਆਦਿ ਪੁਰਖਿ ਤੇਰਾ ਅੰਤ ਨ ਪਾਇਆ,
ਕਰਿ ਕਰਿ ਦੇਖੇ ਵੇਸੁ ।
ਜਦੋਂ ਸਈਆਂ ਵਇਆਹੀਆਂ,
ਲਾੜੇ ਸੋਹਿਨ ਪਾਸਿ ।
ਹਿੰਡੋਲੀ ਚੜ੍ਹ ਆਈਆ,
ਦੰਦ ਖੰਡ ਕੀਤੇ ਰਾਸਿ ।
ਉਪਰੋਂ ਪਾਣੀ ਵਾਰੀਏ,
ਝੁਲੇ ਝਿਮਕਨ ਪਾਸਿ ।
ਇਕ ਲਖਿ ਲਹਿਨ ਬੈਠਿਆਂ,
ਲਖਿ ਲਹਿਨ ਖੜਿਆਂ ।
ਗਰੀ ਛੁਹਾਰੇ ਖਾਂਦੀਆਂ
ਮਾਨਨ ਸੇਜੜੀਆਂ ।
ਤਿਨ ਗਲ ਸਿਲਕਾਂ ਪਾਈਆਂ,
ਟੁਟਨ ਮੋਤਸਰੀਆਂ ।
ਧਨ ਜੋਬਨਿ ਦੁਇ ਵੈਰੀ ਹੋਇ,
ਜਿਨ੍ਹੀ ਰਖੇ ਰੰਗਿ ਲਾਇ ।
ਦੂਤਾਂ ਨੂ ਫੁਰਮਾਇਆ,
ਲੈ ਚਲੇ ਪਤਿ ਗੁਆਇ ।
ਜੇ ਤਿਸ ਭਾਵੈ ਦੇਇ ਵਡਿਆਈ,
ਜੇ ਭਾਵੇ ਦੇਇ ਸਜਾਇ ।
ਅਗੋ ਦੇ ਜੇ ਚੇਤੀਏ,
ਤਾਂ ਕਾ ਹਿਤੁ ਮਿਲੇ ਸਜਾਇ ।

P. T. O.

III

Where are the prancing steeds and stables?
  Where are the trumpets and horns?
Where are the swords and woollen belts?
  Where are the liveries scarlet?
Where are the mirrors reflecting lovely faces?
  Alas, here they are not!

ਸਾਹਾ ਸੁਰਤਿ ਗੁਆਈਆ;
ਰੰਗ ਤਮਾਸੇ ਚਾਇ।
ਬਾਬਰਵਾਨੀ ਫਿਰ ਗਈ,
ਕੋਇਰ ਨ ਰੋਟੀ ਖਾਇ।
ਇਕਨਾ ਵਖਤ ਖੁਆਏ,
ਇਕਨਾ ਪੂਜਾ ਜਾਇ।
ਚੌਕੇ ਬਿਨ ਹਿੰਦਵਾਨੀਆਂ,
ਕੋ ਟਿਕੇ ਕਿਹੜੇ ਨਾਇ।
ਰਾਮ ਨ ਕਿਹੁ ਚੇਤਿਓ,
ਹੁਣਿ ਕੈਹਨ ਨ ਮਿਲੇ ਖੁਦਾਇ।
ਇਕ ਘਰ ਆਵਹਿ ਆਪਨੇ,
ਇਕ ਮਿਲ ਮਿਲ ਪੁਛਹਿ ਸੁਖ।
ਇਕਨਾ ਇਹੁ ਲਿਖਿਆ,
ਬਹਿ ਬਹਿ ਰੋਵਨ ਦੁਖ।
ਜੋ ਤਿਸ ਭਾਵੈ ਸੋ ਥੀਐ,
ਨਾਨਕ ਕਿਆ ਮਾਨੁਖ।

Thine is the Universe, O Lord,
In a moment is it made and unmade ;
Thus is gold circulated from man to man;

Where are the mansions, gates and canopies ?
Where are the comfortable houses for rest ?

Where are the beds of down,
Charming damsels on which would rest not ?

Where are the beetles, the beetle sellers and luring damsels ?
All have vanished in dust !

For gold all have wandered,
Gold hath tempted all :

Without sinful means cometh it not,
After death it accompanies not ;

Who wandereth after it thus
Loseth all nobility ; so the Creator ordains !

Countless *Peers* have preached against it ;
Mir* has heard of it and rushed inspite !

---

*Refers to Babar.

Towns, cities and palaces have perished,

And princes have been cut up and rolled in dust :

No Mughal hath, however, lost his sight,

And none hath stopped the Event.

Mughals and Pathans have fought,

Matched their swords on the field of battle ;

One fired guns accurate,

Other rushed elephants forward ;

Those whose misdeeds merited fall

Have suffered Death, my brother.

The Hindu bride and the Muhammadan bride,

The Bard's bride and the Noble's bride,

Each is bleeding head to foot, torn her raiments are ;

Each wandereth about amongst the dead!

Whose bridegrooms have returned not home,
How may they rest over-night.

All hath happened as ordained by Thee ; O Creator,

To whom may one complain ?

Pain and happiness are in Thy Gift,
To whom else may one appeal :
Thou, O Ordainer, ordereth as pleaseth Thee,
Thy Will must take effect.*

---

* **Asa M. 1. Ashtpadi, 12.**

ਕਹਾਂ ਸੁ ਖੇਲ ਤਬੇਲਾ ਘੋੜੇ.
ਕਹਾ ਭੇਰੀ ਸਹਨਾਈ।
ਕਹਾ ਸੁ ਤੇਗ ਬੰਦ ਗਾਡੇਰੜਿ,
ਕਹਾ ਸੁ ਲਾਲ ਕਵਾਈ।
ਕਹਾ ਸੁ ਆਰਸੀਆ ਮੁਹ ਬੰਕੇ,
ਐਥੈ ਦਿਸਧਿ ਨਾਹੀ ।੧॥
ਇਹ ਜਗ ਤੇਰਾ ਤੂੰ ਗੋਸਾਈ।
ਏਕ ਘੜੀ ਮਹਿ ਥਾਪ ਉਥਾਪੇ.
ਜਰੁ ਵੰਞ ਦੇਵੈ ਭਾਈ ॥ ਰਹਾਉ ॥
ਕਹਾ ਸੁ ਘਰ ਦਰ ਮੰਡਪ ਮਹਲਾ
ਕਹਾ ਸੁ ਬੰਕ ਸਰਾਈ
ਕਹਾਂ ਸੁ ਸੇਜ ਸੁਖਾਲੀ ਕਾਮਣਿ.
ਜਿਸੁ ਵੇਖਿ ਨੀਦ ਨ ਪਾਈ।
ਕਹਾਂ ਸੁ ਪਾਨ ਤੰਬੋਲੀ ਹਰਮਾ,
ਹੋਈਆ ਛਾਈ ਮਾਈ ॥ ੨॥
ਇਸੁ ਜਰੁ ਕਾਰਣਿ ਘਣੀ ਵਿਗੁਤੀ,
ਇਨਿ ਜਰੁ ਘਣੀ ਖੁਆਈ।
ਪਾਪਾ ਬਾਝਹੁ ਹੋਵੈ ਨਾਹੀ,
ਮੁਇਆ ਸਾਥਿ ਨ ਜਾਈ।

P. T. O.

During these songs, many were the peopl that had collected, and it is recorded that Babei

---

ਜਿਸ ਨੋ ਆਪ ਖੁਆਏ ਕਰਤਾ,
ਖੁਸਿ ਲਏ ਚੰਗਿਆਈ ॥ ੩ ॥
ਕੋਟੀ ਹੂ ਪੀਰ ਵਰਜਿ ਰਹਾਏ,
ਜਾ ਮੀਰ ਸੁਣਿਆ ਧਾਇਆ ॥
ਥਾਨ ਮੁਕਾਮ ਜਲੇ ਬਿਜ ਮੰਦਰ,
ਮੁਛਿ ਮੁਛਿ ਕੁਇਰ ਰੁਲਾਇਆ
ਕੋਈ ਮੁਗਲ ਨ ਹੋਆ ਅੰਧਾ,
ਕਿਨੇ ਨ ਪਰਚਾ ਲਾਇਆ ॥ ੪ ॥
ਮੁਗਲ ਪਠਾਣਾ ਭਈ ਲੜਾਈ,
ਰਣ ਮੈ ਤੇਗ ਵਗਾਈ ।
ਓਨ੍ਹੀ ਤੁਪਕ ਤਾਣ ਚਲਾਈ,
ਓਨ੍ਹੀ ਹਸਤ ਚਿੜ੍ਹਾਈ ।
ਜਿਨਕੀ ਚੀਰੀ ਦਰਗਹ ਫਾਟੀ,
ਤਿਨ੍ਹਾ ਮਰਣਾ ਭਾਈ ॥ ੫ ॥
ਇਕ ਹਿੰਦਵਾਣੀ ਅਵਰ ਤੁਰਕਾਣੀ,
ਭਟਿਆਣੀ ਠਕੁਰਾਣੀ ।
ਇਕਨ੍ਹਾ ਪੇਰਣ ਸਿਰ ਖੁਰ ਪਾਟੇ,
ਇਕਨਾ ਵਾਸੁ ਮਸਾਣੀ ।
ਜਿਨ੍ਹ ਕੇ ਬੰਕੇ ਘਰੀਂ ਨ ਆਇਆ,
ਤਿਨ੍ਹ ਕਿਉ ਰੈਣਿ ਵਿਹਾਣੀ ॥ ੬ ॥
ਆਪੇ ਕਰੇ ਕਰਾਏ ਕਰਤਾ,
ਕਿਸ ਨੋ ਆਖਿ ਸੁਣਾਈਐ ।
ਦੁਖੁ ਸੁਖੁ ਤੇਰੇ ਭਾਣੈ ਹੋਵੈ,
ਕਿਸ ਥੈ ਜਾਇ ਰੂਆਈਐ ।
ਹੁਕਮੀ ਹੁਕਮਿ ਚਲਾਏ ਵਿਗਸੈ,
ਨਾਨਕ ਲਿਖਿਆ ਪਾਈਐ ॥ ੭ ॥

in whose camp the songs were sung by a "Captive," heard of it and also came up. The Emperor also listened and saw "God in the face of the Holy Man" The last song that he had heard thrilled his soul and he prayed for forgiveness. The Master asked him to set at liberty the non-combatant people of Syedpur, who had been captured by his Officers and soldiers, and return to them what they had lost if he could do so. All captives were thereupon released. Baber then ventured to ask the Master if he was a Muhammadan Faqir and accepted the mediation of God's holy and last Prophet, Muhammad. To this the Master replied thus :

There is but One God, Omnipotent, True
and Un-knowable ;

Millions of Muhammads are waiting at His
Court that cannot be counted !

Prophets sent come into this world,

Whenever He so desireth, they are sent
for in chains ;

This, I, Nanak, His slave, have ascer tained :

God alone is holy ; All others are profane.*

Baber was so much influenced by the fearless manner in which the reply was given that he immediately offered rich presents and asked what he could do to please him. The Master then replied as follows :

I am gifted by One God ;
  Whose gifts every one enjoyeth.
Whoso looketh up to human support,
  Loseth both matter and his Soul.

There is but One Giver, all others only beg.
  Those who forget Him and look to others, lose all honour.
Kings and Sultans are all made by Him ;
None can equal Him.

**Bhai* Bala's *Janamsakhi.*

ਲਖ ਮੁਹੱਮਦ. ਏਕ ਖੁਦਾਇ।
ਅਲਖ ਸਚਾ ਹੈ ਬੇ ਪਰਵਾਹਿ।
ਕਈ ਮੁਹੱਮਦ ਖੜੇ ਦਰਬਾਰ।
ਸ਼ੁਮਾਰ [illegible] ਪਾਵੈਂ ਬੇਸ਼ੁਮਾਰ।
ਰਸੂਲ ਰਸਾਲ ਦੁਨੀਆ [illegible] ਆਇਆ।
ਜਬ ਚਾਹਿਆ ਤਬ ਪਕੜ ਮੰਗਾਇਆ।
ਇਉ ਸਹੀ ਕੀਆ ਹੈ ਨਾਨਕ ਬੰਦੇ।
ਪਾਕ ਖੁਦਾਇ ਅਉਰ ਸਭ ਗੰਦੇ।

Hear, O Baber Mir, what Nanak saith :
Foolish is the Faqir who begs of thee.*

Baber thereupon prayed to the Master for blessing him with a lasting kingdom in Hindustan. The Master, however, in the words of Bhai Santokh Singh, blessed him and his descendants with the power to rule the country "so long as they governed with justice" and added that "when they departed from justice they shall lose the Empire."

During another brief trip, the Master visited Pakpattan, where he had a long discourse with Sheikh Ibrahim, the *Sajjadanashin* of the Shrine of Sheikh Farid, who on account of his holy life and austerities was himself called Farid the second, and then saw Pir Bahawal-Hak at Multan and went on to Uch, in the present territories of the Bahawalpur State, of whose head he had made acquaintance at Mecca.

---

* *Bhai* Bala's *Janamsakhi*.

ਈਮਾ ਦੀਆ ਏਕ ਖੁਦਾਇ ।
ਜਿਸ ਕਾ ਦੀਆ ਸਭ ਕੋਈ ਖਾਇ ।
ਬੰਦੇ ਦੀ ਜੋ ਲੇਵੇ ਓਟ ।
ਦੀਨ ਦੁਨੀਆ ਹੈ ਤਿਸਕਉ ਤੋਟ ।
ਇਕ ਦਾਤਾ ਸਭ ਜਗਤ ਭਿਖਾਰੀ ।
ਤਿਸਕ ਛਾਡ ਅਵਰ ਕੋ ਲਾਗੇ,
ਉਨ ਸਗਲੀ ਪਤ ਹਾਰੀ ।
ਸ਼ਾਹ ਸੁਲਤਾਨ ਸਭ ਤਿਸ ਕੇ ਕੀਏ ।
ਉਸਕੇ ਸਾਥ ਨ ਕੋਇ ਰਲਈਏ ।
ਕਹੇ ਨਾਨਕ ਸੁਨ ਬਾਬਰ ਮੀਰ ।
ਤੁਝ ਤੇ ਮਾਂਗੇ ਸੁ ਐਹਮਕ ਫਕੀਰ ।

Before returning home from this trip, he also paid a visit to Bawa Wali at Kandhar, whom he had met a few years before at Hassan Abdal.

It was in the reign of Ibrahim Lodhi, as stated in the *Walaitwali* Janamsakhi, that the Master came to Delhi and stayed on a mound, now known as Majnun's Tilla, after the name of a local Sikh*. The Sultan's elephants were stabled not far from it. The Master heard the painful cries from that direction, and sent for information as to the cause of them. One of the elephant drivers came and said that an elephant whom he had tamed and to which he was attached had died and that he would lose his appointment and means of subsistence in consequence and was therefore much grieved. The Master remarked that he should remember God and see if the elephant is not really alive. The driver went back, uttered the name of God, and, when he looked at the carcase of the elephant, it moved, and eventually the elephant rose up in perfect health. The news reached the Sultan, who sent for the Master. In the meanwhile, the Sultan's sattelites used considerable misrepresentation to inflame him against the Master. A charge of heresy and sorcery

---

* In the Janamsakhi this visit is described to have taken place in the beginning of the First Udasi. Sikandar Lodhi, however, was ruling on the throne of Delhi during the First three Udasis of the Master, and Ibrahim Lodhi succeeded his father only in 1517 of Christ. The mention of the name of the Emperor as Ibrahim who had imprisoned the Master shows that this event took place after the Master's main trips were concluded.

was laid against him. Religious bigotry and fanaticism, which characterised, with few honourable exceptions, the Mohammadan rule in India, was of the worst type during the period of Lodhi dynasty, and Sultan Ibrahim was probably the worst of his tribe. When the Master appeared before the Sultan, he was first questioned about his having revived the elephant. The Master, however, replied that it was only God who had the power to revive the dead. None else had that power. The Sultan asked him to kill the animal again ; but the Master remarked that God alone had that power also. The news came shortly after that the animal had again died. The Sultan now insisted the Master to revive it again. The Master, however, disclaimed any power to do so. Then further questions were put, in answer to which the Master openly denied that any incarnations of God could be possible or any prophets could mediate to obtain salvation for a sinful man. " In the Court of the Almighty Father, there are Lacs of Muhammads, Lacs of Brahmas, of Vishnus and of Maheshas ; there are Lacs upon Lacs of Ramas the Great, and lacs of other way-farers in lacs of different garbs."* On this declaration, the whole Darbar

---

* *Bhai* Banno's copy of Granth Sahib *shlok* M. 1, at the end of the volume. This copy has not yet been printed.

ਜਿਤ ਦਰ ਲਖ ਮੁਹੱਮਦਾ ਲਖ ਬ੍ਰਹਮੇ ਬਿਸ਼ਨ ਮਹੇਸ.

ਲਖ ਲਖ ਰਾਮ ਵਡੀਰੀਏ ਲਖ ਰਾਹੀ ਲਖ ਵੇਸ।

was furious, and the charge of heresy was thus held to have been established out of the Master's own mouth. He was peremptorily ordered to be imprisoned. When he was being taken out of the Darbar Hall, he addressed the Sultan thus :

> Beautiful features and clothes wilt thou leave behind ;
> Thy own good and bad deeds will go with thee.
> Order here as thou wilt, narrow is the way by which thou shalt have to go.
> When thou art taken naked to hell, verily, thou shalt look horribly ugly :
> Thou wilt then repent for thy bad deeds.*

It was thus that the Master was sent to imprisonment by Sultan Ibrahim Lodhi some time before he was defeated by Baber at Panipat. The Master, however, commenced his work inside the Jail, and many were the people who were reclaimed from there. It is recorded that the labour which was allotted to the Master in the Jail used to be performed by itself. The

---

* **Asa di Var, M. 1.** *Pauri* **14.**

ਕਪੜ ਰੂਪ ਸੁਹਾਵਣਾ ਛਡਿ ਦੁਨੀਆਂ ਅੰਦਰਿ ਜਾਵਣਾ,
ਚੰਗਾ ਮੰਦਾ ਆਪਣਾ ਆਪੇ ਹੀ ਕੀਤਾ ਪਾਵਣਾ,
ਕਮ ਕੀਏ ਮਨ ਭਾਂਵਦੇ ਰਾਹਿ ਭੀੜੇ ਅਗੇ ਜਾਵਣਾ;
ਨੰਗਾ ਦੋਜਖਿ ਚਾਲਿਆ ਤਾਂ ਦਿਸੈ ਖਰਾ ਡਰਾਵਣਾ।
ਕਰ ਅਉਗਣ ਪਛੋਤਾਵਣਾ ।

mill would grind the corn without being driven. When the Emperor Baber defeated Ibrahim at Panipat and installed himself as King of Hindustan at Dehli, he visited the Jail and immediately recognised him and released him, and with him a large number of others, who had received the Master's instruction and protection. Ibrahim's own cousin, Nawab Daulat Khan Lodhi of Sultanpur, who was the Governor of the Sirhind Province at Sultanpur where the Master had been his *Modi* for ten years, was one of the Ministers of the Sultan, who had invited Baber to invade India and rid the country from the tyrannous rule of the Lodhis.

In 1529, the Master visited Achal-Batala where he had a hot and long contest with the Yogis. This discourse is described at some length by Bhai Gur Das, and the discourse entitled as *Sidh-gosht*, as well as many songs that were sung on this occasion by the Master, are included in the Granth Sahib.

The Master then paid a visit to Hardwar and its vicinity, in 1530, when he was found throwing the Ganges water to the West, while the pilgrims assembled there were offering water to the sun and their ancestors to the east. A large crowd of astonished people gathered round him and enquired what he was doing. "I am watering my fields at Kartarpore; they are getting parched by the scorching heat of the sun, for want of rains." "Where be thy fields and thy Kartarpore," asked a voice. "They are on the Ravi in the Punjab," said Guru Nanak. On this they burst forth into laughter, and said, "How can thy fields be watered from such a long distance? Fool shouldst thou be to think of it." "And bigger fools are you, my friends. If this water in such a large quantity cannot reach my fields on this very earth, some three hundred miles away, how can a handful of it satiate your ancestors and the sun, so far off, you know not where? Leave off these idle pursuits, and worship God who creates, feeds and waters all. Useless are these ceremonies and formalities. The Ganges water cannot wash away your sins, but that may be done by *Bhakti* and Devotion. Change your hearts, perform good deeds, and be saved."

In between these trips the Master resided at Kartarpur, where most of the Sikhs, whose number had by this time much increased, used to visit him. After the conclusion of his Fourth Migration, the Master had abandoned his special journey garments of a Faqir, and had taken to ordinary Punjabi clothes of his time. No more long tours were contemplated, and he reappeared as a householder as he originally was. His son, Sri Chand, however, had by this time adopted an ascetic life and became the reputed Head of the Order of *Udasis* among the Sikhs, so called because Guru Nanak's own Four principal Migrations were known in the local parlance, as recorded in the *Janam-sakhis*, as *Udasis*. Bhai Gurdas in his Ballads, which are the most authentic and earliest extant Sikh records of the time, says that the Master himself started the order of *Udasis*, when he started on his journies. Sri Chand followed the same line and as he never married and kept going about all his life, teaching the creed his Father had given to the world, he seems to have been accepted as the head of our *Udasi* order, more particularly as the Master had rechanged on the termination of his Journeys into ordinary garments.

XII.

SIDH-GOSHTA OR DISCOURSES WITH YOGIS.

The ascetic Order of Yogis exercised considerable influence in Upper India, at the time of the Master's advent. The Order drew its inspiration from Patanjal's School of Philosophy, but, in its outer form and esoteric doctrines, it was founded by Gorakh Nath, and, besides him, acknowledged the leadership of 84 Sidhs, who were supposed to have possessed supernatural powers. These people seem to have considerably indulged in spiritualistic exercises, and often used lower spirits, which were incapable of tearing themselves off from their earthly cares, to produce spectacular effect on the unsophisticated populations to increase the number of their followers. In their outer form, they made a long cut in the lobe of their ears, in which they wore large thick rings of various materials, wood, glass, silver, gold, &c., which were called *Mundra*. They rubbed ashes on their bodies, shaved their heads clean, blew horn, and carried a staff and a begging bag, called *Jholi*. They greeted all by their salutation of "*Adesh*; *Adesh to Gorakh Nath*, *Adesh to* 84 *Sidhs*;" and generally lived outside habitations, visited places of pilgrimage, travelled in distant lands, and used all sorts of intoxicants, smoked opium and ate flesh. The word *Adesh*, which they used as a term of greeting, literally meant order or command, which in its origin might have been adopted to remind of the injunctions of their founder, Gorakh Nath, supplemented by those of the 84 Sidhs or spiritualists.

The Master seems to have had several meetings with monks of this Order. One such meeting, which probably was the first, occurred at a place, then called Gorakhmata, and since known as Nanakmata, in the present district of Nainital, in the United Provinces. About twenty miles further away from Nanakmata, in a very thick forest, stands the Master's Soapnut tree, bearing on one of its branches sweet fruit, while the other branches still yield their usual bitter and pungent nuts. It was here, under the soapnut tree, that the Yogi Machhinder Nath was converted.

At Nanakmata, the Master sat, on his arrival, under an old dry *peepal* tree, where a

Gurudwara now exists. The tree grew fresh sprouts and became green. This attracted notice, and some of the Yogis came and accosted the Master with their usual greetings. The Master acknowledged the greetings by saying, "*Yea, Adesh to the Primeval Lord.*" The Yogis enquired who he was, whose disciple, and wherefrom he had come. He had revived the tree that used to be dry, what further powers he possessed, the Yogis questioned. The Master replied that he was the disciple of the True Lord, than whom none greater existed or could exist, that from Him he had received instruction in the True Word, which had led to his emancipation from all bonds, but that he was an humble man, claiming no supernatural powers, and was roaming about to see the condition of God's creation. After some further talk the Yogis retired to their Yard. At about nightfal, Mardana went to the Yogis to beg of them some fuel and fire, to warm himself and the Master during the night, but the Yogis would not let him have any from their stack. The Master, however, some how, made a fire and the Yogis began blowing severe winds to extinguish the fire. The winds, however, blew out all the fires which Yogis had and left the Master's *Dhuni* untouched. On the morrow, the Yogis, including Bharthar Nath, Bhangar Nath, Shambhu Nath and Machhinder Nath, came to the Master, and, after a brief talk, they invited the Master to accept the Order of Gorakh Nath, and the Master sang thus in reply :

Yog* consists not in the *Khinta* (monk's surplice) ;
Yog consists not in the *Danda* (staff);
Yog consists not in the ashes ;
Yog lieth not in clean shaving,
Yog lieth not in the blowing of horn :
Yog may be obtained by living passionless midst passions !

Yog cannot be attained by mere talk :
Whoever hath attained equilibrium is the true Yogi.

Yog consists not in living in cremation grounds ;
Yog consists not in closing eyes ;
Yog lieth not in wandering abroad ;
Nor lieth it in bathing in holy waters :

* Literally *Yog* means Union with Lord.

Yog may be obtained by living passionless midst passions.*

After this, the Master shifted about twenty miles further into the forest, and was followed by Machhinder Nath Yogi. Machhinder Nath here asked the Master for some food, and the Master asked Mardana to shake the branch of the soapnut tree under which the Master was sitting. The Master asked Machhinder Nath to eat as much as he wanted, and lo, they were sweet nuts. Machhinder himself tried to get more fruit from the other branches, but their fruit he was disappointed to find as bitter as ever.† The Master then

---

* Rag Suhi, M. 1, Sh. 8.

ਜੋਗੁ ਨ ਖਿੰਥਾ, ਜੋਗੁ ਨ ਡੰਡੈ, ਜੋਗੁ ਨ ਭਸਮ ਚੜਾਈਐ ।
ਜੋਗ ਨ ਮੁੰਦੀ ਮੂੰਡ ਮੁੰਡਾਈਐ ਜੋਗੁ ਨ ਸਿਙੀ ਵਾਈਐ ।
ਅੰਜਨ ਮਾਹਿ ਨਿਰੰਜਨ ਰਹੀਐ, ਜੋਗ ਜੁਗਤਿ ਇਵ ਪਾਈਐ ।
ਗਲੀ ਜੋਗੁ ਨ, ਹੋਈ,
ਏਕ ਦ੍ਰਿਸਟਿ ਕਰਿ, ਸਮਸਰਿ ਜਾਣੈ ਜੋਗੀ ਕਹੀਐ ਸੋਈ ।
ਜੋਗੁ ਨ ਬਾਹਰਿ ਮੜੀ ਮਸਾਣੀ, ਜੋਗੁ ਨ ਤਾੜੀ ਲਾਈਐ ।
ਜੋਗ ਨ ਦੇਸਿ ਦਿਸੰਤਰਿ ਭਵੀਐ, ਜੋਗੁ ਨ ਤੀਰਥ ਨਾਈਐ ।
ਅੰਜਨ ਮਾਹਿ ਨਿਰੰਜਨ ਰਹੀਐ, ਜੋਗ ਜੁਗਤ ਇਵ ਪਾਈਐ ।

† The present writer has also had the honour of tasting a piece of these soapnuts, brought by some of the Sikh pilgrims from Nanakmata forest, and he can testify as regards the sweet taste of the nuts. It is said that sweet soapnuts have now multiplied in the forest, from the seed of this branch, while the other branch and trees still bear bitter nuts.

addressed Machhinder Nath thus, while Mardana played the tune and the Master sang his song :

I

Wake up thy Gorakh, O man,

*Go-rakh** he, who protecteth *Go* (earth), and delayeth not in so doing.

Controling mind by the Lord's Word is the horn, which shall so sound, that all shall listen ;

The alms of the Lord's Name are thus received in the beggar's bag.

He hath given water, the air thou breathest, and the sun and the moon as lamps ;

In life and in death, thou hath the earth-O man.

Forgettest thou these gifts ?

Numerous are the Sidhs, Yogis, Jangam and Peers ;

I shall go to them, if in their company I may sing of the Lord, and obtain contentment of mind.

In butter, paper perisheth not, nor salt ;

In water, lotus wetteth not ;

**Go-Rakh*, literally means protector of the earth.

Meet such devotees, saith Nanak,

Yama shall then touch thee not.*

---

* Rag Ram Kali, M. 14.

ਸੁਰਤਿ ਸਬਦੁ ਸਾਖੀ ਮੇਰੀ ਸਿਙੀ,
ਬਾਜੇ ਲੋਕ ਸੁਣੇ ।
ਪਤੁ ਝਲੀ ਮੰਗਣ ਕੈ ਤਾਈ,
ਭੀਖਿਆ ਨਾਮ ਪੜੇ ॥ ੧ ॥

ਬਾਬਾ, ਗੋਰਖ ਜਾਗੈ ।
ਗੋਰਖ ਸੋ ਜਿਨ ਗੋਇ ਉਠਾਲੀ,
ਕਰਤੇ ਬਾਰ ਨਾ ਲਾਗੈ ॥ ਰਹਾਉ ॥
ਪਾਣੀ, ਪ੍ਰਾਣ, ਪਵਨਿ ਬੰਧਿ ਰਾਖੇ,
ਚੰਦ ਸੂਰਜ ਮੁਖਿ ਦੀਏ ।
ਮਰਣ ਜੀਵਣ ਕੋ ਧਰਤੀ ਦੀਨੀ,
ਏਤੇ ਗੁਣ ਵਿਸਰੈ ॥ ੨ ॥

ਸਿਧ, ਸਾਧਿਕ, ਜੋਗੀ ਅਰੁ ਜੰਗਮ,
ਪੀਰ ਪੁਰਸ਼ ਬਹੁਤੇਰੇ ।
ਜੇ ਤਿਨ ਮਿਲਾ ਤਾ ਕੀਰਤਿ ਆਖਾਂ,
ਤਾਂ ਮਨ ਸੇਵ ਕਰੇ ॥ ੩ ॥

ਕਾਗਦ ਲੂਣ ਰਹੇ ਘ੍ਰਿਤ ਸੰਗੇ,
ਪਾਣੀ ਕਮਲ ਰਹੈ ।
ਐਸੇ ਭਗਤ ਮਿਲਹਿ ਜਨ ਨਾਨਕ,
ਤਿਨ ਜਮੁ ਕਿਆ ਕਰੇ ॥ ੪ ॥

II

Listen, O Machhinder, what Nanak saith :

Control thy five cardinal passions, waiver not.

Follow such course of *Yog*,

Mayst thou be saved and all thy generations.

Such ascetic learneth the Course,

Absorbeth he, night and day, in stable contemplation.

Obtaineth he the alms of living in love, in devotion, and in dread of God ;

No more wants hath he, contented inestimably he ;

In steady and deep contemplation of the Lord he ;

In True Name fixeth his mind he.

Nanak speaketh of the ambrosia of the Word,

Listen, O Machhinder, of the Yogi garb:

Be detatched midst expectations ;

Verily, thus mayst thou meet the Lord.

Listen, for Nanak speaketh of the Secret Doctrine,

He admitteth thee in the chain of the Master and the Disciple,

Giveth thee instruction as cure and as food :
No more philosophies shalt thou need.*

These and quite a number of more songs which are duly preserved in the *Granth Sahib*, were sung on this occasion and led to the conversion of Machhinder Nath in spirit.

---

* Ram Kali, M. 1, 5.

ਸੁਣ ਮਾਛਿੰਦ੍ਰਾ, ਨਾਨਕ ਬੋਲੈ ।
ਵਸ ਗਤਿ ਪੰਚ ਕਰੈ ਨਹ ਡੋਲੈ ।
ਐਸੀ ਜੁਗਤਿ ਜੋਗ ਕਉ ਪਾਲੇ ।
ਆਪਿ ਤਰੈ ਸਗਲੇ ਕੁਲ ਤਾਰੇ ॥੧॥
ਸੋ ਅਉਧੂਤੁ ਐਸੀ ਮਤਿ ਪਾਵੈ ।
ਅਹਿਨਿਸਿ ਸੁੰਨਿ ਸਮਾਧਿ ਸਮਾਵੈ ॥ਰਹਾਉ॥
ਭਿਖਿਆ ਭਾਇ ਭਗਤਿ ਭੈ ਚਲੈ ।
ਹੋਵੈ ਸੁ ਤ੍ਰਿਪਤਿ ਸੰਤੋਖਿ ਅਮੁਲੈ ।
ਧਿਆਨ ਰੂਪਿ ਹੋਇ ਆਸਣ ਪਾਵੈ ।
ਸਚਿ ਨਾਮਿ ਤਾੜੀ ਚਿਤੁ ਲਾਵੈ ॥੨॥
ਨਾਨਕੁ ਬੋਲੈ ਅੰਮ੍ਰਿਤ ਬਾਣੀ ।
ਸੁਣਿ ਮਾਛਿੰਦ੍ਰਾ, ਅਉਧੂ ਨੀਸਾਣੀ ।
ਆਸਾ ਮਾਹਿ ਨਿਰਾਸੁ ਵਿਲਾਏ ।
ਨਿਹਚਉ ਨਾਨਕ ਕਰਤੇ ਪਾਏ ॥੩॥
ਪ੍ਰਣਵਤਿ ਨਾਨਕੁ ਅਗਮ ਸੁਣਾਏ ।
ਗੁਰ ਚੇਲੇ ਕੀ ਸੰਧਿ ਮਿਲਾਏ ।
ਦੀਖਿਆ ਦਾਰੂ ਭੋਜਨ ਖਾਏ ।
ਛਿ ਦਰਸਨ ਕੀ ਸੋਝੀ ਪਾਏ ॥੪॥

The next meeting of the Master with the Yogis, and monks of various other orders, took place in the Himmalayan mountains. It appears that it was at the Mansarowar Lake where the Master held these discourses with the Monks. The Yogis and Sidhs questioned the Master how it was that he had been able to reach such difficult heights. It must be remembered that in the time of the Master travelling into the higher Himmalayan ranges, difficult as it in all times must be, was simply incredible, except perhaps by those who had no desire for life. The Master, however, told them that he had reached there by the force of Lord's Name, which alone he meditated on. The Yogis then questioned him about the happenings in and condition of India and other countries. *Bhai* Gur Das has described the Master's answer to his enquiry thus :

> The darkness of falsehood prevaileth all round, O Nath ;
>
> I have set out to find out the moon of truth.
>
> The Earth is heavy with the load of sins, and hath cried out.
>
> The Sidhs have taken shelter in mountains: Who should redeem the earth ?
>
> The Yogis are absolutely ignorant, and indulge merely in rubbing ashes, day and night :
>
> The whole world is suffering for want of the Master.

It is Kaliyuga there : people act like dogs, and eat what is prohibited ;

The Kings commit crimes ; the fence is eating up the crop ;

The subjects, ignorant of any knowledge, speak untold lies ;

Disciples play the tune, and the preceptors dance to it ;

Those sit at home and these visit them there ;

Kazis are corrupt and accept bribes and do injustice ;

For money is the love between man and woman ; they meet and depart at will :

Sin prevaileth all round.*

---

* Vars of Bhai Guru Das, I, 29, 30.

ਬਾਬੇ ਕਹਿਆ ਨਾਥ ਜੀ, ਸੱਚ ਚੰਦ੍ਰਮਾ ਕੂੜ ਅੰਧਾਰਾ।
ਕੂੜ ਅਮਾਵਸ ਵਰਤਿਆ, ਹਉਂ ਭਾਲਣ ਚੜ੍ਹਿਆ ਸੰਸਾਰਾ।
ਪਾਪ ਗਿਰਾਸੀ ਪਿਰਥਮੀ, ਧੌਲ ਖੜਾ ਧਰ ਹੇਠ ਪੁਕਾਰਾ।
ਸਿਧ ਛਪ ਬੈਠੇ ਪਰਬਤੀਂ, ਕੌਣ ਜਗਤ ਕੋ ਪਾਰ ਉਤਾਰਾ।
ਜੋਗੀ ਗਿਆਨ ਵਿਹੂਣਿਆ, ਨਿਸਦਿਨ ਅੰਗ ਲਗਾਇਨ ਛਾਰਾ।
ਬਾਝ ਗੁਰੂ ਡੁਬਾ ਜਗ ਸਾਰਾ ॥ ੨੯ ॥

ਕਲ ਆਈ ਕੁੱਤੇ ਮੁਹੀ ਖਾਜ ਹੁਆ ਮੁਰਦਾਰ ਗੁਸਾਈ।
ਰਾਜੇ ਪਾਪ ਕਮਾਂਵਦੇ, ਉਲਟੀ ਵਾੜ ਖੇਤ ਕਉ ਖਾਈ।
ਪਰਜਾ ਅੰਧੀ ਗਿਆਨ ਬਿਨ, ਕੂੜ ਕੁਸੱਤ ਮੁਖਹੁ ਆਲਾਈ।
ਚੇਲੇ ਸਾਜ ਵਜਾਇੰਦੇ, ਨੱਚਨ ਗੁਰੂ ਬਹੁ ਬਿਧ ਭਾਈ।
ਸੇਵਕ ਬੈਠਨ ਘਰਾਂ ਵਿਚ, ਗੁਰ ਉਠ ਘਰੀਂ ਤਿਨਾੜੇ ਜਾਈ
ਕਾਜ਼ੀ ਹੋਏ ਰਿਸ਼ਵਤੀ, ਵਢੀ ਲੈਕੇ ਹੱਕ ਗਵਾਈ।
ਇਸਤ੍ਰੀ ਪੁਰਖੇ ਦਾਮ ਹਿਤ, ਭਾਵੇ ਆਇ, ਕਿਥਾਊਂ ਜਾਈ।
ਵਰਤਿਆ ਪਾਪ ਸਭਸ ਜਗ ਮਾਂਹੀ ॥ ੩੦ ॥

There then followed a discourse between the Yogis of the various sections and the Master, in the course of which they are said to have considerably tested the Master's knowledge of things spiritual, and after all their efforts at converting him to their Order had failed, the Master preached to them the True path by which alone they could attain salvation, as distinct from the attainment of powers of spiritualism, in which they were evidently stuck-up. There are a large number of hymns in the *Granth Sahib*, which were sung by the Master there, in preaching to the members of the various ascetic Orders, whom he found collected round the Mansarowar Lake. He was finally offered a cup of liquor, an intoxicating drug which the Yogis were very fond of drinking, and thaught that intoxication helped them in the concentration of mind. The Master, however, declined the offer and told them that he had already had his intoxication. Thus :

I have made knowledge the molasses, contemplation the fermenting agent, and pure deeds the leaven ;

My body is the retort, and love the sealer :

Thus have I distilled liquor.

My mind is thus primed, my friend, it hath drunk the ambrosia of the Name : Steady is its intoxication,—

Night and day, it lasts—in Love is mind absorbed and enjoyeth the music of unbeaten strains.

This cup of steady intoxication, the Lord of Perfect

Truth giveth him, whom He favoureth with His Grace,

For he is the seeker of Ambrosia, and careth not for frivolous drinks.

By the Guru's instruction, drinketh he the nectar of the Word, honoured is he as he drinketh ;

Loveth he the Sight of the Lord's Door ; and careth not for the heaven, nor for salvation.

Steeped is ever such hermit in Praise of the Lord ; gambles not he his life away ;

Listen thou, O Bharthar Yogi, Such one drinketh the Ambrosia, ever and ever, saith Nanak.*

---

* Asa M. 1.

ਗੁੜ ਕਰਿ ਗਿਆਨੁ, ਧਿਆਨੁ ਕਰ ਧਾਵੈ,
ਕਰ ਕਰਣੀ ਕਸੁ ਪਾਈਐ
ਭਾਠੀ ਭਵਨੁ, ਪ੍ਰੇਮ ਕਾ ਪੋਚਾ
ਇਤੁ ਰਸੁ ਅਮਿਉ ਚੁਆਈਐ ॥ ੧ ॥
ਬਾਬਾ ਮਨ ਮਤਵਾਰੋ, ਨਾਮ ਰਸੁ ਪੀਵੈ,
ਸਹਜ ਰੰਗ ਰਚਿ ਰਹਿਆ ।
ਅਹਿਨਿਸਿ ਬਨੀ ਪ੍ਰੇਮ ਲਿਵ ਲਾਗੀ,
ਸਬਦੁ ਅਨਾਹਦ ਗਹਿਆ ॥ ਰਹਾਉ ॥
ਪੂਰਾ ਸਾਚੁ ਪਿਆਲ ਸਹਜੇ,
ਤਿਸਹਿ ਪੀਆਏ ਜਾਕਉ ਨਦਰਿ ਕਰੇ ।
ਅੰਮ੍ਰਿਤ ਕਾ ਵਾਪਾਰੀ ਹੋਵੈ,
ਕਿਆ ਮਦਿ ਛੂਛੈ ਭਾਉ ਧਰੇ ॥ ੨ ॥
ਗੁਰ ਕੀ ਸਾਖੀ ਅੰਮ੍ਰਿਤ ਬਾਣੀ,
ਪੀਵਤ ਹੀ ਪਰਵਾਣੁ ਭਇਆ ।
ਦਰ ਦਰਸਨ ਕਾ ਪ੍ਰੀਤਮੁ ਹੋਵੈ,
ਮੁਕਤਿ ਬੈਕੁੰਠੈ ਕਰੈ ਕਿਆ ॥ ੩ ॥
ਸਿਫਤੀ ਰਤਾ ਸਦ ਬੈਰਾਗੀ,
ਜੂਐ ਜਨਮੁ ਨ ਹਾਰੈ ।
ਕਹੁ ਨਾਨਕ, ਸੁਣਿ ਭਰਥਰਿ ਜੋਗੀ,
ਖੀਵਾ ਅੰਮ੍ਰਿਤ ਧਾਰੈ ॥ ੪ ॥

The last meeting with the Yogis which must be mentioned is the one which took place in 1529 of the Christian era, when the Master visited the annual Sheoratri fair at one of the principal seats of the Order at Achal near Batala, in the present district of Gurdaspur. Some years before this occasion, the Master had abandoned his *Udasi* clothes and had settled down at Kartarpur. At Achal, the Master had his own camp, where he was visited by the Yogis, and the first question put to him by the ascetics was why he had re-adopted the householder's life. In the words of Bhai Gur Das the question was put thus by Bhangar Nath :

> Why hast thou mixed acid in milk ?
>
> Whey hath separated and thou canst now have no butter by churning it :
>
> Why hath thou put off the *Udasi* garbs ;
>
> Why hath thou restarted the life of a layman ?*

---

* Vars of Bhai Gurdas.

ਪੁਛਨ ਜੋਗੀ ਭੰਗਰ ਨਾਥ,
ਤੁਹਿ ਦੁੱਧ ਵਿੱਚ ਕਿਉਂ ਕਾਂਜੀ ਪਾਈ ?
ਫਿੱਟਿਆ ਚਾਟਾ ਦੁੱਧ ਦਾ,
ਰਿੜਕਿਆ ਮੱਖਣ ਹੱਥ ਨ ਆਈ ।
ਭੇਖ ਉਤਾਰ ਉਦਾਸ ਦਾ,
ਵਤ ਕਿਉਂ ਸੰਸਾਰੀ ਰੀਤ ਚਲਾਈ ?

The Master's answer was :

> Thy mother, O Bhangar Nath, knew not how to clean the vessel ;
>
> Want of Knowledge hath thus led to the putrefaction of thy soul.
>
> Thou gave up thy home, and adopted asceticism ;
>
> Why shouldst thou be wandering from door to door at the houses of the lay people to beg thy food ?*

He explained to them that adoption of simple *Udasi* garbs was but the means to an end and not the end itself. Asceticism is meant to purge the soul of its filth of ego, but it could not in itself be enough for emancipation. One must subjugate the temptations of the world but not flee from them for ever. The Yogis upon this began exhibiting their super-

---

* *Ibid.*

ਨਾਨਕ ਆਖੇ, ਭੰਗਰ ਨਾਥ,
ਤੇਰੀ ਮਾਂਉ ਕੁਚੱਜੀ ਆਹੀ।
ਭਾਂਡਾ ਧੋਇ ਨ ਜਾਤਿਓਨ,
ਭਾਇ ਕੁਚੱਜੇ ਫੁੱਲ ਸੜਾਈ।
ਹੋਇ ਅਤੀਤ ਗ੍ਰਿਹਸ੍ਤ ਤਜ,
ਫਿਰ ਉਨਹੂੰਕੇ ਘਰ ਮੰਗਨ ਜਾਈ।

natural powers, and, having done so, they asked the Master to exhibit his. The Master, however, said that beyond The True Name of the Omnipotent Lord he claimed no miraculous powers and could exhibit none :

May I wear clothes of fire, may I live in perpetual snows, may I feed myself on steel,

May I drink all pains as water, may I drive the chariot of earth,

May I weigh up the universe in the scales, may I prove it equal to the weight of a dram,

May I develope to be so great that universe be insufficient to contain me, may I control and drive all,

May I have all these powers within me, to do all these and to order all these being done :

Great is the Lord and great are His Gifts, He giveth what he willeth, but

Him on whom He bestoweth His Grace
He granteth the Honour of the True Name.*

After this followed the main Discourse, entitled the *Sidh-Goshta*, contained in Rag Ramkalee of the *Granth Sahib*. It is a long discourse, which it is not within the scope of the present work to translate. In it the Master explained to the Yogis the relative position of asceticism and a spiritual life of development, and he taught to the Yogis the Principal Doctrines of the Message he had brought from

---

* Shlok M. 1.

ਪਹਿਰਾ ਅਗਨਿ, ਹਿਵੈ ਘਰੁ ਬਾਧਾ,
ਭੋਜਨੁ ਸਾਰ ਕਰਾਈ ।
ਸਗਲੇ ਦੂਖ ਪਾਣੀ ਕਰਿ ਪੀਵਾਂ,
ਧਰਤੀ ਹਾਕ ਚਲਾਈ ।
ਧਰਿ ਤਾਰਾਜੀ ਅੰਬਰ ਤੋਲੀ,
ਪਿਛੈ ਟੰਕ ਚੜ੍ਹਾਈ ।
ਏਵਡ ਵਧਾ ਮਾਵਾਂ ਨਾਹੀ,
ਸਭਸੈ ਨਥਿ ਚਲਾਈ ।
ਏਤਾ ਤਾਣੁ ਹੋਵੈ ਮਨ ਅੰਦਰਿ,
ਕਰੀ, ਭਿ ਆਖਿ ਕਰਾਈ ।
ਜੇਵਡ ਸਾਹਿਬੁ ਤੇਵਡ ਦਾਤੀ,
ਦੇ ਦੇ ਕਰੇ ਰਜਾਈ ।
ਨਾਨਕ ਨਦਰਿ ਕਰੇ ਜਿਸੁ ਉਪਰਿ,
ਸਚਿ ਨਾਮਿ ਵਡਿਆਈ ॥

on High. It is enough to close this chapter with one song which the Master sang to the Yogis, also contained in Rag Ramkallee :

Abide in Steadiness, O Yogi, This is thy course.

May the One Lord look on thee once, He shall grant thee Love and satiate thee with the Divine Word.

Thou wandereth about begging food and raiment ;

Evil of hunger consumeth thee and paineth thee.

Guru's instruction thou hath obtained not ;
In Evil course thou hath lost thy honour.

By Guru's instruction, thou mayst yet obtain the path of Devotion.

Five cardinal evils drive the cart of thy body.

God's Powers alone might save thy honour.
The axle of thy cart shall break, the cart shall tumble down,

Thy substance, aged and scattered, shall be lost in the wilderness of the worldliness.

Meditate, O yogi, on the Guru's Word,.

Be Uniform in pain and in pleasure,

Be sorry only for thy separation from the Lord ;

Make the Name Divine thy food : meditate on it under the Guru's instruction ;
Stability thou shalt attain by abiding in the Name.
Tie up the cloth of Stability, freed from bonds thou shalt be,
Thy passions and thy anger shall vanish under the Guru's instruction.
Let the shelter at the feet of the Lord-Guru be the rings worn by thy mind :
By Devotion to God, saith Nanak, thou shalt find Salvation.*

---

* Ramkalli, M. 1, (11).

ਛਾਦਨ ਭੋਜਨੁ ਮਾਗਤੁ ਭਾਗੇ ।
ਖੁਧਿਆ ਦੁਸਟ ਜਲੈ ਦੁਖੁ ਆਗੇ ।
ਗੁਰ ਮਤਿ ਨਹੀ ਲੀਨੀ, ਦੁਰਮਤਿ ਪਤਿ ਖੋਈ ।
ਗੁਰਮਤਿ ਭਗਤਿ ਪਾਵੈ ਜਨੁ ਕੋਈ ॥ ੧ ॥
ਜੋਗੀ, ਜੁਗਤਿ ਸਹਜ ਘਰਿ ਵਾਸੈ ।
ਏਕ ਦ੍ਰਿਸਟਿ ਏਕੋ ਕਰਿ ਦੇਖਿਆ,
ਭੀਖਿਆ ਭਾਇ ਸਬਦਿ ਤ੍ਰਿਪਤਾਸੈ ॥ਰਹਾਉ॥
ਪੰਚ ਬੈਲ ਗਡੀਆ ਦੇਹ ਧਾਰੀ ।
ਰਾਮ ਕਲਾ ਨਿਬਹੈ ਪਤਿ ਸਾਰੀ ।
ਧਰ ਤੂਟੀ ਗਾਡੋ ਸਿਰ ਭਾਰਿ ।
ਲਕਰੀ ਬਿਖਰਿ ਜਰੀ ਮੰਝ ਭਾਰ ॥ ੨ ॥
ਗੁਰ ਕਾ ਸਬਦੁ ਵੀਚਾਰ, ਜੋਗੀ ।
ਦੁਖੁ ਸੁਖੁ ਸਮ ਕਰਣਾ ਸੋਗ ਬਿਓਗੀ ।
ਭੁਗਤਿ ਨਾਮ ਗੁਰ ਸਬਦਿ ਬੀਚਾਰੀ ।
ਅਸਥਿਰੁ ਕੰਧੁ ਜਪੈ ਨਿਰੰਕਾਰੀ ॥ ੩ ॥
ਸਹਜ ਜਗੋਟਾ ਬੰਧਨ ਤੇ ਛੂਟਾ ।
ਕਾਮੁ ਕ੍ਰੋਧੁ ਗੁਰ ਸਬਦੀ ਲੂਟਾ ।
ਮਨ ਮਹਿ ਮੁੰਦ੍ਰਾਂ ਹਰਿ ਗੁਰ ਸਰਣਾ ।
ਨਾਨਕ, ਰਾਮ ਭਗਤਿ ਜਨ ਤਰਣਾ ॥ ੪ ॥

XIII.

SUFI MUHAMMADANS.

The Sufi Mystics of Persia, following a simple system founded originally by a woman. named Rabi'a, in the words of a writer in the Encyclopaedia Brittanica, appeared to have borrowed the practice of monastic life, in order to devote themselves exclusively to meditation and contemplation, from India, and, thus influenced, their compositions became unequivocally pantheistic. As remarked by Prof. Andrew Seth, the movement marked a kind of reaction against the rigid monotheism and formalism of Islam, and, in its speculative aspect, in which nature and beauty and earthly satisfaction appeared as a vain show, it presented the counterpart of the former mood of sensuous enjoyment. Prof. Stanislas Guyard remarks that, under the colour of Sufism, opinions entirely subversive of the faith of Islam were professed by these mystics, and, having drawn adepts from the ranks of heterodoxy, Sufism departed from its original purpose, and entered on discussions respecting the Divine nature, which finally led to Pantheism.

Mortification of the material body, as practised by some of these Sufi Muslims, paled into insignificance the severe austerities of the Hindu Yogis and ascetics, and found a very fertile soil when these Muhammadan *Faqirs* established themselves in India. The Master met several of them during his tours. Reference has already been made to Syed Ahmad Mir Taqi and Hamza Ghous in the Sixth Chapter and a few others in the ninth. He had a talk with Sheikh Sharaf of Panipat practically at the commencement of his First *Udasi*. He made acquaintance of a few others, including Makhdum Rukn-ul-Din, Abul Fateh, Syed Jallal and Pir Baha-ul-Din Haqani of Uch, and Sheikh Ibrahim Farid II of Pakpattan, during his visit at Mecca. On his return to the Punjab he had several discourses with some of these *Faqirs*, which are described in the *Janamsakhis*, and are, in more or less detail, incorporated also in the *Granth Sahib*.

At Mithankot, Sheikh Mitha was bold enough to call upon the Master to accept Islam, thus :

> Name of God first and that Of His Prophet Muhammad next ;
> Read the *Kalma*, O Nanak, that thou mayst be accepted in the Divine Court.*

---

* Janamsakhi Shlok.

ਅਵਲਿ ਨਾਉ ਖੁਦਾਇ ਕਾ, ਦੂਜਾ ਨਬੀ ਰਸੂਲ ।
ਨਾਨਕ ਕਲਮਾ ਜੇ ਪੜਹਿ ਤਾ ਦਰਗਹਿ ਪਵੈ ਕਬੂਲੁ ॥

The Master's reply is recorded in the *Janamsakhi* as follows :

> Name of God First, numerous are the prophets at His door.
>
> Purify thy mind, O Sheikh, that thou mayst be accepted in His Court.*

" But how can the lamp be lighted without oil in it ?" retorted the Sheikh. The Master, thereupon, sang to him the following song :

> How may the lamp be lighted without oil ?
> The *Maya* shall deceive thee not ;
> Nor will the dagger produce the cut ;
> Live as the Lord willeth thee to live ;
> The ambitious must but waiver.
>
> Read up the books, O man ;
> Live in fear of the Lord ; this shall be the wick in the lamp of thy body ;
> Knowledge of the Truth shall feed the same.
>
> This shall be the oil and that the lamp :
> Light it up, and the Lord shall meet thee.
>
> The arrows of cravings are piercing thy soul ;
> Render humble service that thou mayst attain bliss.
> Life in this world is but ephemeral.

---

* *Ibid.* Shlok M. 1.

ਅਵਲਿ ਨਾਉ ਖੁਦਾਇ ਕਾ ਦਰਿ ਕੇਤੜੇ ਰਸੂਲ ।

ਸੇਖਾ, ਨੀਅਤਿ ਰਾਸਿ ਕਰਿ, ਤਾ ਦਰਗਹਿ ਪਵਹਿ ਕਬਲ ।।

Render humble service in this world,
O man ;
Thus shalt thou obtain entrance in the
Divine Court,
Thou shalt then attain Bliss, saith Nanak.*

Sheikh Ibrahim Farid the Second put a straight question to the Master, there being one Lord and two paths, which of the latter two should be followed and which rejected.† The Master answered that there was One Lord and there was but one path ; follow the one

---

* Sri Rag M. 1, G. L. 5 33.

ਅਛਲ ਛਲਾਈ ਨਹ ਛਲੈ,
ਨਹ ਘਾਉ ਕਟਾਰਾ ਕਰਿ ਸਕੈ ।
ਜਿਉ ਸਾਹਿਬ ਰਾਖੈ ਤਿਉ ਰਹੈ,
ਇਸ ਲੋਭੀ ਕਾ ਜੀਉ ਟਲਪਲੈ ॥ ੧ ॥
ਬਿਨੁ ਤੇਲ ਦੀਵਾ ਕਿਉ ਜਲੈ ॥ ਰਹਾਉ ॥
ਪੋਥੀ ਪੁਰਾਣ ਕਮਾਈਐ,
ਭਉ ਵਟੀ ਇਤੁ ਤਨਿ ਪਾਈਐ ।
ਸਚੁ ਬੂਝਣੁ ਆਣਿ ਜਲਾਈਐ ॥ ੨ ॥
ਇਹੁ ਤੇਲੁ ਦੀਵਾ ਇਉ ਜਲੈ ।
ਕਰਿ ਚਾਨਣੁ ਸਾਹਿਬ ਤਉ ਮਿਲੈ ॥ਰਹਾਉ॥
ਇਤੁ ਤਨਿ ਲਾਗੈ ਬਾਣੀਆ ।
ਸੁਖੁ ਹੋਵੈ ਸੇਵ ਕਮਾਣੀਆ ।
ਸਭ ਦੁਨੀਆਂ ਆਵਣ ਜਾਣੀਆ ॥ ੩ ॥
ਵਿਚ ਦੁਨੀਆ ਸੇਵ ਕਮਾਈਐ ।
ਤਾ ਦਰਗਹ ਬੈਸਣੁ ਪਾਈਐ ।
ਕਹੁ ਨਾਨਕ ਬਾਹ ਲੁਡਾਈਐ ॥ ੪ ॥

† *Ibid.*

ਹਿਕ ਸਾਹਿਬ ਦੋ ਹਦੀਂ,
ਕੇਹੜਾ ਸੇਵੀਂ, ਕੇਹੜਾ ਰਦੀਂ ॥

path and reject all else.* Sheikh Ibrahim then put several questions, to which the Master replied thus :

Sheikh Ibrahim ;

> Farid saith, tear up thy silks, and put on the rough garments :
> Thus may I adopt the garb, which may obtain for me the Union with my Lord.†

The Master :

> The Bride is at home, and the Bridegroom away ;
> The Bride liveth in remembrance and repineth ;
>
> Should her intentions and life be pure,
> The Lord would come in no time and meet her.‡

---

* *Ibid.*

ਹਿਕੋ ਸਾਹਿਬ. ਹਿਕੋ ਹੱਟ ।
ਹਿਕੋ ਸੇਵੇ, ਦੂਜਾ ਰੱਦ ॥

† Shlok Farid ji.

ਫਰੀਦਾ ਪਾੜਿ ਪਟੋਲਾ ਧਜਿ ਕਰੀ,
ਕੰਬਲੜੀ ਪਹਿਰੇਉ ।
ਜਿਨੀ ਵੇਸੀਂ ਸਹੁ ਮਿਲੈ
ਸੇਈ ਵੇਸ ਕਰੇਉ ।

‡ *Ibid.*

ਘਰ ਹੀ ਮੁੰਧਿ ਵਿਦੇਸਿ ਪਿਰ,
ਨਿਤ ਝੂਰੇ ਸੰਮਾਲੇ ।
ਮਿਲਦਿਆਂ ਢਿਲ ਨ ਹੋਵਈ,
ਨੀਅਤਿ ਰਾਸਿ ਕਰੇਇ ॥

Sheikh Ibrahim :

I have enjoyed not the Union with the Lord, when young,
Aged hath this mortal frame now become ;
Shall the Bride bewail and moan in the grave :
Ha, I have met not the Bridegroom '?*

The Master :

The Bride hath known not the path, hath lived in vanities of the earth, hath a black and impure mind ;
She shall still meet the Lord by abandoning these vices and acquiring virtues.†

Sheikh Ibrahim :

What Word to meditate on ? What virtues to acquire ? What Mantram to adopt ?
Which garb may I adopt that the Bridegroom may favour me ?‡

---

* *Ibid.*

ਫਰੀਦਾ ਨੰਢੀ ਕੰਤੁ ਨ ਰਾਵਿਓ,
ਵਡੀ ਥੀ ਮੁਈਆਸੁ ।
ਧਨਿ ਕੂਕੇਂਦੀ ਗੋਰ ਮੇ,
ਤੇ ਸਹ ਨਾ ਮਿਲੀਆਸੁ

† *Ibid.*

ਮਹਲ ਕੁਚੱਜੀ ਮੜਵੜੀ,
ਕਾਲੀ ਮਨਹੁ ਕਸੁਧ ।
ਜੇ ਗੁਣ ਹੋਵਨਿ ਤਾ ਪਿਰ ਰਵੈ
ਨਾਨਕ ਅਵਗਣ ਮੁੰਧ ॥

‡ *Ibid.*

ਕਵਣੁ ਸੁ ਅਖਰੁ, ਕਵਣ ਗੁਣੁ,
ਕਵਣੁ ਸੁ ਮਣੀਆ ਮੰਤੁ ।
ਕਵਣੁ ਸੁ ਵੇਸੋ ਹਉ ਕਰੀ,
ਜਿਤੁ ਵਸਿ ਆਵੈ ਕੰਤੁ ।

The Master :

Humility is the word, Forgiveness the virtue, meekness the jewel of Mantram :
These three shouldst thou, O sister, adopt as thy garb, and the Bridegroom will favour thee.*

Sheikh Ibrahim :

I fitted not my boat when I had the time ;
My days are now full, how shall I swim across ?
Touch not the fire for it doth but burn.
Some have pleased the Bridegroom and obtained honour :
I however may meet Him not : milk shall return not to the teats.
Farid saith, O friends, The Bridegroom's call cometh :
The soul shall depart from hence, and the body shall mix in dust.†

---

* *Ibid.*

ਨਿਵਣੁ ਸੁ ਅਖਰੁ, ਖਿਵਣੁ ਗੁਣ,
ਜਿਹਬਾ ਮਣੀਆ ਮੰਤੁ ।
ਏ ਤੇ ਭੈਣੇ ਵੇਸ ਕਰਿ,
ਤਾ ਵਸਿ ਆਵੀ ਕੰਤੁ ॥

† Rag Suhi Farid Ji.

ਬੇੜਾ ਬੰਧ ਨ ਸਕਿਓ ਬੰਧਨ ਕੀ ਵੇਲਾ ।
ਭਰਿ ਸਰਵਰੁ ਜਬ ਊਛਲੈ, ਤਬ ਤਰਣ ਦੁਹੇਲਾ ।
ਹਥੁ ਨ ਲਾਇ ਕਸੁੰਭੜੈ, ਜਲਿ ਜਾਸੀ ਢੋਲਾ ।
ਇਕ ਆਪੀਨੈ ਪਤਲੀ ਸਹ ਕੇਰੇ ਬੋਲਾ ।
ਦੁਧਾ ਥਣੀ ਨ ਆਵਈ. ਫਿਰਿ ਹੋਇ ਨ ਮੇਲਾ ।
ਕਹੈ ਫਰੀਦ, ਸਹੇਲੀਹੋ, ਸਹੁ ਅਲਾਏਸੀ ।
ਹੰਸੁ ਚਲਿਆ ਉਠ ਡੁਮਣਾ ਅਹਿ ਤਨੁ ਢੇਰੀ ਥੀਸੀ ।

The Master.

Fit up thy boat now with meditation on
  the Name :
  Easy shall be thy voyage.
No waters and no waves shall beset thy path.
  Easy shall it be.
Let the Lord's Name be the dye in which
  thy raiment is dyed red—ever red.
The Friend goeth hence, O dear me, how
  shall the meeting take place :
Souldst thou acquire virtue, God himself
  will bless thee with Union.
After Real Union, separation shall not be.
The True One ruleth when migration ceaseth.
Dress thyself in the suppression of vanity :
By the Guru's instruction thou reapeth the
  fruit of the ambrosia of the Word.
The Bridegroom is beloved and loving,
  O friend, saith Nanak,
We are the slaves of the Lord, the True
  Lord of us all.

Rag Suhi, M. 1.

ਜਪ ਤਪ ਕਾ ਬੰਧ ਬੇੜਲਾ, ਜਿਤੁ ਲੰਘਹਿ ਵਹੇਲਾ ।
ਨਾ ਸਰਵਰ, ਨਾ ਊਛਲੈ, ਐਸਾ ਪੰਥ ਸਹੇਲਾ ।
ਤੇਰਾ ਏਕੋ ਨਾਮ ਮਜੀਠੜਾ ਰਤਾ ਮੇਰਾ ਚੋਲਾ, ਸਦ ਰੰਗ ਢੋਲਾ ।
ਸਾਜਨ ਚਲੇ ਪਿਆਰਿਆ, ਕਿਉ ਮੇਲਾ ਹੋਈ ।
ਜੇ ਗੁਣੁ ਹੋਵਹਿ ਗੰਠੜੀਐ, ਮੇਲੇਗਾ ਸੋਈ ।
ਮਿਲਿਆ ਹੋਇ ਨ ਵੀਛੁੜੈ, ਜੇ ਮਿਲਿਆ ਹੋਈ ।
ਆਵਾਗਾਉਣੁ ਨਿਵਾਰਿਆ, ਹੈ ਸੱਚਾ ਸੋਈ ।
ਹਉਮੈ ਮਾਰਿ ਨਿਵਾਰੀਆ ਸੀਤਾ ਹੈ ਚੋਲਾ ।
ਗੁਰ ਬਚਨੀ ਫਲ ਪਾਇਆ, ਸਹ ਕੇ ਅਮ੍ਰਿਤ ਬੋਲਾ ।
ਨਾਨਕ ਕਹੈ, ਸਹੇਲੀਹੋ, ਸਹੁ ਖਰਾ ਪਿਆਰਾ ।
ਹਮ ਸਹ ਕੇਰੀਆ ਦਾਸੀਆ, ਸਾਚਾ ਖਸਮੁ ਹਮਾਰਾ ।

Sheikh Ibrahim :

Should the blooms come early,
May the fruit be gathered later.

Those that are awake may obtain
Gifts from the Lord.*

The Master :

Gifts are within the power of the Lord
With Him no diplomacy shall succeed.

Some are not gifted though awake ;
Others are favoured even when asleep.†

The questions and answers in this discourse show that, in spite of the considerable merit which the Sheikh had richly earned by his spiritual exercises and development, he was despairing of his salvation, and had occasions when he became sceptic. The Master brought him consolation and faith in the goodness of the Lord, who, ever and always, draweth His little ones into Himself.

---

* Shlok Farid ji.

ਪਹਿਲੈ ਪਹਿਰੈ ਫੁਲੜਾ,
ਫਲੁ ਭੀ ਪਛਾ ਰਾਤਿ ।
ਜਾਗੰਨਿ, ਲਹੰਨਿ ਸੇ,
ਸਾਈਂ ਕਨੋ ਦਾਤਿ ॥

† *Ibid.*

ਦਾਤੀ ਸਾਹਿਬ ਸੰਦੀਆ,
ਕਿਆ ਚਲੈ ਤਿਸੁ ਨਾਲਿ
ਇਕ ਜਾਗੰਦੇ ਨਾ ਲਹੰਨਿ,
ਇਕਨਾ ਸੁਤਿਆ ਦੇਇ ਉਠਾਲਿ

There are a large number of Sufi shrines in Multan. Many were the Sufi Faqirs living there when the Master visited it. Makhdum Rukn-ud-Din Bahawal Haq was one of them who had probably met the Master at Mecca. When the Master arrived in Multan, these Faqirs sent him a brimful cup of milk, indicating that the place was so full of holy men that there was no room there for the Master. The Master, however, picked up a Jessamine flower, full of fragrance, and placed it floating on the milk, indicating that he had not come to be a burden to any one and yet could find a place even in that overflowing place of saintliness. Upon this, the Master was invited to stay there for some days, and he had many discourses with most of the Faqirs. Makhdum Rukn-ud-Din Bahawal Haq complained that in spite of his severe austerities he had not been able to control his mind; and the Master told him that the snake could not be killed by crushing the barrow. So too by austerities the mind could not be controlled. On the other hand, these enhance its wanderings by further cravings for being respected and worshipped. It was only the contemplation of the Lord's Name, under the instructions of the Guru, that could effectively subjugate the human cravings and help in the mind-control.

Peer Rukn-ud-Din Bahawal Haq is recorded to have died forty days before the Master's ascension. Finding his end approaching, he wrote a chit and sent it through a messenger to the Master who was then at Kartarpur. The Master opened the slip, and it read thus :

> My load is full ; am ready to depart ;
>
> Pray grant me thy Grace.*

The Master wrote back a message of consolation to him thus :

> Whose load is full shall depart,
>
> For the Will of the Lord is above all.
>
> They are honoured by the Lord, saith Nanak,
>
> Who have lived in Truth.†

With this answer, he mentioned that the Peer was emancipated and he must depart, and that the Master shall also come forty days later.

---

* Janamsakhi.

ਅਸਾ ਜੋ 'ਲਦਣੁ ਲਦਿਆ,
ਅਸਾੜੀ ਭ ਕਰਿ ਕਾਇ ।

† Janamsakhi.

ਭਰਿਆ ਸੋ ਲਦਸੀ,
ਸਭਨਾਂ ਖਸਮੁ ਰਜਾਇ ।

ਨਾਨਕ ਤੇ ਮੁਖ ਉਜਲੇ,
ਚਲੇ ਹਕ ਕਮਾਇ ।

XIV.

Ascension.

The Master returned to Kartarpur for the last time in about the year 1531 of the Christian era, and undertook no more journeys of an important nature. He had proclaimed His Message in many parts of southern Asia, from Arabia and probably Turkey and Egypt in the west, to Burma in the east, from Kashmere and Tibbet, and possibly China, in the north to Ceylon in the south. About thirty *Manjis*, scattered over all these vast countries, seem to have been established by him to continue the work of evangelisation after him, each placed in charge of a competent *Bhaiji*, and at Kartarpur he provided a centre where the disciples could occasionally gather round him to replenish their spiritual stock at the Fountain Head.

Life in the holy colony of Kartarpur was of one continuous communion with God. Three hours before daybreak, people bathed and recited their prayers, and uptil after sunrise continued their morning service of

Asa-Di-Var. The Divine songs having finished, they engaged in the various duties, which they had allotted to themselves. The Master had farms of his own, on which crops to supply food for the devotees were grown. The Master himself also worked in the Farm. *Langar* was then ready and all fed at the Guru's Kitchen. Whether at Kartarpur or away in their own villages, people worked for the common weal of the Community, and those larger numbers who lived at their own homes brought their earnings into the common kitchen when they came to the Master for a usual visit. They farmed for the Guru, they spun for the Guru and they wove for the Guru. Guru to them included the Guru's Sikhs, wherever they were. In communion with the Guru they spent their whole time, right upto and through the evening service and the bedtime service of the Wedding songs.

This institution of the Guru's Langar or Kitchen, or the Temple of Bread, as the Prose-poet Puran Singh has so beautifully rendered the expression, has been described by him in a language which it is difficult for the present writer to surpass or imitate, and no apology seems necessary to quote it here. It runs thus :

"What is a home, but a hospitable feasting of children with bread and love and faith ? What is spiritual life in the temple of flesh, without a full meal first ? The very first temple made by Guru

Nanak, therefore, was the Temple of Bread, or Guru's Langar. In one common Temple of Bread, the bread of God was made free to the children of man. Let none be hungry where the spirit of God prevails. The Guru's people and the Guru were one home and one family; but it was no utopian idea, as of the modern socialism or the democracy of labour; it was the democracy of soul, so gloriously invoked in the temple of the human heart by the genius of the Guru. The sacrifice of selfishness was made for the gladness of soul that the act gave to the people who came round Guru Nanak. The soul of the people was so fully nourished and satisfied that they could not entertain feelings of difference and duality. We are not selfish when we are in the deep repose of a dewy slumber. We are never selfish when we are in love. The people came and laid their selfishness at his feet, and begged a little of it for his service. To serve the devotees was serving the Master. This Union was so spiritually co-operative that none knew if his own hands were his own or of the Guru or of the devotees of the Guru. The bodies and hearts and minds were mingling with each other and with those of the Master, by the magic of his presence amongst them. Here was a religion that made love and labour the common property of man.

"Today no Sikh, with a grain of that faith in him, can possibly think that he owns the Bread. "Bread and water belong to the Guru." No man who is initiated into the path of the Guru can own a home without being ready to share it with the Guru's people.

"The fruits of his labour also belong to them. Such was the Master's foreshadowing of the future ; and in this lay all the difference between him and the centuries of the purely Brahmanical culture before him. "The people are more than myself," says the Guru. "Religion is inspiration of love." The Beloved is in His people, and the service of people is the service of God. And it is through service that love is realised. The spark of love is found by chance by some fortunate one in the company of His saints, and it is the reward of those who have surrendered themselves, head and heart, to the Divine."

"The Master chose out his family of God's disciples ; they served him and he served them. Real service of people is serving them with *life*, and the one who is *alive* can give life to others. So the Master says that the opportunity to serve God in humanity is His gift. They alone serve, whom He gives the authority to do so.

"Guru Nanak's passion for farming is a true index of his creative mind. We must labour to create the grain to feed people with. All other needs that we have are secondary ; there is only one physical distress, and that is hunger. We all must labour on the land and sweat for our bread. Guru Nanak chose finally the life of a farmer for himself. The gardening and farming are the outward symbols of the genius of art. We see in his disciples a rare combination of labour and spiritual vision, of a home life and a cave life : not in a spirit of compromise, but in the spirit of that sweet reconciliation with which the flying bird flaps both his wings for his balance in the blue sky. Guru Nanak poured song into the heart of labour ; and his greatest men were farmers, or the help-mates of the farmers, such as masons who made huts, carpenters who made ploughs, smiths who made tools, and weavers who made garments for the saints. The entrance to this spiritual humanity lay through a small lowly door where selfishness could not pass. If the people could not drop their selfishness of their own accord, then the Guru's personality softly stole into theirs and helped them from within to drop it, without their knowledge."*

The future careers of two out of the numerous people who came to him at Kartarpur and were the recipients of his grace, entitle them to special mention. One of them was one, Bura, of village Ramdas, a few miles away from Kartarpur. He was young in years, more a boy than a man, when he came to the Master, and bowing down before Him said "A few days ago, some powerful Pathans forcibly cut and carried away our crops, ripe as well as unripe, and we were all helpless. It then struck me, O Master, that if we could not save our crops, ripe and unripe, from these Pathans, who can possibly save us, when the all-powerful hand of death seizes us, whether old or young. I have heard of Thee, O Great

* The Book of the Ten Masters.

Master, and have come unto thee. Pray show me the way of emancipation from the hands of Death." The Master replied to him saying, "It is the Almighty God alone who can be the support of all on the day of reckoning, O Bura, SERVE GOD SO THAT GOD MAY SAVE THEE." These words had a magic effect on Bura. His young and innocent heart was completely converted, and Bura spent most of his time thereafter in the Master's service. He was, though young in years, deemed to be a wise man and earned by his spiritual wisdom the name of Buddha, or Old man, and was allowed a place in the assemblies of old and experienced men of the Faith. In a few years he made such spiritual progress that before His ascension, the Master appointed him to perform the sacred ceremony of installation of Guru Angad Dev on the Chief Manji, and after this Bhai Buddha had the honour of performing similar function at the installation of the Third, Fourth, Fifth and Sixth Masters as well, before he himself passed away from his earthly existence.

The Second man to be mentioned was one who was destined to be the embodiment of the Master's Spirit and thus succeed the Master. His name was Lehna, who originally belonged to a village, named Mate ki Sarai, about three miles from the present town of Muktsar in the District of Ferozepur. On the village being plundered by dacoits, Lehna had migrated to and settled at Khadur, many years before the story of his life with which we are concerned began. He was a worshipper of Durga, as most of the other people of Khadur were, and he used every year to lead the village assembly for a pilgrimage to the famous Temple of Jawala Mukhi, in the Kangra District. These pilgrims used to travel, stage by stage, on foot, to pay homage to the goddess of Flame in that temple. There was, however, one Sikh also living in Khadur, and one day Lehna heard him singing the Master's song. He asked him for instruction in those songs, and Lehna consequently learnt to recite them himself. These songs made such an impression on him that he decided to visit the Master at Kartarpur, when on his way to Jawalamukhi next. When the time approached for the annual pilgrimage, he was able to prevail upon his companions to make a *detour* and pass close to Kartarpur to enable him to see the Master, when going to Jawala Mukhi. Having on this occasion left his companions a little away from Kartarpur, he wended his way to the holy colony, and met an old man in the fields. He asked the path to the Master's Temple, and the old man quietly led the way, Lehna following him on horseback. Near the Temple, the old man asked Lehna to dismount, tie up the mare to a peg stuck up in the ground there and enter the temple, in front of him. The old man preceded Lehna into the Temple. When

Lehna entered into the Master's presence, he was astonished to find that it was no other than the old man he had been led by. The Master, however, consoled him and enquired from him what his name was. "My name is Lehna, O Satguruji." *Lehna* in Punjabi means what is due to one from another. "Thy *Lehna* is from me, and I have to pay thee. Where-else hast thou been wandering for it, O Lehna." The Master's Songs had already made strong impression on Lehna, and this short play upon word, uttered in a tone of love and compassion, had such an effect on the heart of Lehna that he would go no further towards Jawalamukhi. The Master's words and the Master's look sank deep into his soul. He sent away his companions to Jawalamukhi, and himself stayed behind. He became a very frequent visitor to Kartarpur since then, and some time later used to stay there for much longer intervals. Legend says that on one occasion when Lehna came to the Temple somewhat earlier than usual, he saw the goddess sweeping the floor, and was told on questioning her that she was an humble one of the maids at the door of the Master. Lehna's conversion was of the completest character. His steady and unflinching faith stood many a hard test. To the Master these tests were of no importance, because he knew where his spirit was to incarnate, when his time was ended. Others than Him, who had not His Vision, had to be convinced. Lehna imbibed the spirit of the Master's teachings in an astonishingly brief space of time, and his extreme devotion was eventually rewarded with the highest Gift of the Divine Spirit, in the lunar month of Asuj, Sambat 1596, corresponding to September 1539 of Christ.

Once the Master's followers asked him whether the usual ceremony of lighting the lamp to light the soul's path to the hereafter, and offering *pind* and *pattal*, as cakes of oblation,* were to be performed after him, and whether his ashes and bones were to be carried to the Ganges. He answered thus :

> Light up the lamp of the Name of One God,
> In which is consumed all pain for oil ;
> That giveth Light, and this soaketh up ;
> Thus will meeting with *Yama* be avoided.
>
> Be no sceptics, O people,
> Collect lacs of stacks of fuel,
> A grain of fire must consume all.
> God himself shall be my *pind* and *pattal*,
> Remembrance of the Name of the
> Creator my funeral obsequies ;

---

*Hindus light a lamp after a man's death, and think that it lights the path of the deceased through the infernal regions. They also offer *Pind* and *Pattal*, a kind of oblations and food, in the name of the deceased to the Brahmans, through whom they hope the deceased to get satisfied of his hunger, etc., during his voyage through those regions. These oblations are of two sorts: one called heavenly and the other earthly. They also cast the ashes and the bones of the deceased in the Ganges at Hardwar, and themselves bathe in the sacred river, there as well as at Benares, in the hope of benefiting the soul of the deceased.

Here and there, in future as in past ;
He alone is my support.
Song of God's Praise is my Ganges and Kashi,
Wherein my spirit bathes and bathes ;
True bath shall it be,
Should one have Love of God, night and day.
Heavenly and earthly oblation cakes,
Brahman maketh and eateth up ;
Cakes of the Grace of God, saith Nanak,
Remain ever and ever of use.*

---

* Rag Asa, M. 1, Gh. 3, Sh. 32.

ਦੀਵਾ ਮੇਰਾ ਏਕੁ ਨਾਮੁ, ਦੁਖੁ ਵਿਚਿ ਪਾਇਆ ਤੇਲੁ ।
ਉਨ ਚਾਨਣ, ਇਨ ਸੋਖਿਆ, ਚੂਕਾ ਜਮ ਸਿਉਂ ਮੇਲੁ ।
ਕਾ, ਮਤ ਕੋ ਫਕੜੁ ਪਾਇ ।
ਲਖੁ ਮੜਿਆ ਕਰਿ ਏਕਠੇ, ਏਕ ਰਤੀ ਲੇ ਭਾਇ ।
ਪਿੰਡੁ ਪਤਲੁ ਮੇਰੀ ਕੇਸਉ, ਕਿਰਿਆ ਸਚੁ ਨਾਮੁ ਕਰਤਾਰੁ ।
ਏਥੈ, ਓਥੈ, ਆਗੈ, ਪਾਛੈ, ਇਹੁ ਮੇਰਾ ਆਧਾਰੁ ।
ਗੰਗੁ ਬਨਾਰਸਿ ਸਿਫਤਿ ਤੁਮਾਰੀ ਨ੍ਹਾਵੈ ਆਤਮ ਰਾਉ ।
ਸਾਚਾ ਨਾਵਣ ਤਾ ਥੀਐ ਜਾਂ ਅਹਿ ਨਿਸ ਲਾਗੈ ਭਾਉ ।
ਇਕ ਲੋਕੀ, ਹੋਰ ਛਮਛਰੀ, ਬ੍ਰਹਮਣ ਵਟ ਪਿੰਡ ਖਾਇ ।
ਨਾਨਕ ਪਿੰਡ ਬਖਸੀਸ ਕਾ, ਕਬਹੂ ਨਿਖਟਸ ਨਾਇ ॥

Time was approaching for the Master's Ascension. One day, *Bhai* Lehna had come to visit the Master, who was working in the paddy crop he had sown, and the Master asked him to carry a large bundle of grass, that had been weeded out of the field, to the cattle shed. Bhai Lehna immediately obeyed and brought the bundle on his head, mud dripping from the wet grass and staining his costly silk garments. Mother Sulakhni remarked to the Master, "see, Sire, how his costly clothes are stained with mud." The Master looked back, and said, "Mud! Seest thou not, good lady, he bears the burden of suffering humanity. They are not mud Stains. They are the sacred saffron anointings. Heaven anoints him. He is the Guru."

The Master asked Bhai Buddha Ji to instal Bhai Lehna as the Guru, and Bhai Buddha Ji having put the anointing of saffron on the forehead of Bhai Lehna, and seated him on the *Manji*, the Master placed the offering of a cocoanut and five coppers before him, and going round him five times, bowed before his Disciple. "Hail to the Guru. Hail to the Guru. Hail to the Guru Angad." And Lo, Bhai Lehna was no longer there. It was Guru Angad, the Master made of The Master's Own Essence. The Spirit of the Master that had come unto him from above had entered a new body, and Guru Nanak was bowing to it before his own ascension. The entire assemblage followed the Master in bowing down before the Master in the Second Form, and the proclamation went out that Divine Spirit had manifested itself in Guru Angad.

The Master then prepared to depart. He sang the Divine Wedding Song :

Sing ye, my comrades, sing now my Wedding Song.

Sing the Song of His Praise.

Sing the Song of my Creator.

Sing the Song of Him, who knoweth no fear.

I would be a sacrifice to this wedding Song ;
For in this Song lieth the everlasting Bliss.
My Lord careth for the smallest life,
The Bounteous Giver meeteth needs of each.

Invaluable are His Gifts ;
Who can appraise Him.
The Auspicious Day has dawned,
The Hour of Wedding is come.
Come, comrades, and anoint the Bride
Pour your blessings, O Comrades,
For the Bride meeteth her Lord.
Take this message to all,

For this Call cometh for All.

Ever and always remember Him, Who sendeth down the Call ;

When the Time for the Call arrives.*

---

* Sohila Rag Gauri Dipki, M. 1.

ਜੈ ਘਰਿ ਕੀਰਤਿ ਆਖੀਐ,
ਕਰਤੇ ਕਾ ਹੋਇ ਬੀਚਾਰੋ ।
ਤਿਤੁ ਘਰਿ ਗਾਵਹੁ ਸੋਹਿਲਾ,
ਸਿਵਰਹੁ ਸਿਰਜਣ ਹਾਰੋ ॥ ੧ ॥
ਤੁਮ ਗਾਵਹੁ ਮੇਰੇ ਨਿਰਭਉ ਕਾ ਸੋਹਿਲਾ,
ਹਉ ਵਾਰੀ ਜਿਤੁ ਸੋਹਿਲੈ,
ਸਦਾ ਸੁਖੁ ਹੋਇ ॥ ਰਹਾਉ ॥
ਨਿਤ ਨਿਤ ਜੀਅੜੇ ਸਮਾਲੀਅਨਿ,
ਦੇਖੈਗਾ ਦੇਵਣ ਹਾਰੁ ।
ਤੇਰੇ ਦਾਨੈ ਕੀਮਤਿ ਨਾ ਪਵੈ,
ਤਿਸੁ ਦਾਤੇ ਕਵਣੁ ਸੁਮਾਰੁ ॥ ੨ ॥
ਸੰਬਤਿ ਸਾਹਾ ਲਿਖਿਆ,
ਮਿਲਿ ਕਰਿ ਪਾਵਹੁ ਤੇਲੁ ।
ਦੇਹੁ ਸਜਣ ਅਸੀਸੜੀਆਂ,
ਜਿਉ ਹੋਵੈ ਸਾਹਿਬ ਸਿਉ ਮੇਲੁ ॥ ੩ ॥
ਘਰਿ ਘਰਿ ਇਹੋ ਪਾਹੁਚਾ,
ਸਦੜੇ ਨਿਤ ਪਵੰਨਿ ।
ਸਦਣ ਹਾਰਾ ਸਿਮਰੀਐ,
ਨਾਨਕ ਸੇ ਦਿਹ ਆਵੰਨਿ ॥ ੪ ॥

Many were those who were shedding tears of love and thankfulness, but there were also those present who were waiting for an opportunity to ask the Master how his body was to be disposed of. Those who had been converted from amongst the Hindus said they would cremate it, and those who had followed the Master from amongst the Muhammadans said they would bury it. When the Master was asked about it, He said let each place some fresh flowers on his sides. Whosoever's flowers remained fresh should do as pleaseth them. The Master covered himself with a clean white sheet and slept. And Lo! when the sheet was removed, there was no body there, and flowers of both sections were still fresh.

They search for the Master in vain,
Who search him on this earth,

The old father of his people is not to be found,

Neither in the grave nor in the cremation flame.

He is in the heart of Guru Angad.

Puran Singh.

XV.

The Master's Creed.

Were the men who comprehended God best Deists or Pantheists? Renan, in his Life of Christ, holds this question to be meaningless. Physical or metaphysical proofs of the existence of God, he says, would have been quite indifferent to these great men. They felt the Divine within themselves. The paltry discussions about deism and pantheism have stifled all fertile ideas of the Divine in the breast of modern rationalism. In trying to comprehend and explain the incomprehensible problem of Existence, man does but suspend for the time being his emotional and divine sentiments, and gets busy with intellectual gymnastics. His intellect eventually fails him and he gets bewildered. The emotional part of him has already been crushed, and the soul, marred by learning and perhaps wealth, becomes incapable of an uplift.

The Master never indulged in philosophical discussions, and never gave utterance to the sacrelegious idea that he was God. He set up no visions. He always called himself the servant or Slave of God, and dwelt in His bosom by direct and constant communion with Him. From his heart he drew all that he taught of the Divinity. He felt God within him and with him, and thus spoke of Him with the authority of an eye-witness. He never argued about Him. God conceived as Father or Bridegroom: such was the simple theology of Guru Nanak. This was not with him a theoretical principle, a doctrine, more or less proved, which he sought to inculcate in others. He never reasoned about it and he exacted from his disciples no effort of attention. "Beyond the Vedas, the Korans and the Universes, is manifestly visible the Monarch of Nanak."* Thus does he declare the existence of God, and he commands the disciples to accept it as a Reality.

Nor did he ever formulate an elaborate system of philosophy. He never cared to make an effort to convince others, by a connected reasoning, as to how the universe was created, and which things or elements in it were eternal and which were transitory. Here also he declared that God is the Creator, and "from

---

* ਵੇਦ, ਕਤੇਬ, ਸੰਸਾਰ, ਹਬਾਹੂੰ ਬਾਹਰਾ ।

ਨਾਨਕ ਕੇ ਪਾਤਸ਼ਾਹ, ਦਿਸੈ ਜ਼ਾਹਰਾਂ ॥

Word, He hath manifested All ".* With this declaration, he takes up the world as it exists and begins to teach and instruct. In his teachings, he has attended more to what the disciple ought to be and cared not so much as to what he had been. He drew from within the inspiration, which the world needed, and, out of his extreme love for all humanity, he taught to save it from utter destruction of the spirit within it.

"There is much in the character and teaching of Nanak," says Sir Lepel Griffin, " which reminds the student of the life and teaching of the great Budhist reformer, whose devotion to the cause of humanity and the general enlightenment of whose doctrine have had so vast an influence upon a quarter of the human race."† To use the words of Mr. Muhammad Latiff,‡ Guru Nanak's best endeavours during his long public career were directed towards removing, or reducing to a minimum, those religious and social differences which had sprung up between the two great religious sects of India,

* Japji.

ਕੀਤਾ ਪਸਾਉ, ਏਕੋ ਕਵਾਉ ।

Again :—

ਏਕ ਕਵਾਵੈ ਤੇ ਸਭ ਹੋਆ ।

† *Ranjit Singh*, 'Rulers of India' series.

‡ *History of the Punjab.*

the Hindus and the Muhammadans, and to reconciling them both, and to a great extent he was successful. He viewed with disfavour the intolerance of the Mussalmans towards the Hindus, and the precepts of his religion inculcated peace to all mankind, brotherly love to one another, and living virtuously and harmoniously. "He set himself to teach men the way of salvation, not as a ruler, but as a servant of God, to whom the Light had been shown, coming to bring, not strife among men, but peace."*

Trevaskis has compared the Master with Budha thus:—"Nanak and Budha alike revolted against a religion overladen with ceremonial and social restrictions; both rebelled against the sore burdens which the priests would have them bear. But the form which the doctrines of each assumed was largely influenced by his surroundings. Budha lived in the centre of Hindu India, and among the many gods of the Brahmans; these he rejected; he knew of nought else; and he preached that there was no God. Nanak was born in the Province which then formed the border land between Hinduism and Islam; he was brought up under the shadow of the monotheism of Muhammad, and he taught that there was One God. But that God was neither the God of the Muhammadan, nor of the Hindu

---

* Sir C. Gough's *The Sikhs And The Sikh Wars.*

but the God of the Universe, of all mankind and of all religions. The burthen of his teaching was, " there is no Hindu and no Muhammadan." He rejected the wisdom of the Scribes and the mint and anise and cummin of the Pharisees, and taught that salvation lay in repentance and in pure and righteous conduct. He believed in transmigration, but held that successive stages were but purifications, and that at the last the soul, cleansed from its sin, went to dwell with its Maker. He did not despise or attack the Hindu and Muhammadan teachers; he held, indeed, that they too had been sent from God; but he preached a higher and purer religion, embracing all that was best in both, but purged from much of evil that had been allowed in either, because of the hardness of the men's hearts."*

The essential character of the Master was that of a Prophet in the highest and truest sense of the word. With reference to the religious system prevailing in the country, his aim seems to have been to raise both Hinduism and Islam alike from the lowest depths of polytheism and aggressive unitarianism, of barren ceremonialism and mechanical conventialism, into which they had fallen, and to preach to them, in addition, a more exclusive mono-theism, a nobler doctrine and a purer morality, based on solid

* *The Land Of The Five Rivers*, by H. K. Trevaskis, I.C.S., Page 165.

foundations of Divine Grace. The religion that he taught possessed a noble ideal and a practical and social meaning. It was based on the Two fundamental principles of the Unity of God and Brotherhood of Man. In the words of Sir Charles Gough, "he penetrated beneath the crust of observances and conventions, and found the root of the matter in the Unity of God and Equality of men before him."*

The Fundamental *mantram* of the Sikh religion saith :

"There is but One God, whose name is True, the Creator, the All-pervading, devoid of fear and enmity, Immortal, Unborn, Self-begotten ; Realise by the Master's Grace. Worship Him.

He was True in the beginning. He was True in the primal age. He is True now, and He will ever be True, says Nanak,"†

---

* *The Sikhs and Sikh Wars.*

† Japji Sahib. *Pauri* 1.

੧ ਓ, ਸਤਿ ਨਾਮੁ, ਕਰਤਾ, ਪੁਰਖ, ਨਿਰ ਭਉ,
ਨਿਰ ਵੈਰ, ਅਕਾਲ ਮੂਰਤ, ਅਜੂਨੀ, ਸੈਭੰ, ਗੁਰ, ਪ੍ਰਸਾਦਿ ॥
ਜਪੁ ॥ ਆਦਿ ਸਚੁ ਜੁਗਾਦਿ ਸਚੁ, ਹੈਭੀ ਸਚੁ, ਨਾਨਕੁ,
ਹੋਸੀ ਭੀ ਸਚੁ ॥

"Why worship the second, who takes birth and dies; worship the One alone who pervades the lands and the waters."*

"Whom shall I call the second? There is none. In all there is that Spotless One"†

Numerous Muhammads have there been, and multitudes of Brahmas, Vishnoos and Shivas, thousands of peers and prophets, and lacs of saints and holy men: "But the Chief of Lords is the One Lord, Creator, God of the True Name, O Nanak! His qualities, with out and beyond reckoning, are beyond comprehension."‡ "Do not fall in useless struggles,

---

* *Shlok* M. 1.

ਦੂਜਾ ਕਾਹੇ ਸਿਮਰੀਐ, ਜਮੇ ਤੇ ਮਰ ਜਾਇ,

ਏਕੋ ਸਿਮਰੇ ਨਾਨਕਾ, ਜੋ ਜਲ ਥਲ ਰਹਿਆ ਸਮਾਇ ।

† **Rag** Gowree, Go-araree M. 1: Asht. Sh. 5 (*Rahao*).

ਦੂਜਾ ਕਉਨ ਕਹਾਂ ? ਨਹੀ ਕੋਈ ।

ਸਭ ਮੈ ਏਕ ਨਿਰੰਜਨ [illegible]ਈ ।

‡ *Bhai* Banno's manuscript copy of *Granth Sahib*, *Shlok* **M.** 1.

ਜਿਤ ਦਰ ਲਖ ਮੁਹੰਮਦਾ, [illegible]ਖ ਬ੍ਰਹਮੇ, ਵਿਸ਼ਨ ਮ[illegible]ਸ਼ ।

ਲਖ ਲਖ ਰਾਮ ਵਡੀਟੀਏ, ਲਖ ਰਾਹੀ, ਲਖ ਵੇਸ ।

ਸਿਰ ਨਾਥਾਂ ਕੇ ਏਕ ਨਾਥਿ ਸਤਿ ਨਾਮ ਕਰਤਾਰ ।

ਨਾਨਕ, ਤਾਕੀ ਕੀਮਤ ਨਾ ਪਵੈ ਬੇਅੰਤ ਬੇਸ਼ੁਮਾਰ ।

worship not another than God, bow not to the dead." *

The Master combined the excellencies of preceding reformers, says Cunningham, in his *History of the Sikhs*, and he avoided the more grave errors into which they had fallen. Instead of the circumscribed divinity, the anthropomorphous God of Ramanand and Kabir, he loftily invokes the Lord as the One; the Sole, the Timeless being, the Creator, the Self-existent, the Incomprehensible and the Everlasting. He likens the Deity to Truth, which was before the world began, which is, and which shall endure for ever, as the ultimate idea or cause of all we know and behold. He addresses equally the *Mullah* and the *Pandit*, the *Dervaish* and the *Sannyassee*, and he tells them to remember *that* Lord of Lords who had seen come and go numberless Muhammads, Vishnus and Shivas."

" For Nanak," says Frederic Pincot, in his essay on ' Sikhism ' in *The Religious Systems of the World*, " there was no such thing as a God for the Hindus, a god for the Muhammadans, and

---

* Rog Sorath, M. 1, Asht., Sh. 1 (1).

ਦੁਬਿਧਾ ਨ ਪੜਉ, ਹਰਿ ਬਿਨੁ ਹੋਰੁ ਨ ਪੂਜਉ,

ਮੜੈ ਮਸਾਣਿ ਨ ਜਾਈ ।

a god or gods for the outer heathen; for him there was but one God, not in the likeness of man, like Rama, not a creature of attributes and passions, like the Allah of Muhammad; but one, sole, indivisible, self-existent, incomprehensible, timeless, all pervading,—to be named, but otherwise indescribable and altogether lovely. Such was Nanak's idea of the Creator and Sustainer of the phenomenal world, and it was a conception which at once abrogated all petty distinctions of creed, and sect, and dogma, and ceremony. The realisation of such a God shatters the sophistries of the theologian and the quibblings of the dialectitions, it clears the brow from the gloom of abstruse pondering over trifles, and leaves the heart free for the exercise of human sympathies."

The great philosophers of the world have immensely exercised their brains, and numerous ascetics have performed penances and austerities and mortified their bodies in the vain attempt to fully comprehend and describe God's nature, but were utterly lost in the immensity of their subject, and were no wiser than when they started. By the exercise of their developed intellects, they were able merely to find different schools of philosophy, and stifled their souls, wherein lay the Kingdom of God. "Brahma, born of Vishnu's navel, studied all the Vedas and recited them with a musical throat, and yet he comprehended not His Greatness and, to him also metempsichosis remained in mist."* Even the great Budha himself spent many of his years of research in the vain pursuit of comprehending God, but, honest to his conviction, he gave up the effort, baffled as he was by the immensity of the Divinity and His creation, and contented himself to speak no more of Him. He was forced by his intellect to declare Four axioms that Life was full of ceaseless pain, that Pain was due to human cravings, that the cessation of cravings would lead to happiness, and that the eight fold path of righteous conduct would result in the negation of cravings and therefore to the negation of all pain. The problem of existence he described as the result of the eternal law of cause and effect, and, positively acknowledging no God, no soul and no matter, merely because he could comprehend their existence not, he took shelter in the doctrine of Nothingness, out of which, on account of the law of causation, life and matter had come into existence and into which all life was aimed to lapse. Not comprehending the nature of Divinity through his intellect, circumscribed as it was by the limitations of time, space and

* Rag Goojri, M. 1, Gh. 1, Sh. 2 (1).

ਨਾਭਿ ਕਮਲ ਤੇ ਬ੍ਰਹਮਾ ਉਪਜ,
ਵੇਦ ਪੜਹਿ ਮੁਖਿ ਕੰਠ ਸਵਾਰਿ ।
ਤਾਂਕੋ ਅੰਤੁ ਨਾ ਜਾਈ ਲਖਣਾ,
ਆਵਤ ਜਾਤ ਰਹੇ ਗੁਬਾਰਿ ॥

causality, it became inconvenient to him to acknowledge the existence of the Maker of the Eternal Laws, which he himself had found to govern the Universe. And yet, it must be added, he never openly denied the Existence of God either, in spite of the fact that, under the system founded by him, the highest aim of man must be to make himself extinct and thus freed from the pain of birth, to attain *Nibban* as he called it. Other sages of Old have also similarly been arguing and reasoning, with the result that six recognized system of Indian philosophy, and numerous other theories and dogmas, about the existence of Life and a higher power, came to contest supremacy in human brain. These good, honest and highly intellectual people, however, did not stop to realize that merely because their intellects were limited and God was beyond those limits is no reason why, on account of their own limitations, they should shirk acknowledging the Great Truth and not make an effort to immerse their souls into that infiniteness and then make no attempt to describe.

In the Master's creed, as taught by him, it is God's nature to be beyond comprehension and beyond description by the human intellect. That which may be comprehended and may be described and explained *is not God*

" Invisible, Infinite, Incomprehensible, Un-
" perceivable, Timeless, Without Destiny,

" Without Caste, Without Birth, Self-Exist-
" ent, Without Attachment and Without
' Apprehensions."*

Such is the Deity to be worshipped in the Master's religion, and is not to be denied or simply ignored, because of these His Attributes.

'He is neither established, nor created. He Himself is the Pure One. They who have served him have obtained honour. Sing of Him, the Sum-total of all virtues, saith Nanak. Sing, hear, and put His love into your hearts. Thus shall your sorrows be removed and beatitude attained."† God is ever true, He is the True Lord, and of True Name. He who made

* Rag, Sorath, M. 1, Gh. 1, Sh. 6 (1).

ਅਲਖ, ਅਪਾਰ, ਅਗਮ, ਅਗੋਚਰੁ, ਨਾ ਤਿਸੁ ਕਾਲੁ ਨ ਕਰਮਾ,
ਜਾਤਿ ਅਜਾਤਿ, ਅਜੋਨੀ, ਸੰਭਉ, ਨਾ ਤਿਸੁ ਭਾਉ, ਨ ਭਰਮਾ,

† Japji Sahib, *Pauri* 5.

ਥਾਪਿਆ ਨ ਜਾਇ, ਕੀਤਾ ਨ ਹੋਇ

ਆਪੇ ਆਪ ਨਿਰੰਜਨ ਸੋਇ ।

ਜਿਨ ਸੇਵਿਆ ਤਿਨ ਪਾਇਆ ਮਾਨ ।

ਨਾਨਕ, ਗਾਵੀਐ ਗੁਣ ਨਿਧਾਨ

ਗਾਵੀਐ, ਸੁਣੀਐ ਮਨ ਰਖੀਐ ਭਾਉ ।

ਦੁਖ ਪਰ ਹਰ ਸੁਖ ਘਰ ਲੈ ਜਾਉ ।

the Universe, is and will be, is neither seen nor will pass away. He alone who with his hands created all things of different colours, descriptions and species beholds his handiwork, which attests of His Greatness. He will do what pleaseth Himself; no order may be issued to Him. He is the King, the King of Kings, and all remain subject to His will, saith Nanak."* Thus the Deity, under whatever name known, as Brahm, Hari, Ram, Govind, Allah, &c., &c., is incomprehensible, invisible, uncreated, eternal, and alone possessing real existence.

The Master often referred to the philosophical systems of his countrymen, says Cunningham,† and regarded bliss as the dwelling of the soul

---

* Japji Sahib, *Pauri* 27.

ਸੋਈ ਸੋਈ ਸਦਾ ਸਚ ਸਹਿਬ ਸਾਚਾ ਸਾਚੀ ਨਾਈ।

ਹੈ ਭੀ, ਹੋਸੀ, ਜਾਇ, ਨ ਜਾਸੀ, ਰਚਨਾ ਜਿਨ ਰਚਾਈ।

ਰੰਗੀ ਰੰਗੀ ਭਾਂਤੀ ਕਰ ਕਰ ਜਿਨਸੀ ਮਾਇਆ ਜਿਨ ਉਪਾਈ।

ਕਰ ਕਰ ਵੇਖੇ ਕੀਤਾ ਆਪਣਾ, ਜਿਉਂ ਤਿਸਦੀ ਵਡਿਆਈ।

ਜੋ ਤਿਸ ਭਾਵੈ ਸੋਈ ਕਰਸੀ, ਫਿਰ ਹੁਕਮ ਨ ਕਰਨਾ ਜਾਈ।

ਸੋ ਪਾਤਸਾਹਾਂ, ਸ਼ਹਾ ਪਾਤਸਾਹਿਬੁ ਨਾਨਕ ਰੈਹਨ ਰਜਾਈ।

† *History of the Sikhs.*

with God. He makes the constant use of the current language or notions of the time on good many other subjects, and says that 'he who remains bright amid darkness, unmoved amid deception, that is, perfect amid temptations, should attain happiness.' He referred to the Arabian prophet, and to the Hindu Incarnations, not as impostors and the diffusers of evil, but as having been truly sent by God to instruct mankind, and he lamented that sin should nevertheless prevail. Such references to the Hindu incarnations and to the Hindu philosophy have led many a writer to hold that the Master believed in them as objects of worship and faith. Dr. Ernest Trump openly commits himself to this mistaken notion, and says, "we should be wrong in assuming that Nanak forbade the worship of other gods on the ground of the unity of the Supreme. Far from doing so, he took over the whole Hindu Pantheon, with all its mythological back ground, with the only difference that the whole was subordinated to the Supreme Brahm. The position of the popular gods was, thereby, though not openly attacked, naturally lowered, and their service must needs appear less important, yet even useless, for the attainment of the highest object of mankind." A little further on, Dr. Trump remarks that 'it is a mistake if Nanak is represented as having endeavoured to unite the Hindu and Muhammadan idea about God. Nanak remained a thorough Hindu, according to all his views, and if he had communionship with Mussalmans and many of these became his disciples, it was owing to the fact that Sufism, which all these Muhammadans were professing was in reality nothing but a Pantheism, derived directly from Hindu sources, and only outwardly adapted to the forms of Islam."* The whole of this lengthy discussion of the German Translator of a portion of the *Adi Granth* is based on his attempt to evolve a comprehensive system of philosophy out of the *Granth Sahib*, without trying to enter into its spirit, and, strange as it may appear, he himself somewhat rightly observed that "Guru Nanak was not a speculative philosopher." All his criticism of what appeared to him defective in the train of philosophical thought, as he tried to gather out of the *Granth*, has been vain. He ought to have remembered that if the Master used the prevailing philosophical systems of the country in his arguments to illustrate his meaning, this does not justify the charge laid against him of believing in the Hindu Pantheon. He had to employ the common terminology of the language in which he preached and in order to comprehend His meaning, a deeper study of His teachings was necessary than Dr. Trump could afford to do.

---

* Translation of the *Adi Granth*, pp. Ci—Cii.

Professor Wilson* also would, with Dr. Trump, appear to think slightingly of the Master's doctrines as being mere metaphysical notions founded on the abstractions of Soofeeism and the Vedant philosophy. "But, it is difficult," says Cunningham, "for any one to write about the omnipotence of God and the hopes of man, without laying himself open to the charge of belonging to one speculative school or another." Cunningham quotes certain epigrams and sayings of St. Paul and others, and says that such expressions as 'Doth not the Lord fill heaven and earth,' 'God in whom we live and move and have our being,' and 'of Him, and to Him, and through Him are all things,' might be used to declare the Prophet and the Apostle to the Pantheists or Materialists. But it nevertheless seems plain that Jeremiah and Paul, and likewise Nanak, had another object in view than scholastic dogmatism, and that they simply desired to impress mankind with exalted notions of the greatness and goodness of God, by a vague employment of general language which they knew would never mislead the multitude."

"It is to be remembered," says Cunningham, "that the Sikhs regard the mission of Nanak and Govind as the consummation of other

---

* As. Res. XVII, 233; and Continuation of Mills' *History of India*, VII, pp 101. 102; quoted in Cunningham's *History of the Sikhs*.

dispensations including that of Mahomed, and their talk, therefore, of Brahma and Vishnus and various heavenly powers, is no more unreasonable than the deference of Christians to Moses and Abraham, and to the arch-angels Michael and Gabriel. Such allusions are perhaps more excusable in the Sikhs, than the 'singular polytheism of Christian mediæval divines, which they grafted on the language, rather indeed the principles of Christianity."

"Nanak, indeed, refers continually to Hindu notions, but he was not therefore an idolator," says Cunningham,* "and it should further be borne in mind that as St. John could draw illustrations from Greek philosophy, so could St. Paul make an advantageous use of the Greek poets, as was long ago observed, in a right spirit by Milton (Speech for the Liberty of Unlicensed printing). In the early age of Christianity, moreover, the sybilline leaves were referred to as foretelling the mission of Jesus, but although the spuriousness of the passages is now admitted, the Fathers are not accused of Polytheism, or of holding Amalthea, a nurse of Jupiter, to be a real type of the Virgin Mary."

It would thus appear that if Guru Nanak has sometimes drawn illustrations from the Hindu sources, it does not follow from it that

---

* Middle ages, iii, 345, quoted in Cunningham's *History of the Sikhs.*

he himself cherished the exact ideas, contained in those illustrations, as objects of his faith. For let it be remembered that he has likewise drawn upon the Muhammadan sources for his sermons. For this purpose the reader may only be referred back to Guru Nanak's sermon in the Musjid at Sultanpore, where he does not denounce Islam, but has only tried to express a better and holier view thereof.

It must be remembered that, at the time of the Master's advent, the religious atmosphere was surcharged with formalities and ceremonialism, divorced from the spirit. Among the Hindus, the ascetic Yogis with all their pretensions of miraculous powers, held the supreme control, while the Muhammadans mostly, and indeed professedly, revered the Sufi Faqirs, who had established a number of shrines and mausoleums in Upper India, and exercised considerable influence in the country. As stated by Professor Stanlas Guyard,* these Sufis borrowed certain ideas about meditation and contemplation from the Hindus of India and drew their adepts mostly from the ranks of heterodoxy. Under these influences, their practices had very much departed from the original purpose, with which Sufism was founded amongst the Moslems of Persia by

* Encyclopaedia Britlanica (Ninth Edition), Vol. XVI, page 594).

Ra'bia; and they finally drifted into pantheistic beliefs. These latter they appear to have engrafted on the monotheistic doctrines of Islam, without, however, acknowledging the source to which they were indebted for these new ideas. They had mostly adopted monastic life, like the *Yogis*, and their austerities and mortification of the body may well pale those of the Hindu anchorites into insignificance. Both Yogis and Sufi *derveshes* of Upper India claimed supernatural powers, and, as much by the exhibition of these pretensions as by the human sympathies excited for their bodily mortificacations, they were able to collect hordes of credulous followers from amongst the unsophisticated and illiterate masses, to lead them to nowhere. This superficially spiritual atmosphere, the Master had to tackle as much as the purely irreligious and profane lives of the people around him. He had to use language, therefore. which they could easily understand, and through that language to divert the trend of religious thought from the intellect to the spirit.

The second Fundamental principle of the Master's Creed is the Brotherhood of Man. without distinction of colour, race, caste or tribe. Distinction of caste is one of the fundamental institutions, resting on religious sanction, of the Hindus, amongst whom the Master had to preach. "Caste may be generally described as the theory and practice of hereditary social distinctions, carried to the extremest limits, and confirmed by the sanction of religion. The spirit is more or less present in most societies which have attained a high organization; but carried to an extreme, it is a barrier to all progress, since in effect it is an enormous system of privilege."* The Master knew that spiritual development, religious reform and social progress could not be possible under a system of privileges, which vested the monopoly of spiritual evolution and religious sanctity in the higher castes, and debarred those of the lower castes from these advantages. While the latter could, in their humility at any rate, save their souls from getting hardened, and were easy for the Master to approach, with his message, the vanity of the higher castes, who enjoyed extraordinary social privileges, shut them away from the light that was being sent down to them. These wasted their freedom and opportunities in becoming slaves to things. The Master had pity for these privileged classes, for the rich and noble, as much as he had for the *Chandal*, the Pariah, the pauper and the criminal. The social privileges, the riches and the pleasures of life seemed to him to be greater tragedies than the untouchability, the poverty and the sorrow.

The Master emphatically denounced caste in most unmistakable terms, and established the

* Sir C. Gough.

equality of man before God, who only wanted the purity of thought and action in human beings, endowed with the Divine Spark, to favour them with a Realization of Him and the ultimate Emancipation.

> Caste and Birth will not be of avail ;
> Go and ask those who know the Truth ;
> That's the caste and that descent,
> Which is defined by deeds.*
>
> What can the caste do ? Ascertain Truth. †
>
> Value the light within, ask not of caste ;
> For caste there is none hereafter.‡

" Just as the grand idea of the Incomprehensible Unity, which could only be named and adorned, levelled all distinctions of creed and caste, so did the great truth of the Brotherhood of man sweep away the barriers of nation, tribe and station. Nanak taught that all men are equal before God ; that there is no high, no low, no dark, no fair, no privileged, no outcaste, all are equal both in race and in creed, in political rights and in religious aspirations .§

---

* Rag Parbhati, M. 1, Sh. 6.

ਜਾਤ ਜਨਮ ਨ ਪੁਛੀਐ, ਸਚ ਘਰ ਲਿਹੁ ਬਤਾਇ।
ਸਾ ਜਾਤ, ਸਾ ਪਤ ਹੈ, ਜੇਹੇ ਕਰਮ ਕਮਾਇ।

† Var Majh, M. 1, Pauri 9.

ਜਾਤੀ ਦੈ ਕਿਆ ਹਥ? ਸਚ ਪਰਖੀਐ।

‡ Rag Asa, M. 1, Sh. 3.

ਜਾਨ ਜੋਤ, ਨ ਪੁਛਹੁ ਜਾਤੀ, ਅਗੇ ਜਾਤ ਨ ਹੇ।

§ Prederic Pincot.

Dr. Trump remarks that the institution of caste was not directly assailed by Nanak; but, immediately after this remark, he quotes the last-mentioned *shabad* of the *Asa Rag* and goes on to say that "emancipation is not confined to the higher castes, but made accessible to all men, even to the *chandal*. Different stories are therefore cited in the *Granth*, that even the lowest men attained to salvation by muttering the name (of God), Nanak received all men as his disciples without any regard to caste, recognising in all the dignity of human birth and thus laid the foundations of a popular religion." This shows how a mere superficial study of the *Granth Sahib* has led Dr. Trump to record inconsistent expressions. He has, in fact, in more than one place, expressed contradictory views, and, laudable though his attempt of translating *Guru Granth Sahib* may have been, his hasty conclusions and unwarranted opinions, point to his scanty information and want of keen insight, and, therefore, are deeply to be regretted.

"Those two ideas, the Unity of God and the Brotherhood of man," says Pincot, "while uniting all classes on a common basis, at the same time, separated those who accepted them from the rest of their countrymen as an association of God-fearing republicans; for what Nanak claimed was *Liberty from prescribed trammels, Equality before God, and the Fraternity of Mankind.* The practical application of the doctrines thus taught led to the formation of a new nationality, the disciples of the great teacher becoming a republican fraternity, which gradually consolidated into a separate nation by the necessity for struggling for the liberty they claimed."

Thus unity of God and unity of mankind were the two fundamental doctrines of the Master's Creed. "Unison is the word," says Isaac Taylor, "which characterises true religion and describes the upper world." This was the Master's religion and this he preached to his followers. "Oneness," both of God and of mankind, was his motto, and he preached that whereas God is One, it will be the principal source of eternal beatitude for all brethren (*Bhais*, Sikhs) to dwell together in perfect unity. As God Himself is One, so is He pleased with Oneness. Produce concord and avoid discord; love all, despise none and produce Oneness; believe in One, love One and Oneness, and be One.

Next to the above fundamental principles come the means of man's salvation. But, before proceeding to explain the means of salvation, it seems necessary to know what constituted salvation, as taught by the Master. It has already been remarked that the Master nowhere entered upon metaphysical or philosophical discussions, and that, in interpreting his teachings, we are to keep all subtleties of the Hindu philosophy out of our consideration, and must put only popular construction upon the words used by him. That the Master believed in the transmigration of souls is doubtless true. He did teach of a previous birth and did consider the present as the result of the deeds of the past. The present life is sure to be followed by another, whose nature will be determined by our own good or bad actions. This apprehension of a future birth is what troubles the soul of man, and thus it is to get rid of this *apprehension*, which is a source of happiness to the soul.

No man but is striving hard to be happy. The attainment of everlasting happiness, the end which every man is trying to achieve, is what the Master believed to be the salvation. In what form that eternal beatitude is attained is not discussed. But the Master did teach that it could be reached, even in this life, and consisted of living *with* God and in God.* "Rare are such holy men in whose pure hearts lives the True one; seek the Lord's protection, and let the spirit meet the Divine, saith Nanak.†

---

* Cunningham, however, says that Nanak regarded bliss as the dwelling of the soul with God, after its punitary transmigration should have ceased.

† Rag Sorath, M. 1. Sh. 6,

ਸਚੇ ਭਾਂਡੇ ਸਾਚ ਸਮਾਵੇ ਵਿਰਲੇ ਸੂਚਾ ਚਾਰੀ ।

ਤੰਤੇ ਕੋ ਪਰਮ ਤੰਤ ਮਿਲਾਇਆ, ਨਾਨਕ ਸਰਨ ਤੁਹਾਰੀ

One enjoys eternal happiness when God is constantly *with* him : and in which form he himself would then be, the Master has not cared much to discuss.

Those are saved with whom the Father is pleased, on whom He bestows His favours. " He whom God favours, O Nanak, finds the Lord." The effort of the human soul is to be directed to the single purpose to please the Lord and win His favours. Cunningham says that " the extension of Grace is linked with the exercise of our will and the beneficent use of our faculties. God, says Nanak, places salvation in good works and uprightness of conduct ; the Lord will ask of man, " What has he done," and the Teacher further required timely repentance of men, saying, " if not until the day of reckoning the sinner abaseth himself, punishment shall overtake him."

It is the training of one's *Surt* (Soul-Consciousness) for constant communion with the Supreme that may lead to the unfoldment of the soul ; and this training cannot come so long as the mind, indulged in earthly cravings and low appetites, is dragging the *Surt* down from its spiritual ideal. It is in this training that Devotion to Him, Meditation of His True Name with a heart full of Faith, and pure moral deeds, become the means, by which the Grace of the Almighty may be deserved. It is for this training that the need of the Guru or Preceptor is essential. It is by complying with the instruction received from the Guru that one may train his Soul-Consciousness and prepare his Spirit for the reception of Grace. This obviously implies strict obedience to the Guru's Word.

Some Western writers have misunderstood the injunction to render implicit obedience to the Guru and have been led to remark that the "chief duty of the disciple is blind obedience to his Guru."* Compliance with the instructions of the Guru, and rendering manual service to him, with the clear and conscious end in view of humble self-abasement and reception of Grace, is by no means a *blind* obedience to be so lightly and contemptuously spoken of. For, "without the Guru, Love cannot be inspired, and the filth of ego cannot be removed."† It is in love and devotion that services are performed and obedience rendered. How else may the filth of ego be washed away, and how else may lessons in humility be learnt. This is but a mode in which one may melt his soul and pour it out at the Lord's feet. In receiving ordinary education of the world, a pupil in

---

* Dr. Trump Adi Granth, p. cx.

† Sri Rag, M. 1, Asht, Sh. 11.

ਬਿਨ ਗੁਰ ਪ੍ਰੀਤ ਨ ਉਪਜੈ, ਹਉਮੈ ਮੈਲ ਨ ਜਾਇ ॥

his elementary stages has to accept a lot from his teacher, without questioning why and wherefor in respect of the lessons he receives; and it seems strange how in one's spiritual training, acceptance of the Guru's word, without question, regarding the development of one's character and soul for being fitted to receive the Lord's Grace, may be contemptuously mentioned by people who might have known better. Such remarks merely betray spiritual bankruptcy.

> O man, how canst thou obtain emancipation without Love?
> Through Guru's Word, shall He manifest Himself within thee and grant thee Treasures of Devotion.
> O man, love God as lotus loves the water:
> The more it is beaten by the waves, the more it unfolds itself;
> Having received its life in water, it dies without it.
> O man, love God as fish loves the water:
> The more the water, the more joyous is it and contented in mind and body,
> Without water, liveth not for a moment: God knoweth its heartache.
> O man, love God as the *Chatrik* loves the rain:
> The tanks full, the lands green, are of no avail, without a single drop of rain from above.
> O man, love God as the *Chakwi* loves the sun:

Sleepeth not for a moment, liveth close to what is so distant.*

---

* Sri Rag. M. 1. (11);

ਰੇ ਮਨ ਐਸੀ ਹਰਿ ਸਿਉ ਪ੍ਰੀਤਿ ਕਰਿ,
ਜੈਸੀ ਜਲ ਕਮਲੇਹਿ ।
ਲਹਰੀ ਨਾਲਿ ਪਛਾੜੀਐ,
ਭੀ ਵਿਗਸੈ ਅਸਨੇਹਿ ।
ਜਲ ਮਹਿ ਜੀਅ ਉਪਾਇ ਕੈ,
ਬਿਨੁ ਜਲ ਮਰਣੁ ਤਿਨੇਹਿ ॥ ੧ ॥
ਮਨ ਰੇ ਕਿਉ ਛੂਟਹਿ ਬਿਨੁ ਪਿਆਰ ।
ਗੁਰਮੁਖਿ ਅੰਤਰਿ ਰਵਿ ਰਹਿਆ,
ਬਖ਼ਸੇ ਭਗਤਿ ਭੰਡਾਰ ॥ ਰਹਾਉ ॥
ਰ ਮਨ ਐਸੀ ਹਰਿ ਸਿਉ, ਪ੍ਰੀਤਿ ਕਰਿ
ਜੈਸੀ ਮਛੁਲੀ ਨੀਰ ।
ਜਿਉ ਅਧਿਕਉ ਤਿਉ ਸੁਖੁ ਘਣੋ,
ਮਨਿ ਤਨਿ ਸਾਂਤਿ ਸਰੀਰ ।
ਬਿਨੁ ਜਲ ਘੜੀ ਨ ਜੀਵਈ,
ਪ੍ਰਭੁ ਜਾਣੈ ਅਭ ਪੀਰ ॥ ੨ ॥
ਰੇ ਮਨ ਐਸੀ ਹਰਿ ਸਿਉ ਪ੍ਰੀਤ ਕਰਿ
ਜੈਸੀ ਚਾਤ੍ਰਿਕ ਮੇਹ ।
ਸਰ ਭਰਿ ਥਲ ਹਰੀਆਵਲੇ,
ਇਕ ਬੂੰਦ ਨ ਪਵਈ ਕਹ
ਕਰਮ ਮਿਲੈ ਸੋ ਪਾਈਐ,
ਕਿਰਤੁ ਪਇਆ ਸਿਰਿ ਦੇਹ ॥ ੩ ॥
... ...
... ...
ਰੇ ਮਨ ਐਸੀ ਹਰਿ ਸਿਉ ਪ੍ਰੀਤਿ ਕਰਿ,
ਜੈਸੀ ਚਕਵੀ ਸੂਰ ।
ਖਿਨੁ ਪਲੁ ਨੀਦ ਨ ਸੋਵਈ,
ਜਾਣੈ ਦੂਰਿ ਹਜੂਰਿ ।
... ...
... ...

In his devotion to the Lord, the Master likens the disciple to a bride, preparing herself for the reception of the Bridegroom. It is by self-surrender that she pleaseth her Beloved. But she must attend to her toilet and so look as to inspire love at first sight. So must the disciple prepare his soul for receiving Lord's Grace.

All are the Husband's brides ; all adorn themselves

When they come for estimates, fancy dress is declared un-natural :

By hypocrisy the Bridegroom's affection is not gained : Counterfeit overguilding is but miserable.

O God, thus may the Bride enjoy the Bridegroom :

Whomso Thou favoureth are the accepted wives, those thou adornest of Thy Own Grace.

Those that are adorned with the Guru's Word, live in body and mind with Thee, the Bridegroom ;

With folded hands they stand and wait for Thee, to Truth they pray and pray :

Steeped in the colour of Devotion, ever living in fear of the Truth, they are dyed in the true colours of Love.

The Bride shall never be widow that abideth with Sat Guru.

The Bridegroom is ever delightful, young, true, neither dieth nor divorceth,

Ever sports with the Bride : genuine is His Grace and will.

Amongst women is she beautiful, on whose forehead is the Jewel of Love ;

Her beauty and wisdom are charming, on account of her infinite Love of the True One ;

Without the Bridegroom she knoweth no man : Such is her love and affection for the True Master.

O thou, that art asleep in the dark night; how shall thy night pass without the Bridegroom.

Thy bosom burns, thy body is on fire, and thy heart too, O lady, is consumed

In vain is thy beauty, O lady, for the Bridegroom meeteth thee not.

Bridegroom is in thy bed, thou, O bride knoweth it not, so asleep thou art.

Bridegroom is awake, thou art asleep, who may wake thee up.

May the True Guru meet thee, Mayst thou live in Fear of Him, Love shall be thy companion, saith Nanak.*

---

* Sri Rag. M. 1, Asht, Sh. 2.

ਸਭੇ ਕੰਤ ਮਹੇਲੀਆਂ ਸਗਲੀਆਂ ਕਰਹਿ ਸੀਗਾਰ,
ਗਣਤ ਗਣਾਵਣ ਆਈਆ ਸੂਹਾ ਵੇਸੁ ਵਿਕਾਰ,
ਪਾਖੰਡ ਪ੍ਰੇਮ ਨ ਪਾਈਐ ਖੋਟਾ ਪਾਜ ਖੁਆਰ।
ਹਰਿ ਜੀ ਇਉ ਪਿਰ ਰਾਵੈ ਨਾਰਿ,
ਤੁਧ ਭਾਵਨ ਸੋਹਾਗਣੀ ਆਪਣੀ ਕਿਰਪਾ ਲੈਹਿ ਸਵਾਰ।
ਗੁਰ ਸਬਦੀ ਸੀਗਾਰੀਆ ਤਨ ਮਨ ਪਿਰ ਕੈ ਪਾਸਿ,
ਦੋਇ ਕਰ ਜੋੜ ਖੜੀ ਤਕੈ ਸਚ ਕਹੈ ਅਰਦਾਸਿ।
ਲਾਲ ਰਤੀ ਸਚ ਭੈ ਵਸੀ ਭਾਇ ਰਤੀ ਰੰਗ ਰਾਸਿ।
ਸਾਧਨ ਰੰਡ ਨ ਬੈਸਈ ਜੇ ਸਤਿ ਗੁਰ ਮਾਹਿ ਸਮਾਇ,
ਪਿਰ ਰੀਸਾਲੂ ਨਉਤਨੋ ਸਾਚਉ ਮਰੈ ਨ ਜਾਇ,
ਨਿਤ ਰਵੈ ਸੋਹਾਗਣੀ ਸਾਚੀ ਨਦਰ ਰਜਾਇ।

... ...

ਨਾਰੀ ਅੰਦਰ ਸੋਹਣੀ ਮਸਤਕਿ ਮਣੀ ਪਿਆਰੁ,
ਸੋਭਾ ਸੁਰਤਿ ਸੁਹਾਂਵਣੀ ਸਾਚੈ ਪ੍ਰੇਮਿ ਅਪਾਰ,
ਬਿਨ ਪਿਰ ਪੁਰਖ ਨ ਜਾਣਈ, ਸਾਚੇ ਗੁਰ ਕੈ ਹੇਤਿ ਪਿਆਰਿ।
ਨਿਸ ਅੰਧਿਆਰੀ ਸੁਤੀਏ ਕਿਉ ਪਿਰ ਬਿਨੁ ਰੈਣਿ ਵਿਹਾਇ,
ਅਕ ਜਲਉ ਤਨ ਜਾਲੀਓ ਮਨ ਤਨ ਜਲਿ ਬਲਿ ਜਾਇ,
ਜਾ ਧਨ ਕੰਤ ਨ ਰਾਵੀਆਂ ਤੇ ਬਿਰਥਾ ਜੋਬਨੁ ਜਾਇ।
ਸੇਜੈ ਕੰਤ ਮਹੇਲੜੀ ਸੂਤੀ ਬੂਝ ਨ ਪਾਇ,
ਹਉ ਸੁਤੀ ਪਿਰ ਜਾਗਣਾ ਕਿਸ ਕਉ ਪੂਛਉ ਜਾਇ,
ਸਤਿ ਗੁਰਿ ਮੇਲੀ ਭੈ ਵਸੀ ਨਾਨਕ ਪ੍ਰੇਮੁ ਸਖਾਇ,

In another hymn the Master remarks what should the innocent girl, who has known no union with the Bridegroom, do, and he answers that she may go and enquire from those that have obtained the bliss of Union, as to how they have acheived it, and then declares :

Accept as good whatever He doth ;
  Leave off thine own wisdom ;
By His love thou shalt possess thy soul ;
  Ever think of His Feet.
Do as He biddeth thee to do,
  Give up thy body and soul to Him ·
Such should be thy perfumery :
  Thus says the United Bride to thee,
    O sister,
  So shalt thou meet thy Lord*.

---

* Tilang M. 1.

ਜੋ ਕਿਛ ਕਰੇ ਸੁ ਭਲਾ ਕਰ ਮਾਨੀਏ,
  ਹਿਕਮਤ ਹੁਕਮ ਚੁਕਾਈਐ ।
ਜਾ ਕੇ ਪ੍ਰੇਮ ਪਦਾਰਥ ਪਾਈਐ,
  ਤਉ ਚਰਣੀ ਚਿਤੁ ਲਾਈਐ ।
ਸਹੁ ਕ ਸੁ ਕੀਜੈ, ਤਨ ਮਨੋ ਦੀਜੈ,
  ਐਸਾ ਪਰਮਲ ਲਾਈਐ ।
ਏਵ ਕਹੇ ਸੁਹਾਗਣੀ ਭੈਣੇ,
  ਇਨੀ ਬਾਤੀਂ ਸ਼ਹੁ ਪਾਈਐ ॥

Surrender thyself, so mayst thou meet
  thy Lord,

No other wisdom can be of avail.

The day He looks on thee shall count,
  For the bride has then gained all treasures.

Whoso is loved by the Lord is the wedded
  one,

  She is also the queen of all, saith Nanak.

Dyed in this colour, blissful in peace,

  Living day and night in Love,

Thou shalt attain the perfection of beauty,
  and of Love, and of Wisdom.*

---

*Tilang, M. 1.

ਆਪ ਗਵਾਈਐ, ਤਾਂ ਸਹੁ ਪਾਈਐ,
ਅਵਰ ਕੈਸੀ ਚਤਰਾਈ ।

ਸ ਨਦਰ ਕਰ ਦੇਖੇ, ਸੋ ਦਿਨ ਲੇਖੇ,
ਕਾਮਣਿ ਨੌਨਿਧ ਪਾਈ ।

ਆਪਣ ਕੰਤੁ ਪਿਆਰੀ ਸਾ ਸੁਹਾਗਣਿ,
ਨਾਨਕ, ਸਾ ਸਭਰਾਈ ।

ਐਸੇ ਰੰਗ ਰਾਤੀ, ਸਹਿਜ ਕੀ ਮਾਤੀ,
ਅਹਿ ਨਿਸ ਭਾਇ ਸਮਾਣੀ ॥

ਸੁੰਦਰ ਸਾਇ ਸਰੂਪ ਬਿਚਖਣ,
ਕਹੀਐ ਸਾ ਸਿਆਣੀ ।

It is in the measure of the effort that a human soul makes to deserve Divine love that God sends down His Grace, and not by thinking or even feeling that one is worthy of that love. Indeed he, who believes that he has, by his life and character, deserved God's Love is hardly worthy of it. It is in utter humility and absolute self-surrender that one may become worthy of His Grace. One must live by love and admiration, and recognize that he is unworthy of God's love, before the sacrament of Love comes to him. The Master says :

> What love is this that takes one to another.
> Those are the approved Lovers, who remain ever absorbed,
> Who accept as good what He doth, not good what He doth not.
> They are not the lovers, who make calculations with Him.*

This constant absorption in the Name, in the Lord of Love, mentioned in this stanza, brings us to the practice of meditation of God's Name, which is such an essential feature of the Sikh religion—" muttering of God's name," as Dr. Trump has so scoffingly translated the word *japna*. The words *japna*, *simarna*, *dhyana*,

---

*Asa di *Var*, Sh. 2).

ਏ ਕਿਨੇਹੀ ਆਸਕੀ ਦੂਜੇ ਲਗੈ ਜਾਇ,
ਨਾਨਕ ਆਸਕੁ ਕਾਢੀਐ ਸਦ ਹੀ ਰਹੈ ਸਮਾਇ ।
ਚੰਗੈ ਚੰਗਾ ਕਰ ਮੰਨੇ ਮੰਦੈ ਮੰਦਾ ਹੋਇ,
ਆਸਕੁ ਏਹ ਨ ਆਖੀਐ ਜਿ ਲੇਖੈ ਵਰਤੈ ਸੋਇ ।

mana are used synonymously by the Master, for the efforts of a human soul to enter into communion with the Divine. It is continuous communion with God that is to be aimed at by the disciple, and his efforts are to continue till it is achieved. When achieved, it would require no effort, but the disciple will then ever abide with Him. " When rising, when sitting, when sleeping, and when waking, ever and always, remember God," saith the Master.*

The word used for worship in the Fundamental *mantram* of the Sikh religion is *Jap*, and that is the title of the Sikh morning prayer, which is also recited at the beginning of all functions. The manner of this worship is explained in various places in the *Granth Sahib*, and it involves eight-fold exercise, which may be summarised thus :

1. Purity of body and mind.
2. Silence.
3. Meditation on the meaning of the *mantram*.
4. Concentration of mind.
5. Patience and contentment.
6. Faith and reverence in intellect.
7. *Santsang* or company of holy men.
8. Conforming life or one's deeds to the sense of the *mantram*.

---

* ਊਠਤ, ਬੈਠਤ, ਸੋਵਤ, ਜਾਗਤ,
ਸਦਾ ਸਦਾ ਹਰਿ ਧਿਆਇਐ ॥

These are the exercises in which the disciple must constantly develop his soul, and whatever detracts him from them must be avoided.

It is now necessary to refer briefly to the basic principle of the Sikh Ethics, as taught by the Master. In this respect also, as in most others to which reference has already been made, Dr. Trump has fallen in a grave error in remarking that in a religion where highest object of life is the extinction of individual existence, there can be no room for a system of moral duties," and in assuming that " Sikhism is not a moralising Deism." The absurdity of these remarks is so apparent that it would have hardly needed refutation, had it not been the fact that more than one European writer, and some of the Indian writers also, who have ever needed something to support a misrepresentation of the Sikh religion, have often drawn upon Dr. Trump's authority. Sikhism nowhere teaches the extinction of individual existence as the object of life, and the reader of this volume appears to stand in no need of being reminded that the Master enjoined the purest morality, both in deed and thought, upon his disciples. He again and again insists on the suppression of earthly cravings and prohibits the soul being subjected to the pleasures of the senses. Indeed these lessons he had begun to inculcate even in his early years, when he denounced the ceremonies of the *Yagoypwit* and purification from *Sutak*. It was in the same strain that throughout his life he addressed all those whom he found engaged in symbolism and formalities.

The ethics of Sikhism are in fact based on the soundest possible foundation. The purity of conduct and the performance of moral duties, however, have not been made an end in itself for human conduct. It is only a means to an end. It has already been explained that salvation according to the Sikh religion lies in the human soul abiding in eternal happiness at the Feet of the Lord, and that it may be achieved only by deserving and obtaining the Grace of God. In order to deserve the bestowal of Grace, self-surrender in the Love of God is absolutely essential. This self-surrender does not necessarily mean extinction of individual existence, but it does mean subordinating one's own will to the will of the Supreme. Man must bring all his actions into line with the Will of the Supreme Lord of the Universe, love of whom is the essential qualification of the disciple.

> Perish all such actions, in the performance
> of which my Supreme Beloved may be
> forgotten.

> That, saith Nanak, is the approved and loving conduct, which may deserve honour in the Court of the Almighty Master.*

What a beautiful maxim is thus laid down to control all human actions and activities. Avoid all such deeds which may distract thee from the Lord. The fundamental principles of the Sikh religion, we have seen, are the Unity of God, to whom all love is due, and absolute equality of man and service of humanity. Under a system like this, there was no necessity for dogmatisation about moral duties of man. The purity of morals, in the performance of both positive and negative duties, is an essential qualification, without which it would not be possible for the mind to attend to his spiritual functions without distraction. These, therefore, may well be described as a means to the means of one's salvation.

It has been explained above that the Master directed all human conduct to be subjected to the One supreme duty of Remembrance of the Lord and Devotion to His Name. He taught

---

* Var Vadihans, M. 4., *Shlok*. M. 1.

ਜਾਲਉ ਐਸੀ ਰੀਤਿ, ਜਿਤੁ ਮੈ ਪਿਆਰਾ ਵੀਸਰੈ,
ਨਾਨਕ ਸਾਈ ਭਲੀ ਪ੍ਰੀਤਿ, ਜਿਤੁ ਸਾਹਿਬ ਸੇਤੀ ਪਤਿ ਰਹੈ ॥

that all human desires and deeds, which lead human soul away from this supreme duty, must be annihilated. But the Master did not confine his moral injunctions to such negative efforts of the human soul. Budha's negation of human cravings having thus, in the Master's teachings, been based on the fundamental duty as above stated to sustain it, the Master draws attention to the further development of the human soul in the performance of its positive functions. The Master has likened the human soul to a trader, who carries his capital into his business, not merely to protect it from wastage, but also to earn further profit and to add to what he had and thereby to augment his resources.

> O man, thou hast come to earn profit ;
>
> What trash art thou engaged in ?
>
> The night is ending.*

God has, in His supreme Beneficence, endowed human soul with a spark of spiritual existence, and this is the capital which has been supplied to the Trader to do his business during this earthly existence.

---

* ਪ੍ਰਾਨੀ, ਤੂੰ ਆਇਓ ਲਾਹਾ ਲੈਣਿ ।

ਲਗਾ ਕਿਤੁ ਕੁਫਕੜੇ ਮਕਦੀ ਚਲੀ ਰੈਣ ॥

Trade, Trade, O merchant, and protect thy goods :
Purchase such goods that may in the end go with thee !
Financier is wise and shall hereafter look for thy stock in trade !
Remember the Lord, O brother mine,
Collect the goods of Lord's Praise, that on seeing thy gains, the Lord may be pleased !
Those that have not the capital of Truth,
How can they be comfortable ?
Trade in false (counterfeit) goods degradeth both mind and body :
Such (trader), like the ensnared animal, Shall suffer extreme pain and shall ever cry in agony :
Counterfeit (goods) shall not be accepted in the Treasury :
Trader in them shall receive no audience from the Lord or the Guru.
Counterfeit shall receive no respect,
Counterfeit shall succeed not,
Counterfeit shall earn but counterfeit ;
Such (trader) shall come and go, with the loss of all honour.
Counsel thy mind with the Guru's word and sing praises of the Lord, saith Nanak;
Be steeped in the Love of Lord's Name thou mayst have no burdens and no doubts :

> Meditate on the Lord : Ample shall be thy profits, and thou shalt march on fearlessly, with the Lord's Name in thy mind :*

Questioned what His profession was and how he spent His Life, the Master sang the following beautiful hymn, in *Rag Gauri Bairagan* :—

> Aye : I am the Trader in the Lord's Name !
> Thy Name, O Lord, I buy as stock in Trade !
>
> 1. Be I a deer, live I in the jungle, and eat I the wild growth ;
>
> May my Master grant me, of His grace, union with the Lord !

---

*Sri Rag. M. 1, 23.

ਵਣਜੁ ਕਰਹੁ, ਵਣਜਾਰਿਹੋ, ਵਖਰ ਲੇਹੁ ਸਮਾਲਿ ।
ਤੈਸੀ ਵਸਤੁ ਵਿਸਾਹੀਐ, ਜੈਸੀ ਨਿਬਹੈ ਨਾਲਿ ।
ਅਗੈ ਸ਼ਾਹੁ ਸੁਜਾਣੁ ਹੈ, ਲੈਸੀ ਵਸਤੁ ਸਮਾਲਿ ॥ ੧ ।

ਭਾਈ ਰੇ, ਰਾਮ ਕਹੁ ਚਿਤ ਲਾਇ ।
ਹਰਿ ਜਸੁ ਵਖਰੁ ਲੈ ਚਲਹ ਸਹੁ ਦੇਖੈ, ਪਤੀਆਇ । ਰਹਾਉ ॥
ਜਿਨਾ ਰਾਸਿ ਨ ਸਚੁ ਹੈ, ਕਿਉਂ ਤਿਨਾ ਸੁਖਿ ਹੋਇ ।
ਖੋਟੇ ਵਣਜਿ ਵਣਜਿਐ, ਮਨੁ ਤਨੁ ਖੋਟਾ ਹੋਇ ।

ਫਾਹੀ ਫਾਥੇ ਮਿਰਗ ਜਿਉਂ, ਦੁਖ ਘਣੋ, ਨਿਤ ਰੋਇ ॥ ੨ ॥
ਖੋਟੇ ਪੋਤੈ ਨਾ ਪਵਹਿ, ਤਿਨ ਹਰਿ ਗੁਰ ਦਰਸ ਨ ਹੋਇ।
ਖੋਟੇ ਜਾਤ ਨ ਪਤਿ ਹੈ, ਖੋਟਿ ਨ ਸੀਝਸਿ ਕੋਇ ।
ਖੋਟੇ ਖੋਟੁ ਕਮਾਵਣਾ, ਆਇ ਗਇਆ ਪਤਿ ਖੋਇ । ੩ ॥

ਨਾਨਕ ਮਨੁ ਸਮਝਾਈਐ, ਗੁਰ ਕੈ ਸਬਦਿ ਸਾਲਾਹ ।
ਰਾਮ ਨਾਮ ਰੰਗਿ ਰਤਿਆ, ਭਾਰੁ ਨ ਭਰਮ ਤਿਨਾਹ ।
ਹਰਿ ਜਪਿ ਲਾਹਾ ਅਗਲਾ, ਨਿਰਭਉ, ਹਰਿ ਮਨ ਮਾਹ ॥ ੪ ॥

My all may then be sacrificed !

2. Be I a *Kokil*, live I in the mango grove, and sound I the *pleasant* notes of meditation !

May I meet my Master, in due course ;

I shall then grow immensely handsome !

3. Be I a fish, live I in water, and know I the secrets of Life ;

May I be surrounded by my Master all round ;

With open arms shall I then meet Him !

4. Be I a *Nagan*, live I in the earth, and fearless I be on hearing the Divine tune ;

May I be, ever and always the *suhagan* (the wedded bride),

Ever absorbed in the Supreme Lord,

Shall I be, saith Nanak !

Gauri Bairagan, M. 1, 19.

ਹਰਣੀ ਹੋਵਾ, ਬਨਿ ਬਸਾਂ, ਕੰਦ ਮੂਲ ਚੁਣਿ ਖਾਉ
ਗੁਰ ਪ੍ਰਸਾਦੀ ਮੇਰਾ ਸਹੁ ਮਿਲੈ:
ਵਾਰਿ ਵਾਰਿ ਹਉ ਜਾਉ ਜੀਉ ॥ ੧ ॥
ਬਨਜਾਰਨਿ ਰਾਮ ਕੀ,
ਤੇਰਾ ਨਾਮੁ ਵਖਰੁ ਵਾਪਾਰ ਜੀਉ ॥ ੧ ॥ ਰਹਾਉ ॥
ਕਕਿਲੈ ਹੋਵਾਂ, ਅੰਬਿ ਬਸਾਂ,
ਸਹਿਜ ਸਬਦ ਬੀਚਾਰੁ ।

P. T. O.

Such is the positive trade which the Master enjoins upon disciples to engage in. Man is not merely to abstain from evil thought and evil deed, however necessary it is for him to do so! Enough it is not for him to think right and do right, essential as these qualities are. He is to base his abstention and his performance on the fundamental principle of Love of God and the realisation of His Name in all his deeds of omission and commission. Upon that fundamental ground work, he is to build up his trade and earn profit, so that the capital, with which he was endowed, may multiply

---

ਸਹਿਜ ਸੁਭਾਇ ਮੇਰਾ ਸਹੁ ਮਿਲੈ,
ਦਰਸਨਿ ਰੂਪਿ ਅਪਾਰੁ ॥ ੨ ॥
ਮਛਲੀ ਹੋਵਾਂ, ਜਲਿ ਬਸਾਂ,
ਜੀਅ ਜੰਤ ਸਭਿ ਸਾਰਿ ।
ਉਰਵਾਰਿ, ਪਾਰਿ, ਮੇਰਾ ਸਹੁ ਵਸੈ,
ਹਉ ਮਿਲਉਗੀ ਬਾਹ ਪਸਾਰ ॥ ੩ ॥
ਨਾਗਨਿ ਹੋਵਾਂ, ਧਰ ਬਸਾਂ.
ਸਬਦੁ ਵਸੈ ਭਉ ਜਾਇ ।
ਨਾਨਕ, ਸਦਾ ਸੋਹਾਗਣੀ.
ਜਿਨ ਜੋਤੀ ਜੋਤਿ ਸਮਾਇ ॥ ੪ ॥

hundred thousand fold, and the Great Capitalist may receive him with open arms :

> Nanak is Thy Merchant, O Lord
>
> Thou art his Capital !
>
> Anxiety must vanish when he praiseth Thee and prayeth to Thee.*

God, conceived as Bridegroom, is to be worshipped and adored. How can the human soul, steeped in sins, be honoured by the Husband, asks the Master ?

> My mind abideth not steadily with the All Merciful :
>
> Avaricious, hypocrite, sinful, fraudulent,
>
> Attached more and more it is to the *Maya*.
>
> 1. The Five (deadly sins) live secretly within,
>
> Mind is not stable, it wandereth about homeless :
>
> 2. (Say we :) Garlands of Flowers shall I put on,
>
> Decorations shall I wear, when the Bridegroom Beloved shall come unto me.

---

* Rag Vadihans, M. 1, Gh. 1, 1 (4).

ਨਾਨਕ ਤੇਰਾ ਬਾਣੀਆ ਤੂੰ ਸਾਹਿਬ ਮੈਂ ਰਾਸਿ ।

ਮਨ ਤੇ ਧੋਖਾ ਤਾ ਲਹੈ, ਜਾਂ ਸਿਫਤਿ ਕਰੀ ਅਰਦਾਸਿ ॥

3. Five companions have I and yet the Bridegroom is alone.

   Fundamental Truth is: the soul shall depart.

4. The soul with its Five companions shall then cry!

   When, carried to the Financier, accounts are rendered, saith Nanak.*

If it were stated that the Master did not dogmatise about Ethics or moral duties of Man, the statement may be tolerated. But to say that there was no room in his teachings for a system of moral duties is simply absurd. With

---

* Asa, Gh. 5, M. 1, 34.

ਭੀਤਰਿ ਪੰਚ ਗੁਪਤ ਮਨਿ ਵਾਸੇ,
ਥਿਰੁ ਨ ਰਹਹਿ ਜੈਸੇ ਭਵਹਿ ਉਦਾਸੇ । ੧ ॥
ਮਨ ਮੇਰਾ ਦਇਆਲ ਸੇਤੀ ਥਿਰ ਨ ਰਹੈ ।
ਲੋਭੀ, ਕਪਟੀ, ਪਾਪੀ, ਪਾਖੰਡੀ,
ਮਾਇਆ ਅਧਿਕ ਲਗੇ ॥ ਰਹਾਉ ॥
ਫੂਲ ਮਾਲਾ ਗਲਿ ਪਹਿਰਉਗੀ ਹਾਰੋ ।
ਮਿਲੈਗਾ ਪ੍ਰੀਤਮੁ ਤਬ ਕਰਉਗੀ ਸੀਗਾਰੋ ॥ ੨ ॥
ਪੰਚ ਸਖੀ ਹਮ ਏਕ ਭਤਾਰੋ ॥
ਪੇਡ ਲਗੀ ਹੈ ਜੀਅੜਾ ਚਾਲਣ ਹਾਰੋ । ੩ ॥
ਪੰਚ ਸਖੀ ਮਿਲਿ ਰੁਦਨ ਕਰੇਹਾ ।
ਸਾ_ ਪਜਤਾ, ਪ੍ਰਣਵਤਿ ਨਾਨਕ, ਲੇਖਾ ਦੇਹਾ ॥ ੪ ॥

regard to those who harangued huge audiences about their moral duties, the Master declared thus :

1. He speaketh lies, he swalloweth what is prohibited ;
   (And yet) he goeth out to preach to others :
   He deceiveth himself, and leadeth others into deception ;
   Such, saith Nanak, seemeth to be the Leader !
2. He himself knoweth not, and preacheth to others,
   Such is the Leader !
3. Blind himself, leadeth he the way ;
   Driveth the whole party into Destruction ;
   Meeteth with utter condemnation in the hereafter :
   Such seemeth to be the Leader !*

---

* Var Majh M. 1, Shlok, M. 1.

ਕੂੜੁ ੋਲਿ, ਮੁਰਦਾਰ ਖਾਇ ।
ਅਵਰੀ ਨੋ ਸਮਝਾਵਣਿ ਜਾਇ ।
ਮੁਠਾ ਆਪਿ ਮੁਹਾਏ ਸਾਥੈ ।
ਨਾਨਕ ਐਸਾ ਆਗੂ ਜਾਪੈ ॥
ਆਪਿ ਨਾ ਬੂਝਾ ਲੋਕ ਬੁਝਾਈ, ਐਸਾ ਆਗੂ ਹੋਵਾਂ
ਨਾਨਕ ਅੰਧਾ ਹੋਇ ਕੈ ਦਸੈ ਰਾਹੈ।
ਸਭਸੁ ਮੁਹਾਏ ਸਾਥੈ ।
ਅਗੈ ਗਇਆ ਮੁਹੇ ਮੁਹਿ ਪਾਹਿ, ਸੁ ਐਸਾ ਆਗੂ ਜਾਪੈ ॥

In another place, the Master beautifully illustrates the condition of those hypocrites who talk a lot about ethics but follow not one line of what they preach. He says :

> Tread I not on the path indicated :
> Yet declare I that I have reached the destination :
> With Thee, my Husband, I am not on speaking terms :
> How can I find comfortable residence at Home ?*

It has already been remarked that the Master grounded all his teachings on the supreme duty of man to please the Almighty Father in order to deserve His Grace, and he directed all deeds to be abandoned which lead one astray from this path. All austerities and all moral deeds, without their ground work, were declared by Him as fruitless. All actions, performed without loss of sight of the ideal to be attained, and which may advance the soul towards that ideal, are declared by the Master to be meritorious. All deeds, in the performance of which the ideal is forgotten and which lead one away from it, are forbidden. The disciple with his mind fixed on the ideal is called

* Rag Vadihans, M. 1. Gh. 1, 2 (3).

ਰਾਹੁ ਦਸਾਈ ਨ ਜੁਲਾ, ਆਖਾਂ ਅੰਮੜੀਆਸੁ ।

ਤੈ ਸਹ ਨਾਲ ਅਕੂਅਣਾ, ਕਿਉਂ ਥੀਵੈ ਘਰ ਵਾਸੁ ।

Gurmukh and one with his mind away fron the same is called *Manmukh*. The latter, notwithstanding his deeds of benevolence, is declared to be the *sakat*, switched off from the ideal, and the former in spite of his extreme poverty and consequent inability to do much worldly good to others, is the *Gurmukh*. With regard to the *sakat* the Master has declared thus :

Don't go near the *sakat*,
Avoid him from a distance :
Touch not a smoked vessel,
Lest it give thee some stain !*

The Master enjoins upon the disciple to keep company with *Gurmukhs*, those who would keep him in touch with the ideal, those whose own souls tend towards the Lord and who can guide the disciple on his march towards the Lord. It is here that the Master declared the disciple's devotion to the *Gurmukh* in the following forceful lines :—

Whoever tells me of Thee, O Lord !
What shall I present him witn ?

---

* ਸਾਕਤ ਸੰਗ ਨ ਕੀਜੀਏ,
ਦੂਰੋਂ ਜਾਈਏ ਭਾਗੁ ॥
ਬਾਸਨ ਕਾਰੋ ਪਰਸੀਏ
ਮਤਿ ਕਿਛੁ ਲਾਗੈ ਦਾਗੁ ॥

I shall sever my head off and offer it to him for a seat :

I shall then serve him, without head on my body.

Why shall I not die ? Why shall I not give up my life ?

It is the Lord that is thus glorified in him !*

The Master in another beautiful stanza called upon the disciple to make the supreme sacrifice, before stepping into the path of discipleship. He says :

Wantest thou to delight in Love ?

Head on the palm of thy hand, come unto my path !

Sacrifice thy head, waiver not !

Then alone step forth into this path.†

---

* Rag Vadihans M. 1, Gh. 1, Sh. 3.

ਤੇ ਸਾਹਿਬ ਕੀ ਬਾਤ ਜਿ ਆਖੇ,
ਕਹੁ ਨਾਨਕ, ਤਿਸ ਕਿਆ ਦੀਜੈ ।
ਸੀਸੁ ਵਢੇ ਕਰ ਬੈਸਣ ਦੀਜੈ,
ਵਿਣੁ ਸਿਰ ਸੇਵ ਕਰੀਜੈ ।
ਕਿਉਂ ਨ ਮਰੀਜੈ, ਜੀਅੜਾ ਨ ਦੀਜੈ,
ਜਾ ਸਹੁ ਭਇਆ ਵਿਡਾਣਾ ॥

† *Shlok (Varan te vadhik)*, M. 1, *Sh.* 20.

ਜੇ ਤਉ ਪ੍ਰੇਮ ਖੇਲਣ ਕਾ ਚਾਉ.
ਸਿਰ ਧਰਿ ਤਲੀ ਗਲੀ ਮੇਰੀ ਆਉ ।
ਸਿਰ ਦੀਜੈ ਕਾਣਿ ਨ ਕੀਜੈ,
ਤਉ ਇਸ ਮਾਰਗ ਪਾਉ ਧਰੀਜੈ ॥

It must be remembered that Sikhism, as taught by the Master, is a religion of individual instruction. Each disciple has to subordinate his ego to the Will of the Master before he can be led along the path of spiritual progress, and consequently there can be no room in such a system of any dogmatic assertion about the actions which all may perform or abstain from. The groundwork of ethics has been laid down in unmistakable terms, and the individual effort to attain the Ideal have to be guided according to the stage to which the soul has already progressed. As this progress must vary with each individual, so must the *Gurmukh* guide him onward.

People have often mortified their bodies in order to develop the spirit. The Master, however, addressed the Lord thus :—

For Thee, O Lord, am steeped in Love !

Numerous Thy Names, Numerous Thy forms !

Indescribable and immeasurable, Thy Attributes !

To see Thee, O Lord,

The gods suffered austerities, starvation and wanderings,

The *Yogis* and celibates adopted rigid conduct,

And they put on ochre clothes.

In search of Thee,

They abandoned homes and palaces, elephants and steeds, countries and domains ;

The preceptors, the prophets and the genuine seekers,

Gave up the world, and then approached Thee !

They abandoned appetites, normal pleasures and delicacies ;

They spurned cloth and put on skins ;

They mortified their bodies with pain, at Thy door !

Steeped in Thy Name is the Dervish !

(Thus) hath he adopted, O Lord !

the skin, the beggar's bowl and the staff, the tuft, the thread and the loin cloth.

I masquerade in Thee,

Thou my Master !

What other caste shall Nanak speak of.*

---

* Asa Gh. 4, M. 1, 33.

ਦੇਵਤਿਆ ਦਰਸਨ ਕੈ ਤਾਈ ਦੂਖ ਭੂਖ ਤੀਰਥ ਕੀਏ ।

ਜੋਗੀ ਜਤੀ ਜੁਗਤ ਮਹਿ ਰਹਤੇ ਕਰਿ ਕਰਿ ਭਗਵੇ ਭੇਖ ਭਏ ॥

ਤਉ ਕਾਰਣਿ ਸਾਹਿਬਾ ਰੰਗਿ ਰਤੇ;

ਤੇਰੇ ਨਾਮ ਅਨੇਕਾ ਰੂਪ ਅਨੰਤਾ,

ਕਹਣੁ ਨ ਜਾਹੀ ਤੇਰੇ ਗੁਣ ਕੇਤੇ ॥੧॥ ਰਹਾਉ ॥

P. T. O.

It is obvious that in a system such as this, where salvation of the human soul is deemed to be a pure matter of Grace, prayer, individual as well as congregational, must find a prominent place ; and on the bestowal of Grace all past sins must be completely washed away. The Master does not ask the disciple to fly away from the world. This indeed the disciple cannot do. Nor does he teach that the world, as we see it, does not exist, that it is all an illusion and much of a dream. Under a belief such as this, there could hardly be a scope for individual effort. On the other hand, the Master declared the universe as the creation of the Lord, and proclaimed that "real was the

---

ਦਰ ਘਰ ਮਹਲਾ ਹਸਤੀ ਘੋੜੇ,
ਛੋਡਿ ਵਿਲਾਇਤਿ ਦੇਸ ਗਏ ।
ਪੀਰ ਪੈਕਾਂਬਰ ਸਾਲਿਕ ਸਾਦਿਕ,
ਛੋਡੀ ਦੁਨੀਆ ਥਾਇ ਪਏ ॥

ਸਾਦ ਸਹਜ ਸੁਖ ਰਸ ਕਸ ਤਜੀਅਲੇ,
ਕਾਪੜ ਛੋਡੇ ਚਮੜ ਲੀਏ ।
ਦੁਖੀਏ ਦਰਦਵੰਦ ਦਰਿ ਤੇਰੇ,
ਨਾਮਿ ਰਤੇ ਦਰਵੇਸ ਭਏ ।

ਖਲੜੀ ਖਪਰੀ ਲਕੜੀ ਚਮੜੀ,
ਸਿਖਾ ਸੂਤੁ ਪੋਤੀ ਕੀਨੀ ।
ਤੂ ਸਾਹਿਬੁ ਹਉ ਸਾਂਗੀ ਤੇਰਾ,
ਪ੍ਰਣਵੈ ਨਾਨਕੁ ਜਾਤਿ ਕੈਸੀ ।

Creation of the *Real* One".* Again, "this universe is the Residence of the True One The True One liveth therein."† It is in this real universe that individual soul has descended to work up its elevation and it is not by spurning it that the elevation can be attained. Let the matter be subservient to the spirit within, let the spirit remain fixed on the Ideal and be guided along the path by the Master's word, and let the spirit continuously remain in communion and pray for Grace, and thus may it be raised. Forgiveness of sins will then come of Divine Grace and in this lies the consolation of Sikhism.

> Born in sins,
> Committing sins,
> Always living in sins :
> The dirt will not go by washing,
> Even though we may wash a hundred times !
> Should He forgive,
> Shall we be forgiven,
> Else, dirt will go on cumulating !‡

---

* Japji. XXXI.

ਨਾਨਕ ਸਾਚੇ ਕੀ ਸਾਚੀ ਕਾਰ ।

† *Asa Di War*, M. 1.

ਏਹ ਜਗ ਸਚੇ ਕੀ ਹੈ ਕੋਠੜੀ,
ਸਚੇ ਕਾ ਵਿਚੁ ਵਾਸਿ ॥

‡ Var Magh, M. 1, Shlok 23

ਖਤਿਅਹੁ ਜੰਮੇ, ਖਤੇ ਕਰ. ਨਿਤਿ ਖਤਿਆਂ ਵਿਚੁ ਪਾਹਿ ।
ਧੋਤੇ ਮੂਲ ਨ ਉਤਰਹਿ, ਜੇ ਸਉ ਧੋਵਣ ਪਾਹਿ
ਨਾਨਕ, ਬਖਸੇ ਬਖਸੀਅਹਿ, ਨਾਹਿ ਤਾ ਪਾਹੀ ਪਾਹਿ ॥

As a huge ocean is full of water,
So are my sins, O Lord !
Be Merciful and Gracious :
Thou hast refloated sunken stones !*

The Master himself declared and consoled all by saying :

Be no sceptics, O people
A grain of fire consumeth lacs of stacks of fuel.†

---

*Rag Gowri, M. 1, Sh. 17.

ਜੇਤਾ ਸਮੁੰਦ ਸਾਗਰ ਨੀਰ ਭਰਿਆ,
ਤੇਤੇ ਔਗਣ ਹਮਾਰੇ ।
ਦਇਆ ਕਰਹੁ, ਕਿਛੁ ਮਿਹਰ ਉਪਾਵਹੁ,
ਡੁਬਦੇ ਪਾਥਰ ਤਾਰੇ ।

† Asa. M. 1, Ghor. 3 (2).

ਲਕਾ ਮਤ ਕੋ ਫਕੜਿ ਪਾਇ ।
ਲਖ ਮੜਿਆ ਕਰਿ ਏਕਠੇ,
ਏਕ ਰਤੀ ਲੇ ਭਾਹਿ ॥

XVI.

THE MASTER'S CHURCH.

They come when sent, O Nanak !
They go back when recalled.*

This is what the Master said about the missions of the Prophets, who have from time to time appeared in this world to teach and reform. They all knew that they had but a brief span of life, within which to perform the task imposed upon them, and yet they found that the world was too big and the work too heavy to be performed singlehanded. Consequently, they trained some of their followers and sent them out to carry their messages to peoples whom they themselves could not approach. It was thus that most of the Churches that we find established in the world came into existence. The great Budha trained his first disciples, and commissioned them thus: "Go out, O Bhikshus, and wander about for the benefit and welfare of the many,

* ਘਲੇ ਆਏ ਨਾਨਕਾ, ਸਦੇ ਹੀ ਉਠ ਜਾਹਿ।

in mercy for the gods and men, and for their advantage. Proclaim, O Bhikshus, the principles of the grand Dhama, and preach the pure and perfect life, that has been taught unto you." He established the congregation, called the Sangha, and the *Mantram* which his disciples adopted was "Om! I take refuge in the Budha: I take refuge in the Sangha; I take refuge in Truth." Thus was the Budhist Church established for the propagation of the creed which he preached, and the construction of numerous *Viharas* for the training of the Bhikshus followed, in the centuries which succeeded Budha's death. Christ also, before his departure from this earth, collected his eleven disciples, for the twelfth was an apostate who had betrayed him, and told them: "Go ye therefore, and teach all nations, baptizing them in the name of the Father, and of the Son, and of the Holy Ghost: teaching them to observe all things whatsoever I have commanded you." These were the early Christian missionaries who preached abroad and established his Church after he himself had gone. Muhammad had similarly a select following, whom he called the Exiles and the Allies, because the former had followed him to Medina and the latter had found him shelter there, when he was virtually driven out of Mecca, and addressed them thus before his death: "The number of believers will increase, but that of the Allies never can. They were my family with whom I found a home. Do good to those who do good to them and break friendship with those who are hostile to them." And his parting command to his followers was:—*First*—Expel all idolators from Arabia. *Second.*—Allow all proselytes equal privileges with yourselves. *Third.*—Devote yourselves to incessant prayer." Following his admonition, and perhaps partly by extending unduly its implications, the followers of Muhammad spread the awe of the scimetar, not only by driving the idolators from Arabia, but also following them and those of other countries abroad. Thus was the Islamic Church also found and spread, as much by preaching, as by the use of the scimetar to back it up.

The Church founded by the Master, however, though after the fashion of Budha in its inception, had a different implication. In His case, the Master's Spirit was to remain incarnate in human body, after the First of the bodies had ended its days on the earth. Before His ascension, the Master transfused his Spirit into the heart of his disciple, Lehna, who was thenceforward called Angad, made of the Master's Own Essence; and this Spirit was ordained to continue to work in Nine more bodies for a period of over two hundred years. The burden of the world was too heavy to be lightened in one earthly existence. Thus the Master remained at the head of the Church he had founded, for nine more generations, after he had left his own body. The Master had ascended to the Divine, but the Master had survived on the earth. Thus He was the Centre of the Sikh Church; and continued as such till time came of His final ascension at the close of the Tenth Mastership, when The Master's Word, as contained in the Granth Sahib, the Holy Book, was installed in the Supreme Command of the Church. "By the Command of the Almighty Lord has the Panth been established: All Sikhs are hereby ordained to believe in the Granth Sahib as the Guru. Yea, believe in the Holy Book, for this is the Manifest Body of the Master. Those, who have a pure heart, may find the Master in His Word."*

Sangat or the Congregation commands respect next to the Master in His Church. It is in the *Sangat* that the *Gurmukh*, *i. e.*, the illumined

---

* Guru Gobind Singhji.

ਆਗਿਆ ਭਈ ਅਕਾਲ ਕੀ ਤਭੀ ਚਲਾਇਓ ਪੰਥ ।

ਸਭਿ ਸਿਖਨ ਕੋ ਹੁਕਮੁ ਹੈ ਗੁਰੂ ਮਾਨੀਓ ਗ੍ਰੰਥ ॥

ਗੁਰੂ ਟੰਥ ਜੀ ਮਾਨੀਓ ਪਰਗਟ ਗੁਰਾਂ ਕੀ ਦੇਹਿ ।

ਜਾਂ ਕਾ ਹਿਰਦਾ ਸੁਧਿ ਹੈ, ਖੋਜਿ ਸ਼ਬਦ ਮੇਂ ਲੇਹਿ ।

soul of the saintly disciple, imparts illumination to the others. It will be remembered that the Master during his travels had established a number of *Manjis* in different parts of southern Asia, where the disciples had to congregate daily and occasionally to sing the sacred songs, to pray to the Almighty Father, and to solve their spiritual difficulties from the *Bhaiji* or the Reverend Brother, who was placed in charge of the *Manji* by the Master Himself. It was here that the Master's work was continued by the Reverend Brother, who always presided at the congregations, and instructed the Brothers in their spiritual, religious, social and moral duties. These early Sikhs, few in number, always made up the deficiency of numbers by their zeal and sincerity, by their piety and love, by their sacrifices and by their service of others. These *Sangats* were the noblest examples in history of assemblies of pious and spiritual enthusiasts, of truthful and mutually confiding seekers after Truth, and of humble and sincere servants of humanity. Men with strong determination and Faith, and yet extremely meek and loving in nature, no nobler specimen of humanitarian organization than of these has ever been in existence or conceived. Each disciple learnt his lessons of Service by serving and obeying the Reverend Brother, as he would serve and obey the Master Himself, and wherever the Sikh went he carried his duty of un-ostenta tious service of the public, of those who needed help and succour, with him. Misery and pain, wherever found or heard of, attracted these God-fearing and God-loving spiritual republicans, to alleviate it. Numerous instances of these are chronicled but this does not appear to be the appropriate place to recount them. The story of Bhai Tara, who ran up to Lahore, when it was in flames, for help, is an instance in point. He told his sister, who, being the only relation he had, tried to prevent him lest he may himself perish in the attempt to render help, thus :

Let me go, let me go , my sister ;
For the opportunity of service is fleeting ;

Being called a Sikh of Guru Nanak,
I cannot keep away on hearing of misery.*

It must be remembered that Sikhism, as taught by the Master, is a religion of the Spirit which must of necessity be a matter of individual instruction. Whatever the stage of spiritual development, a disciple has reached, may be, it is necessary that his spirit may remain *linked* up with that of the Master, and through him, with the Supreme Power-House of Spirituality, for, switched off from Him, the individual soul is helpless and apt to break off as a *Sakat*,

* Kh : Tr : Society.

ਤਾਰਾ ਆਖਦਾ, ਭੈਣਿ ਜੀ ਜਾਣ ਦੇਵੇ,
ਵੇਲਾ ਪੁਰਬੀ ਦਾ ਪਇਆ ਵਿਹਾਂਵਦਾਏ ।
ਨਾਨਕ ਗੁਰੂ ਦਾ ਸਿਖ ਸਦਾਇ, ਭੈਣੇ,
ਦੁਖੀ ਦੇਖ ਕੇ ਰਿਹਾ ਨਹੀਂ ਜਾਂਵਦਾਏ ।

whose very touch, according to the teachings of the Master, would mean pollution. In such a system, the essential means to spiritual development of the human soul must include guidance from a higher Spirit, instruction from an instructed or inspired Soul, and a continuous touch with the Master's teachings through the company of saints and congregational service. The *Bhaiji* or the Reverend Brother, who presided over the *Sangat*, always took up his duties in all humility, deeming it a service imposed upon him by the Master, and not in a spirit of overlording.

At the *Manjis*, which were founded by the Master himself in his tours, *Bhaijis* were nominated by the Master to preside over and instruct the *sangats.* The successor of a *Bhaiji* was subsequently, in each case, nominated by the predecessor, with the approval of the Master. Subsequently, *Bhaiji* came in certain places to be called the *Baba* or Father. This title was originally applied to the Master himself. It is also mentioned in several places in the Granth Sahib, for example, in *Rag* Gauri Cheti, Mohala First, Shabad 13, where the Master's earthly body addressed his Spirit as "*Baba* Nanak." It appears that, after the Master's ascension, the title of *Baba* was applied to the Master's sons, Sri Chand and Lakhmi Chand as an Honorary distinction, while the Embodiment of the Master's Spirit was known only as the Guru or the Master. None of the succeeding Gurus was called *Baba*, after he had succeeded to the highest authority in the Church. Since then, the order of *Babas* came to occupy the same position as that of *Bhaiji* under the Master's dispensation. It may be that, as Guru Angad Dev, in whom the Master's spirit had been transfused before the Master's ascension, had, as desired, removed himself to Khadur Sahib, Kartarpur and the colony of Dera Baba Nanak on the opposite bank of the river were left in charge of the Master's sons, and being thus in charge of these institutions they became entitled to the epithet of *Baba* by virtue of that office. Whatever the reason, the fact remains that both Sri Chand, who was an ascetic and is now known as the founder of the order of *Udasis*, and Lakhmi Chand, who had married and had a family, were included in the higher order of *Baba*, and ever since then the sons of all succeeding Gurus or Masters and their descendants have held the honorific title of *Baba*.

All Sikhs being thus *Bhais*, or brothers-in-Guru, the Sikh social organization has often been called a Brotherhood or Fraternity. No distinction was observed in the *Sangat* or congregation between members of the Brotherhood on the basis of caste, origin, colour or sex. Higher spiritual attainments were the only consideration for the selection of a *Bhai* or brother as a *Baba* or Father, apart from the honorary distinction conferred on the descendants of the Masters.

It is necessary to mention here that, during his four principal *Udasis*, the Master wore scanty clothes, after the fashion of ascetics, barely enough to cover his body, but suited to the climate and other conditions of the countries he had to visit. In the firt two *Udasis* and the fourth, his garb was an admixture of Hindu and Muhammadan dresses. He had a sheet and ropes and *tilak* of the Hindu ascetic, and green or blue garment of a Musalman Faqir. He wore a wooden sandal of the Hindu Sanyasi on one foot and a Muhammadan shoe, made of hide, on the other. In his Third *Udasi*, which, as we know, was taken in the Himmalayan mountains, he wore skins and furs. Bhai Gurdas has referred to these as the foundation by the Master of the Or[illegible] of *Udasis* (*Udasi ki rit chalai*), immediately after he had been instructed by the Lord. When the Master returned from his Four *Udasis*, he put off these garbs, and adopted the simple garb of a layman. Bhai Gurdas specifically refers to this action of hteMaster as well, in the following terms:

> When the Baba came to Kartarpur, he put off the Udasi garbs;

He wore the layman's clothes, sat on the *Manji* and continued his spiritual instruction to all.*

Subsequently, when the Master visited the Yogis at Achal-Batala, the very first objection which the Yogis made against him related to his re-adoption of the clothes of the laity and householder. The Master's object, however, was not to make monks of his disciples. The necessities of the journeys required for the time being the adoption of simpler garbs of monks, but even then he was careful, it appears, to avoid creating an impression that he belonged to any known order of monks. He had no prejudices on the subject, and, as soon as the necessity ceased, he cast away those clothes, and took up once more the ordinary clothes of a *Sansari*, as Bhai Gur Das calls a householder.

It seems convenient to mention here that the elder of the two sons of the Master, Sri Chand by name, had himself adopted the Master's *Udasi* garb, and continued it throughout his life. It appears that he did so when the family were allowed to settle down at the holy colony

---

* Bhai Gurdas, Var 1.

ਬਾਬਾ ਆਇਆ ਕਰਤਾਰ ਪੁਰ,
ਭੇਖ ਉਦਾਸੀ ਸਗਲ ਉਤਾਰਾ।
ਪਹਿਰ ਸੰਸਾਰੀ ਕਪੜੇ,
ਮੰਜੀ ਬੈਠ ਕੀਆ ਅਵਤਾਰਾ ॥

of Kartarpur, after the Master's Second *Udasi*. It was here that Sri Chand was also instructed in the Master's teachings, and, with an early leaning towards spiritual development, Sri Chand seems to have taken to the mood of contemplation with extraordinary zeal, and lived for the rest of his life more or less self-centred. He never married, and on this account he seems to have often been described as the founder of the *Udasi* order of Sikhs. Whether Baba Sri Chand made any disciples or not, does not appear to be on record. At least none of the existing *Udasi Sadhs* trace their spiritual descent direct from Baba Sri Chand, except through Baba Gurditta, the eldest son of The Sixth Master, Guru Har Gobind Sahib. Baba Sri Sri Chand lived till long after the succession of the Sixth Master, and the migration of the family from Amritsar, first to Kartarpur in the present District of Jullundur (not the Kartarpur of the First Master), and then to Kiratpur (the City of Divine Songs) founded by the Sixth Master himself. It is recorded that Baba Sri Chand, before his death, handed over, with the Sixth Master's permission, the *seli* and *topi*, the insignia of the *Udasi* Order, to Baba Gurditta, the eldest son of the Sixth Master, and father and grandfather respectively of the Seventh and Eighth Masters, and himself vanished in the Himmalayan mountains. Baba Gurditta, himself a married man, subsequently established four *Dhunis* by granting certain privileges to his four disciples, Baba Almast, Baba Phul, Baba Gobind and Baba Balu the Cheerful, and these, in course of time, became the four principal sub-divisions of the *Udasi* Order. Baba Gurditta being himself a married man does not appear to be called the Founder of the *Udasi* Order, otherwise it seems that it was he, who adopted the ascetic disciples and granted them privileges to preach and spread the Mission of the Master in other lands. At some period of their development, marriage appears to have ceased to be prohibited amongst the *Udasis*. Perhaps the married life of Baba Gurditta had its influence in this respect. Since the change, whenever it occurred, the *Udasis* have often acknowledged double descent, *nadi* and *bindi*, *i. e.*, spiritual and physical. In addition to these, it appears that special marks of Grace or *Bakhshishs* were extended by the Masters, mostly the Seventh and Tenth, to six other men from among their disciples, and these six became the founders of further sub-divisions of *Udasis*, in addition to the Four *Dhunis*, founded by Baba Gurditta.*

* The question how far the *Udasis* are an order connected with the Sikh Church, and how far they follow the tenets of Sikhism, as preached by the Master, has recently assumed some importance, owing to a conflict between them and the *Akalis* in the matter of control over Sikh Shrines. Self-interest seems to have dictated various allegations and counter-allegations, and unconscious remarks of certain writers, who seem to have either not studied the question or little thought of the misuse which their remarks were apt to be made of, that upon the Master's ascension there was a schism between his disciples, on account of the alleged supersession of Sri Chand in the matter of succession,

It is of interest to add on this subject that all spiritual descendants of *Baba* Sri Chand, that is, all members of the *Udasi* order, were acknowledged to be entitled to the title of *Baba* even as the physical descendants of Lakhmi Chand were given or assumed the same, as honorary distinction.

All Sikhs, whether *Bhais*, *Bhaijis*, or *Babas*, generally worked for their own living, except perhaps the ascetic *Udasis*, who engaged themselves in purely spiritual matters and were supported by others. In many cases, the *Bhaiji's* own house was the place of congregational meetings, for it was there that the Master had originally visited and instructed him and

---

have been seriously misunderstood. It must be remembered that Bhai Gurdas wrote in the time of the Fifth Master, when Baba Sri Chand was still alive and had not yet made over the insignia of the Master's *Udasi* garb to Baba Gurditta. His statement that the Master put them off on his return to Kartarpur at a time when Baba Sri Chand lived with him coupled with the fact that, as recorded by the chroniclers, Baba Sri Chand made over the insignia to Baba Gurditta, seem to invest another fact discovered by the present writer in his visit at Kiratpur with special significance and importance. Those insignia, *seli* and *topi*, are still preserved, in a Gurdwara at Kiratpur, which is in charge of the descendants of a daughter of the Seventh Master and grand-daughter of Baba Gurditta, to whom, along with a book, also respectfully preserved, they were gifted by the Seventh Master at her marriage. Baba Gurditta had started the four *Dhuans*, after the political conflicts to the Sixth Master with the Mughal Emperor, in consequence of which, it appears, he had to retire to the sub-montaine tracts of Kiratpur, and members of this ascetic Order seem to have been later on entrusted with the care of the sacred places and were enjoined to keep themselves aloof from political struggles, which were inevitable under the Tenth Master.

had installed him on the *Manji*. His superiority lay originally in his being selected as the recipient of the Master's Grace, in his extreme devotion to the Master, in his higher spiritual attainments and in his greater capacity to guide others along the Path. There could obviously be no limit to the number of such men. The multiplication of the disciples naturally required and led to the increase in their number also, from time to time, and under the Third Master women were also promoted to the *higher* rank, and as *Mais* or Mothers undertook the task of preaching among their sex.

The Master was thus the greatest Emancipator of humanity. He preached that spiritual eminence was consistent with the performance of household duties. Asceticism, which was considered of such importance among the Hindu *Yogis* and Moslem Sufi *Derveshes*, was not as exalted as it had come to be believed. Married life, which indeed was the law of nature, was no bar to spiritual progress. It perfected human life on the other hand. " A householder, who does no evil, who is ever intent upon good, who continually exerciseth charity, is pure as is the water of the Ganges."* "Householder

---

*Var Ramkallee M. 3.

ਸੋ ਗਿਰਹੀ ਜੋ ਨਿਗ੍ਰਹਿ ਕਰਹਿ ।
ਜਪ, ਤਪ, ਸੰਜਮ, ਭਿਖਿਆ ਕਰਹਿ ।
ਪੁਨ ਦਾਨ ਕਾ ਕਰੇ ਸਰੀਰ ।
ਸੋ ਗਿਰਹੀ ਗੰਗਾ ਕਾ ਨੀਰ ॥

and hermit are equal, whoever meditates on the name of the Lord ?" The Master constantly discouraged the idea that any special virtue was to be gained by the ascetic life. He declared that true religion consisted not in outward ceremonials and the acceptance of prescribed religious formulæ, but in the state of the heart, and that it was possible to meditate with advantage on spiritual things, while engaged in the ordinary business of life, without retreating to the wilderness or the seclusion of a monastery.

The Master was also the greatest emancipator of woman in this country. It has already been mentioned that the Third Master exalted women to the higher ranks of Rev. Mothers and Preceptors. Guru Nanak himself denounced, in unmistakable terms, those who reviled woman. This is what he says in *Asa-di-War* :

> Born of woman, nourished by woman, wedded to woman ;
>
> Of woman is Love born, and woman starts life agoing ;
>
> On death of woman one looketh for another and by woman whole life is regulated :
>
> Why then revile her who giveth birth to heroes.
>
> Of woman is beauty born, none without her exists.

> Unborn of woman is only He, the True One, saith Nanak.*

It has been explained elsewhere that the Master based all. his ethical teachings on the necessity of the remembrance of the Lord and Devotion to His Name. The observances enjoined on those who belonged to his Church were similarly grounded on the same ideal. He set up no ceremonials, and such as were needed after him were ordered to conform to the same principle. For instance, when the prescription of marriage ceremony became necessary under his successors, one was laid down in strict conformity with the ideal set up.

> Thou desirest to perform a function, go and pray to the Lord ;
>
> He will bless thy function, if thou perform it in His Presence.

---

* Asa di Var, M. 1, Pauri 19, Sh. 2.

ਭੰਡਿ ਜੰਮੀਐ, ਭੰਡਿ ਨਿਮੀਐ ਭੰਡਿ ਮੰਗਣ ਵੀਆਹੁ ।

ਭੰਡਹੁ ਹੋਵੈ ਦੋਸਤੀ, ਭੰਡਹੁ ਚਲੈ ਰਾਹੁ ।

ਭੰਡੁ ਮੁਆ ਭੰਡ ਭਾਲੀਐ, ਭੰਡਿ ਹੋਵੈ ਬੰਧਾਨੁ ।

ਸੋ ਕਿਉ ਮੰਦਾ ਆਖੀਐ, ਜਿਤੁ ਜੰਮਹਿ ਰਾਜਾਨ ।

ਭੰਡਹੁ ਹੀ ਭੰਡਿ ਉਪਜ, ਭੰਡੈ ਬਾਝੁ ਨਕੋਇ ;

ਨਾਨਕ ਭੰਡੈ ਬਾਹਰਾ ਏਕੋ ਸਚਾ ਸੋਇ ।

Do it in the company of Saints, and drink of the Nectar of His Name.

He is the remover of all fears, He is Kind and Merciful,

Saveth He the Honour of His Servant.

By praising Him, thou shalt know the knowable, saith Nanak.*

All functions in the Master's Church must conform to this principle, and so should all other questions which may arise from time to time.

The hymns sung on the occasion of a death in a Sikh family are typical of the spirit of Sikhism, in relation to the events of life. The very first of these hymns describes the occasion as a wedding, and all the five songs are entitled as *Kirtan Sohila*, the Wedding Songs, which all Sikhs are enjoined to recite just before retiring to bed each night The first of these was sung

---

* *Shlok* M. V.

ਕੀਤਾ ਲੋੜੀਏ ਕਮ, ਸੁ ਹਰਿ ਪਹਿ ਆਖੀਐ ।

ਕਾਰਜ ਦੇਇ ਸਵਾਰ, ਸਤਿਗੁਰ ਸਚਾ ਸਾਖੀਐ ।

ਸੰਤਾ ਸੰਗ ਨਿਧਾਨ, ਅੰਮ੍ਰਿਤ ਰਸਿ ਚਾਖੀਐ ।

ਭੈ ਭੰਜਨ ਮੇਹਰਬਾਨ, ਦਾਸ ਕੀ ਰਾਖੀਐ ।

ਨਾਨਕ ਹਰਿ ਗੁਣ ਗਾਇ, ਅਲਖ ਪ੍ਰਭ ਲਾਖੀਐ ।

by the Master immediately before his ascension. It would repay repetition :

> Sing, ye, my comrades, sing now my wedding song.
>
> Sing the song of His Praise ;
>
> Sing the song of my Creator.
>
> Sing the song of Him, who knoweth no fear.
>
> I would be a sacrifice to this Wedding Song ;
>
> For in this Song lieth the Everlasting Bliss.
>
> For even the smallest life doth my Lord care ;
>
> The bounteous Giver meeteth needs of each.
>
> Invaluable are His Gifts ;
>
> Who can appraise Him.
>
> The auspicious day hath dawned ;
>
> The hour of Wedding is come.
>
> Come, comrades, and anoint the Bride ;
>
> Pour your blessings, O comrades,
>
> For the Bride meeteth her Lord.
>
> Take the Message to all :
>
> For the call cometh for all.
>
> Ever and always remember Him, who sendeth down the Call
>
> When the time for the Call arriveth.

---

* Sohila Rag Gauri Dipki, M. 1. (see page 227).

Could any thing transcend the ecstasy with which the Sikh is enjoined to meet the final Call? He must feel this ecstasy each night, when going to bed, and he must feel just the same when he goeth in response to the last Call. He must dream of his Union with the Lord each night, and he must finally repose in the happy dream from which he may wake not.

One constantly hears in India questions as to what food a man may eat and what he may eschew. Both Hindus and Muhammadans have their lists of permitted and prohibited articles. The diet to which these questions generally relate is the animal food. The Master, however, declared that "only fools, who know not the reality and think not calmly, quarrel over meat."* "In flesh we are conceived, of flesh we are born, and of flesh we are made. *Gyan* and *Dhyan* (knowledge and calm thinking) thou knoweth not, and yet, O Pundit, thou passeth for a wise man."† It is a long discourse which he addressed to the Brahmans at Kurukhshetra, where they thought that scrupulous abstention from animal food *alone*

---

* Sh. M. 1. (See page 101).

* ਮਾਸ ਮਾਸ ਕਰ ਮੂਰਖ ਝਗੜਹਿ
ਗਿਆਨ ਧਿਆਨ ਨਹੀ ਜਾਣਹਿ ।

† *Ibid.*

† ਮਾਸਹੁ ਜੰਮਹਿ, ਮਾਸਹੁ ਨਿੰਮਹਿ,
ਹਮ ਮਾਸੈ ਕੇ ਭਾਂਡੇ ।
ਗਿਆਨ ਧਿਆਨ ਕਿਛੁ ਸੂਝੈ ਨਾਹੀ,
ਚਤੁਰ ਕਹਾਵੈਂ ਪਾਂਡੇ ।

without following the spirit of religion, was enough to make them pure, and that all those, who abstained not from flesh, were, in spite of their purity of life and high spiritual attainments, doomed to perdition. The sermon, however, should not be understood to mean that the Master preached in favour of flesh-eating. Indeed, he attached little importance to these matters, and left even this question to be tested on the touchstone he had prescribed to regulate all human conduct. "All food is pure, for it hath come from God to all" † "But that eating for pleasure is impure, which produceth ailment in the body or evil thoughts in the mind."† With the variety of climatic and other conditions in different parts of the earth, it would have been simply impossible to lay down a single rigid rule on a non-essential subject like this, and no healthier and more elastic maxim, yet in strict consonance with the Ideal he had brought for the guidance of the human race, could be conceived. The chronicles do not say what food he himself ate, but from the general character of his teachings it seems that he could not have cared for animal diet himself, but assumed no merit on that account. The fact

---

*Asa di Var M. 1.

ਖਾਣਾ ਪੀਣਾ ਪਵਿਤ੍ਰੁ ਹੈ,
ਦਿਤੋਨ ਰਿਜ਼ਕ ਸਬਾਹਿ ।

† ਸੋ ਖਾਣਾ ਖੁਸ਼ੀ ਖੁਆਰੁ ।
ਜਿਤੁ ਖਾਧੇ ਤਨ ਪੀੜੀਏ,
ਮਨਿ ਮੈ ਚਲਹਿ ਵਿਕਾਰੁ ॥

that his immediate successor, Guru Angad. allowed meat to be cooked in his *Langar*, without insisting upon abstainers to eat of it, shows that there was no positive prohibition against it in the Church.

The ceremony of initiation of a novice into Sikhism, as originally instituted by the Master, was a simple one. Sir Lepel Griffin says that the "old Sikh faith had a baptismal ceremony which had fallen into disuse. This was resuscitated by Govind Singh (the Tenth Master), as the necessary initiatory ceremony of Sikhism." With this last proposition it is difficult to agree. Keeping in view the fact that the Master was not a man of conventions, the ceremony instituted by him could not possibly have been of a military character, which the Tenth Master had to institute and now prevails. Before the introduction of this somewhat elaborate Baptism of the Sword, the novitiate was simply instructed in the principles of the faith and administered *Charanghal*, or the water in which the toe of the Master is immersed. This is indeed what *Bhai* Gur Das specifically mentions.

XVII.

The Master's Method.

The Master had a method of teaching, peculiar to himself. He indulged in no speculations nor in lengthy arguments about matters he had to teach. He used no parables to illustrate his meaning, like a school Professor. He laid down no logical premises and drew no conclusions from them. He taught chiefly by example and authority. He was not merely a Teacher of spirituality and religion, which he was in the truest sense of the word, but the disciple found all those lessons that he taught fully illustrated in the Master's own life. He was the exemplar of the Divine principles which he preached. He was the model of the life which he wanted his followers to adopt. There was thus little need to argue. When he spoke, the disciple understood what he meant. Indeed he saw with his own eyes what he was required to do. The Master thus preached with an authority, which seemed so natural with him. He commanded. He had no fear of his adversaries and depended not upon the assistance of his friends. He felt confidence within himself and knew for certain that his words would not be lost. He spoke of God and how to reach Him simply as one who had himself come from on High, and said what he knew; and his simple telling brought to his audience the Reality he spoke of.

They say, example is better than precept. Himself a non-believer in formalism, the Master lost no opportunity to show the absurdities into which it had led the world. The Brahman came to administer to him the *Yagyopwit*, the sacred thread, which he had served out to so many people born of Hindu parents of the *Dwij* or twice born classes, when the Master had reached the suitable age. The Master demonstrated the futility of the proceedings and refused to receive the thread. The Brahman prepared to purify his family and his house of the pollution of *Sutak*, which was supposed to have attached on account of the birth of his son; and he expressed his views on the subject and stopped the ceremony which alone the Brahman could perform. He was asked if oblations of cakes were to be offered after his death and if his path to hereafter was to be lighted by a *ghee*-fed lamp, when his end was approaching, and he declared what might be done and what need not be performed. On none of these occasions, he denounced the words or expressions used.

He was not to destroy and then to leave the subject. He did not like to offend. He gave a new meaning to the words and infused a new sense in the functions. Thread symbolised man's binding down his passions. Yea, administer to me the *Yagyopwit*, O Pandit, which the spirit is in need of, which may neither break nor be soiled, neither be burnt nor get worn out. Blessed is he who weareth it. *Sutak* of a very abominable character is polluting beautiful lives of godly men, O Pandit, for covetousness is the *sutak* of the mind and speaking falsehood is of the tongue, casting a lustful eye at another's wife, beauty and riches is *sutak* of the organs of vision, and hearing false tales is that of the ears. All superstition is *sutak*, O Pundit, pray remove it. Yes, light up the lamp of the Lord's Name, in which all pain will be consumed as oil is burnt in a lamp, and this lamp shall illumine the way hereafter. It is the remembrance of the Creator which will serve as Cakes on the future way to eternity.

To the Mussalman, he never said to cease being a Moslem. Be a true Moslem, O Kazi, for to be one thou must cast off thy vanity and be humble, render submission to God with patience and be kind to all living beings, created by Him. Pray, with honesty as your holy book, on the carpet of sincerity, in the Musjid of Compassion, If thou wantest to be a true

Moslem, my friend. Good deeds shall then be thy *Ka'aba*, truth thy *Kalma*, and charity thy prayer. Thou must have meekness for thy rosary. The Kazi, as much as the Nawab and the Mullah had but to agree. In Mecca, the simple answer, "Turn my feet to where the house of God is not", was enough to set all athinking, and they had but to realise that God lived on all sides and could not be confined only within the four walls of a building, however ancient it was.

In the Temple of Jagannath at Puri. he granted to the High Priests of the Thakurji the Vision of the Sublime *Arti*, which all Nature was performing in front of The Lord of All Universes, and gave an entirely new meaning to the word. Those who had ears to hear and eyes to see heard the message and saw the Grand *Arti* and questioned no more. The deaf and the blind had but to follow. Similar Vision had to be shown to those who believed in seven earths and seven skies as the limits of the Universe, when the Master was to be stoned to death on account of his declaration that in God's Creation there were lakhs upon lakhs of such earths and skies. Did not Bahlol see them and bow?

It was a novel way in which the Master's presence in a place was announced. In Kurukhshetra, the people rushed against him to punish the sacrilege of a pot of meat, while the occasion was one of purification from the Demon's pollution and release of the sun-god from his grip. At Baghdad, he was to be stoned to death for his 'blasphemous' utterances, and the eagerness of the people to acquire merit by murder brought them face to face with Him. At Jaggannath's Temple, he had sinned by sitting down when he ought to have stood up at the *Arti*, and at Mecca he had committed the outrage by lying down with his feet towards the *Ka'qba*. In Hardwar he threw water to the west, to irrigate his fields some three hundred miles away, when the occasion needed offerings of water to the sun-god and the ancestors to the east. All these heterodox actions attracted attention and large audiences, wherever the necessity was to preach openly. In each case the method of collection of audience also served to introduce the subject of the discourse, but from our mundane point of view, it involved risks which one may feel difficult to justify being taken. The Master, however, knew that he ran no risk, for nothing could happen to him as he was under the Protection of Him who had Commissioned Him to proclaim the Kingdom of Love and Devotion to the Name, wherein shall God be Glorified and hypocrisy destroyed.

Through all this fearlessness however, ran a ring of meekness and sincerity, which is so rare to find anywhere else. "Do ye want to strike down innocence? Do so, brothers, and wait no more, for I am but an humble creature of God, who will offer no resistance. If, however, ye want to have a talk, pray calm yourselves and be seated, and I will talk to you;" he said to the furious crowds at Kurukhshetra.

"I have come from afar and was weary and tired. I have but thrown myself down, my friends," he told the people at Mecca, when he asked them to turn his feet to where the House of God was not. The Master was an artist in whom meekness meant a frank acceptance of all experiences, just as love indicated in him the sense of beauty which revealed to the world its soul as well as its body. It always disarmed opposition, and nothing else could happen.

XVIII.

The Master's Personality.

The personality of the Master presents to the student of his life a strange combination of qualities. A number of paradoxes, more apparent than real, seem to strike the imagination, and our timid methods of investigation do not ordinarily afford us a sufficiency of historic explanation. The Master lived at a time when the game of public life is freely played, during a period of human activity when man risks all and gains all. The movement which he started meant unison of the lay mind with the Supreme Spirit and implied Liberty from all trammels. That he met with considerable opposition goes without saying. When in more recent times, laws were passed for the emancipation of slaves, the strongest opposition came from the slaves themselves. So, when the Master raised the banner of Freedom from Spiritual and Moral Slavery of the Nations of the Earth, the greatest opposition came from those who shuddered from the truth being told about their degraded condition. The Master was threatened with death on several occasions; he was called a heretic and his bard could find no place to keep peace with his surroundings; he was sold as a slave and was captured as a prisoner; and finally the apotheosis was reached when he was incarcerated in jail. On all these occasions, circumstances were enough to suppress the conscience of the boldest among men. But the Master's conscience was inspired by the Supreme Consciousness, which refused to be put down. Such obviously adverse events, on the other hand, served the fulfilment of His purpose. Threatened violence changed into meek submission, persecution altered into the vanquishment of the persecutor, sale as a slave led to the abolition of slavery and emancipation of all slaves, and his imprisonment with Criminals in Jail resulted in the downfall of an Empire and evangelisation of the sinners. His adversities proved to be blessing in disguise, and if it is correct that the world has been built of sorrow, it has been well remarked that it has been built with the hands of love. The great Budha saw pain and sorrow around him, and exclaimed, "how could it be that Brahm would make a world and keep it miserable." He little knew that sorrow is the supreme emotion a man is capable of, and the Master whose whole life was that of an artist of the sublimest nature exalted sorrow as a blessing.

How beautifully he declared,

> I sicken at pleasure, the pain healeth me ;
> In pleasure, I forget Thee, O Creator.
>
> Thou ordaineth, I can do nothing ;
> What I do is all an undoing.*

By his fearless calmness in adversity, he has taught us the lessons to appreciate the beauty of sorrow, and to realise, with Goethe, that

> Who never ate his bread in sorrow,
> Who never spent the midnight hours
>
> Weeping and waiting for the morrow,
> He knows you not, ye heavenly powers.

For Guru Nanak, nature had dealt her choicest both in body and mind. Strong healthy physique, beautiful and attractive features, and white rosy colour, his physiognomy always impressed all, who looked at him, with his sacred character and inspired them with spontaneous reverence for him. His adversities seem to be part of the scheme of his life, otherwise his genial and frank nature, and his unlimited capacity for Reform, made troops of followers wherever he went.

---

* Shlok, M 1.

ਦੁਖ ਦਾਰੂ, ਸੁਖ ਰੋਗ ਭਇਆ,
ਜਾ ਸੁਖ ਤਾਮ ਨਾ ਹੋਈਂ ।
ਤੂੰ ਕਰਤਾ, ਕਰਣਾ ਮੈ ਨਾਹੀ,
ਜਾਂ ਹਉ ਕਰੀ, ਨ ਹੋਈ ॥

He is described by one writer as " thorough and consistent, prudent and yet urgent, and as gentle in manner as he was strong in faith." The movement which he started was not the result of a long meditation and deep thought, but had a spontaneous growth from the Master's inborn nature. He had no dogma but a fixed personal resolution, exceeding in intensity every other created will, and men became his followers, not by believing this thing or that thing, but by being attached to his person. His heart burnt within him at the degraded condition of the people around him, and he worked prudently but firmly and always successfully. He laughed very seldom, yet he never produces the impression of austerity, moroseness, sadness or unhappiness. He was always rejoicing in Spirit. At times he was scarcastic but always serious. With strong and forceful expression, and straightforward and bold demeanour, he never allowed an opportunity to slip.

Guru Nanak presents a character thorough and consistent from the very beginning. In his character we do not find any improvements being made. In fact he had no extravagances to prune off and no eccentricities to return from. His character is never modified, it is one and the same throughout. Some western writers have concluded from his habit of giving away in alms what he possessed in material resources, that he was extravagant and careless in money matters. But they do not seem to have realised that he never lived beyond his means, when he was in business, and that when he eventually renounced his *Modikhana*, he left it in good financial stability.

The consistency of the Master's character will be obvious to any one who compared his lessons to his teacher at the village school and to the Pundit at his *Yagyopwit* ceremony, in his early life, with his utterances at Kurukhshetra, Brindaban and Jagannath; or the incident of his restoration of the damaged crops of his village with the event of Bawa Wali at Hassan Abdal. Never hesitating in doing his task, unfaltering in his trials, unshaken amid persecution and undaunted in adversity, Guru Nanak presents a character, thorough and consistent all round, and unparalleled in the history of the world.

Guru Nanak was a man among men. His example inspired us with hopes and aspirations. Nowhere does he produce an impression that his standard is beyond approach by mortal man. He in fact raises his fellow beings towards himself. He indeed tells us, in actions as in words, that every human being is capable of approaching the Divine, only if one would try to do so. He in short does not leave us behind exhausted. Each step that he draws us nearer to himself inspires us with fresher aspirations. Nowhere do his life and teachings mortify us, however low and degraded we may be. His loving hand extends to us even there.

That the Master set up a new dispensation and founded the true religion in its pristine glory and purity goes without saying. As regards other religious systems, he followed none and denounced none. It has already been explained that he gave new meaning to them. His perfect idealism included the highest rule of unspotted and virtuous life, with the sole object of deserving the Lord's Grace. In Him, Supreme Consciousness asserted and, breaking through the barriers of caste, creed and colour, declared the Unity of God and Brotherhood of Man, insisted on the moral Code of Budha and Christ but grounded it on the supreme duty of winning Grace, and he inculcated a continuous exercise of realisation of the Presence of God. It is in the absence of this last realisation that humanity has always been apt to lapse from the path of rectitude.

The foundation of the True Religion was the Master's work. After him all that remained was to develop it and make it fruitful. His great work indeed was to have made himself beloved in the highest degree by his disciples. His doctrine was so little dogmatic that he never thought of its being systematically written. His songs, now preserved in the Granth Sahib, were first written in scattered scraps by his disciples, as they heard them, and were collected immediately after him by the Second Master, Guru Angad, and incorporated in the Holy Book by the Fifth Master, Guru Arjan Dev. These Songs constitute the Master. Music was his life; and His Divine Music still thrills the lives of His numerous followers. That he was inspired is clear from what he himself always said when he was singing. "Play the tune, Mardana, for the song hath come." This is what he always commanded to his bard when he received the inspiration. On one occasion, he told Bhai Lalo in express terms, "As the word cometh to me from the Lord, I impart knowledge thereof, O Lalo." The proof that the Master was God-Commissioned lies clearly in the character of his message and in the influence which he exerted on the lives of his followers, an influence that has lasted through centuries. The Master himself said in his hymns that he was instructed by God Himself.

> Nanak found his Guru in the Supreme Lord
> and found consolation in the True Word*

---

*Ramkali, M. 1, 6.

ਗੁਰ ਪਰਮੇਸਰ ਨਾਨਕ ਭੇਟਿਓ,
ਸਾਚੇ ਸਬਦ ਨਿਬੇਰਾ ।

> The Immeasurable, the Supreme Brahm,
> The Supreme Lord: Nanak had Him as his Guru.*

We have already seen † that when the Master received his baptism, the Supreme Master blessed him with Grace and made this blessing a part of the First Principle of the creed, which Lord Himself prescribed for being broadcast, by saying that He is to be realised by the Master's Grace. There the word "Master" so far as Guru Nanak was concerned, on whom the Grace was bestowed, referred to the Almighty Father Himself.

It is thus that pure Sikhism, the product of a perfectly spontaneous spiritual movement, freed from its birth from all dogmatic restraint, having struggled for four hundred years for liberty of conscience, despite persecutions and attempts at its suppression and extinction, still reaps the fruits of its glorious origin. To refresh itself, it has but to return to the Master the Holy Book.

This Sublime Master we shall call Divine, not of course in the sense that he has absorbed all divinity, or has been identical with it, but in the sense that Guru Nanak is he who came

---

* ਅਪ੍ਰੰਪਰ, ਪਾਰਬ੍ਰਹਮ, ਪਰਮੇਸਰ,
ਨਾਨਕ ਗੁਰ ਮਿਲਿਆ ਸੋਈ ਜੀਉ ।

† Chapter iv.

from the Divine and caused his fellowmen to make the greatest step towards the Divine. He created heaven, upon this earth, of pure souls, and, to find its characteristics, one has only to refer to the state of his disciples in his time and after him. In Guru Nanak, who may legitimately be called a man among men and a god among gods, was concentrated all that was good and lofty in human nature. He was above all passions which we fight against. Never has any man, so much as he, made the interests of humanity predominate in his life over the pettiness of self-love. Unreservedly bound to his mission, he subordinated all things to it, and it was by the intensity of this heroic will that he conquered heaven.

The legend of Guru Nanak's life will always bring into activity the tender feelings of human soul, and all men will proclaim that among sons of men, none was born greater than Nanak. Following the Fifth Master, Guru Arjan Dev, let us sing ਸਭ ਤੋਂ ਵਡਾ ਸਤਿਗੁਰ ਨਾਨਕ ਜਿਨ ਕਲ ਰਾਖੀ ਮੇਰੀ, Greatest of all is the Divine Master Nanak who hath sheltered me from all pain.

> Yes, write it in the rock,.................
> Grave it on brass with adamantine pen.
> 'Tis God Himself becomes apparent, when
> God's wisdom and God's goodness are displayed,
> For God of these His attributes is made.

Matthew Arnold.